DATE DUE

OC 21 '99			
MY 23 '01			
JE 10 '09			
GAYLORD			PRINTED IN U.S.A.

Challenging the Myths of
Fair Employment Practices

Challenging the Myths of Fair Employment Practices

Richard S. Barrett

QUORUM BOOKS
Westport, Connecticut · London

Library of Congress Cataloging-in-Publication Data

Barrett, Richard S., 1924–
    Challenging the myths of fair employment practices / Richard S.
Barrett.
        p.   cm.
    Includes bibliographical references and index.
    ISBN 1–56720–141–5 (alk. paper)
    1. Employee selection—United States.   2. Employment tests—United
States.   3. Discrimination in employment—United States.
    4. Employment tests—Law and legislation—United States.   I. Title.
    II. Title: Fair employment myths.
    HF5549.5.S38B375   1998
    658.3'112—DC21   98–4929

British Library Cataloguing in Publication Data is available.

Library of Congress Catalog Card Number: 98–4929
ISBN: 1–56720–141–5

First published in 1998

Quorum Books, 88 Post Road West, Westport, CT 06881
An imprint of Greenwood Publishing Group, Inc.

Printed in the United States of America

The paper used in this book complies with the
Permanent Paper Standard issued by the National
Information Standards Organization (Z39.48–1984).

10 9 8 7 6 5 4 3 2 1

Copyright Acknowledgment

The author and publisher are grateful for permission to reprint portions of the
following copyrighted material:

"Ethical Principles of Psychologists and Code of Conduct" from *American
Psychologist*, Vol. 47 (1992), pp. 1597–1611. Copyright © 1998 by the
American Psychological Association. Reprinted with permission.

To Shirley, my wife

Contents

Appendixes

Preface

After rereading the rather technical expositions in *Fair Employment Strategies in Human Resource Management* (Barrett 1996), I decided that a more practical guide was needed for human resource managers, attorneys, and students who are not trained in psychometrics. Most of the issues regarding testing and fair employment that seem shrouded in complexity are readily understood, and the more technical psychometric issues yield to discussions with a statistician who is familiar with the field. I have written this book for the benefit of the users of tests and for all those who are concerned with the effective use of tests. My aim is to demystify procedures clouded in unnecessary complexities and to encourage the use of modern, effective selection procedures.

This book is concerned primarily with the employment of minorities, women, and older and disabled workers. In it I explore and, I hope, refute many of the misconceptions about fair employment that have grown up since the passage of Title VII of the Civil Rights Act of 1964. My discussion of legal, professional, and ethical issues relating to testing and other selection procedures is supported by citations to, among others, the following sources:

Title VII of the Civil Rights Act of 1964

Age Discrimination in Employment Act of 1967

Americans with Disabilities Act of 1990

Uniform Guidelines on Employee Selection Procedures

Questions and Answers to Clarify and Provide a Common Interpretation of the Uniform Guidelines on Employee Selection Procedures

Standards for Educational and Psychological Testing of the American Psychological Association

Principles for the Validation and Use of Personnel Selection Procedures of the Society for Industrial and Organizational Psychology (SIOP)

"Ethical Principles of Psychologists and Code of Conduct" of the American Psychological Association

The Ethical Practice of Psychology in Organizations

Affirmative Action Guidelines

The Rights and Responsibilities of Test Takers

Court cases and other governmental and professional policy statements

This book is a distillation of what I have learned in testifying in more than 100 cases in the past 30 years and in developing tests to meet professional, legal, and ethical standards. Three basic threads run through this book. The first is a description of current good practice. The second is validity. Validity is subsumed under the more comprehensive term used by the Supreme Court when it found for the plaintiff in *Griggs v. Duke Power Company* (1971) and said that "the touchstone is business necessity." The third thread is the measurement and reduction of adverse impact against minorities and women, older workers, and the disabled. These main issues are discussed with reference to ethical issues.

This book is intended for human resource managers and other executives who deal with fair employment issues. It can also be an auxiliary text for courses in testing and fair employment. There are several things that this book is not. It is not a text. Many excellent publications cover the selection process, fair employment issues, statistics, and ethical principles. Reference is made to the most useful sources. It is not a review of the literature, although it is based, in part, on published documents. There are comprehensive references to most of the chapters of *Fair Employment Strategies in Human Resource Management*. Nor is it a statistics text. Statistical concepts relevant to fair employment are presented in Chapter 14, but those who avoided statistics in college may have to refer to a text or rely on a statistician to communicate the basic concepts.

The chapters are organized, whenever applicable, by this schema:

Background.

Purpose for which the selection procedure, validation study, or statistical analysis is designed.

Population and sample to which the selection procedure, validity study, or statistical analysis is applied.

Measurement and data collection procedures used.

Analysis and conclusions based on these investigations.

Myths.

Implications.

Fair employment is engulfed in misconceptions that stand in the way of successful selection programs and the integration of minorities, women, and older and disabled workers into the workforce—hence the name *Challenging the Myths of Fair Employment Practices*.

My involvement with fair employment began in the early 1960s, when I did a routine selection study for a large insurance company. Ten percent of my sample was black, so I analyzed the candidates' performance on the tests by race. Although the results were inconclusive, the analysis inspired me to get a grant from the Ford Foundation that resulted in *Testing and Fair Employment* (Kirkpatrick et al. 1968). We concluded that our study did not provide clear evidence for or against differential validity, that is, whether or not tests worked differently for minorities and whites.

On the strength of this study, I was asked to testify in *Griggs v. Duke Power Company* (1971). I received the call on a Tuesday and flew to Durham, North Carolina, on Wednesday. There I met with the attorneys from the NAACP Legal Defense and Education Fund, read some depositions, and testified on Thursday in time to catch a plane home that afternoon. The transcript of my testimony, direct, cross, and redirect, and some interspersed colloquies runs to only 21 pages. After the suit was lost in the District Court and the Appeals Court, the Supreme Court decided in favor of Griggs, 8–0. Such are the modest beginnings of a lifetime involvement.

The three young attorneys from the Legal Defense Fund went on to brilliant careers. Robert Belton became a professor of clinical law at Vanderbilt University, Julius LeVonne Chambers left his law firm to serve as director-counsel of the NAACP Legal Defense Fund, and Gabrielle Kirk MacDonald, after serving as a District Court judge and a professor of law, was appointed chief judge in the Bosnian war crimes trial.

Soon after *Griggs*, the same attorneys asked me to testify in *Moody v. Albemarle Paper Company*, which elaborated the legal basis for evaluating tests. Later, I testified in *Davis v. Washington*. The Supreme Court found for the defendant in *Davis* on the grounds that, since the case was brought under the Constitution, the plaintiffs were required to show intent, which was not required under the doctrine in *Griggs*. Nevertheless, the Court let stand the principles of *Griggs* for Title VII cases.

This effort led to further testimony in more than 100 fair employment cases and participation as a temporary employee of the Equal Opportunity Commission in the writing of the *Uniform Guidelines on Employee Selection Procedures, Questions and Answers to Clarify and Provide a Common Interpretation of the Uniform Guidelines on Employee Selection Procedures, Standards for Educational and Psychological Testing*, and *Principles for the Validation and Use of Personnel Selection Procedures*.

In 1996 I edited and contributed to *Fair Employment Strategies in Human Resource Management* (Barrett 1996), which summarizes the opinions of 28 professionals in the field of fair employment. After thinking about the arcane nature of our contributions, I concluded that a more intelligible book supplementing *Fair Employment Strategies* would help personnel departments, lawyers, and the public to understand the law and the issues more fully.

I am indebted to my daughter, Laura Barrett, my wife, Shirley, and to my colleague, Donald Schwartz, for his careful reading of the manuscript and for his helpful suggestions. I, of course, remain responsible for the content.

Challenging the Myths of Fair Employment Practices

Chapter 1

Law and Regulations

BACKGROUND

Laws governing fair employment issues have been enacted since the Thirteenth and Fourteenth Amendments. Statutes 1981 and 1983 were enacted to implement the Fourteenth Amendment. The more recent and salient laws are covered here. These laws made discrimination illegal with respect to members of minority ethnic or racial groups, adherents of religious doctrines, women, the disabled, and workers more than 40 years of age up to retirement. They reflect a growing consensus in the citizenry that arbitrary discrimination based on non–job-related characteristics violates the premise that all are created equal.

Purpose

The purpose of the Civil Rights Act of 1964 was to eliminate certain practices of employment discrimination based on race, color, sex, religion, or national origin by employers, employment agencies, and labor organizations. Its predecessor, the Equal Pay Act of 1963, prohibits pay differences between male and female workers who are doing equal or substantially equal work.

Much of the ferment of the 1960s focused on civil rights, especially fair employment. Memories of the decision in a case brought under Illinois law, in the now forgotten case of *Myart v. Motorola*, were still fresh. Bryant, the hearing examiner, had made sweeping charges forbidding the use of tests as being instruments of discrimination. When Congress was debating the Civil Rights Act, representatives of employers sought to blunt Bryant's unrealistically restrictive decision. Senator John Tower proposed an amendment to Section 703(h), which was incorporated in the law. The final version of the amendment says:

nor shall it be an unlawful employment practice for an employer to give and act upon the results of any professionally developed ability test provided that such test, its administration, or action upon the results is not designed, intended, or used to discriminate because of race, color, religion, sex, or national origin.

The original amendment proposed by Senator Tower said, "design or intended to discriminate." This amendment was rejected. The words "or used" were added by Senator Humphrey as a compromise, and the amendment was approved.

The first race discrimination case to reach the Supreme Court was *Griggs v. Duke Power Company*. Duke Power had two lines of progression, one for whites who operated the power plant and one for blacks who worked in the coal yard. The highest-paid black earned less than the lowest-paid white. After the passage of Title VII, Duke Power opened the jobs in the white line of progression to those who had a high school education. Realizing that this was a difficult standard for some potentially competent applicants to meet, they offered an alternative route. Employees could be transferred to the more desirable jobs by passing two aptitude tests with a score higher than that of the average high school graduate. A handful of applicants, black and white, took the test and failed. With the backing of the NAACP Legal Defense Fund, Willie Griggs and other affected blacks sued.

Duke Power argued that they did not intend to discriminate, and besides, the tests met the standard of being "professionally developed" because they were developed by professionals. I testified that I could not look into the hearts and minds of the executives of Duke Power but that the phrase "professionally developed" in the Tower amendment could only mean that it met the standards in the then-current *Guidelines on Employment Testing Procedures* of the Equal Employment Opportunity Commission (1965) and the *Technical Recommendations for Psychological Tests and Diagnostic Techniques* (1954) of the American Psychological Association. The Supreme Court, invoking the word "used," said that the effect of the selection procedure, not the intent, was crucial and that the test user had to demonstrate job relatedness if there was an adverse impact on minorities, that is, if there was a demonstration that they were hired or promoted at a substantially lower rate than that of the non-minorities. The plaintiffs lost in the District Court and in the Appeals Court by a vote of 2–1, but won in the Supreme Court, 8–0.

The company's validity study in the next significant case, *Albemarle Paper Company v. Moody*, ran to one and one-half pages, exclusive of charts that illustrate the effect of the reported correlation coefficients. It omitted data from part of the organization, although parallel data from other parts of the organization were included. One sample had six members. The Supreme Court, determining that the company had failed to demonstrate that the tests were job-related, found for the plaintiff.

In the last case in which I testified that reached the Supreme Court, *Davis v.*

Washington, the Court found for the defendant on the grounds that, since the case was brought under the Constitution rather than Title VII, the plaintiffs were required to show intent. Nevertheless, the Court let stand the principles of *Griggs* for Title VII cases.

The standards for determining when a selection procedure should be subject to review by the courts and how the test user should demonstrate the job relatedness of the procedure as it was used were amplified in the *Uniform Guidelines on Employee Selection Procedures* (1978) and *Questions and Answers to Clarify and Provide a Common Interpretation of the Uniform Guidelines on Employee Selection Procedure* (1979). The *Standards for Educational and Psychological Testing* (1985), *Principles for the Validation and Use of Personnel Selection Procedures* (1987), and *The Ethical Practice of Psychology in Organizations* (Lowman 1998) are professional documents concerned with the validity and ethical use of the tests, not with their impact on minorities and women.

These standards differ in significant ways. The *Uniform Guidelines* are the standards by which the federal government, in its administrative and prosecutorial role, judges the legality of selection procedures for hiring, promotion, layoff, discharge, and downsizing under Title VII of the Civil Rights Act. Although the EEOC was not granted the power to make rules under Title VII, the *Uniform Guidelines* have been granted ''great deference'' by the courts and regularly figure in discrimination suits. Since they were written before the Americans with Disabilities Act, they do not address the selection problems facing disabled applicants and workers.

The *Standards* are the formal statement of three national organizations concerned with any kind of testing. They are the American Educational Research Association, the American Psychological Association, and the National Council on Measurement in Education. Part I, *Technical Standards for Test Construction and Evaluation*, covers basic psychometric issues that apply to all tests: validity; reliability; test development and revision; scaling, norming, score comparability, and equating; test publication; and technical manuals and users' guides. Part II, *Professional Standards for Test Use*, covers several uses of tests, of which those relevant to selection are general principles of test use, employment testing, and professional and occupational licensing and certification. Part III, *Standards for Particular Applications*, addresses two issues of concern to employment testing: testing linguistic minorities and testing persons with handicapping conditions. Part IV, *Standards for Administrative Procedures*, concerns test administration, scoring and reporting, and protecting the rights of test-takers.

The *Principles* are concerned only with professional standards in employment testing. Published in 1987, they are an elaboration of the *Uniform Guidelines* and the *Standards*. They emphasize the current procedures of job analysis; criterion-related, content-oriented, and construct-oriented validation strategies; validity generalization; and operational use. Since they were published before the passage of the Americans with Disabilities Act, there was no special concern for testing of the handicapped.

Both the *Standards* and the *Principles* are statements of the testing professions and have no force under law. They were written in response to the promulgation of the *Uniform Guidelines* in 1978. Both committees operated under the stricture that they were to elaborate, but not to contradict, the *Uniform Guidelines*. Because of the status of the *Uniform Guidelines*, litigants and courts rely almost exclusively on them. The professional societies that adopted the *Standards* and the *Principles* have no enforcement powers except where ethical standards have been seriously violated. The *Standards* apply directly to all tests. The *Principles* focus on employment tests. However, the rules that they lay down can be applied, with some extensions, to other selection instruments, such as interviews, performance ratings, and Assessment Centers.

The *Uniform Guidelines* are based on the premises that the purposes of both employment and certifying tests are to:

1. Offer equal employment opportunities to applicants of all racial and ethnic groups, both sexes, older workers, and the disabled.
2. Protect the rights of the test-takers.

The purposes of preemployment tests are to:

1. Identify the applicants who will become the most effective employees.
2. Enhance the profitability or effectiveness of the employer's workforce.

The purposes of licensing and certifying tests are to:

1. Protect the public from inadequately trained practitioners.
2. Enhance the ethical practices of the profession by assessing the applicants' knowledge of the ethical standards.

These objectives are sought with the underlying goal to protect the rights and privacy of the test-takers. Let us examine the objectives, point by point:

Both employment and licensing tests should:

Offer equal employment opportunities to applicants of all racial and ethnic groups, older workers, and the disabled. Society, through the enactment and enforcement of fair employment statutes and executive orders, has demonstrated a commitment to reducing discrimination in employment. There is also concern for the validity and discrimination of licensing and certifying tests, although they generally do not come under the aegis of the Civil Rights Act. Paradoxically, although in many professions employment is denied to those who cannot pass the licensing tests, the courts have often ruled that they are not employment tests covered by Title VII of the Civil Rights Act. Certification testing is subject to *Standards for Educational and Psychological Testing*. The procedures are sufficiently important, and many of them are sufficiently flawed, to merit inclusion here.

Protect the rights of the test-takers. Selection procedures are subject to restraints based on the ethics of the testing profession and, especially in the case of the Americans with Disabilities Act (1990), on the law. The Joint Committee on Testing Practices (1997) is preparing *The Rights and Responsibilities of Test-Takers* (see Appendix 1). Most of the provisions relate to employment testing. Perhaps the provision that is least applicable to preemployment testing is "have the test results explained promptly after taking the test in commonly understood terms." It is often impractical to feed back the results of testing to applicants who are turned down after having left the premises. Otherwise, they should be treated with courtesy, be informed of the test's purposes, and be assured that the test is administered, scored, and interpreted professionally and that the results are confidential.

Employment tests should:

Identify the applicants who will become the most effective employees. Different circumstances determine who are the most effective employees. Generally, the employer is interested in the performance of the employee over a career. Where training is expensive—it can take three years to train a nuclear power plant operator—the ability to absorb the technical aspects of the work may be the basic consideration, when the training emphasizes the development of the essential skills. Where training is less expensive, for example, in the hiring of trained typists, it may be important to hire those who will stay on the job long enough so that they master the routines and amortize the costs of hiring. The difference in the objectives influences the appropriateness of different selection procedures.

Enhance the profitability or effectiveness of the employer's workforce. The value of selecting effective workers generally is obvious, but there are situations, such as assessment centers, in which the cost of the selection procedure limits its effectiveness.

Licensing and certifying tests should:

Protect the public from inadequately trained practitioners. Professions are arcane; that is, people who are not trained in them are not expected to understand their intricacies. Therefore, there has been a trend to set up entrance testing to professions to make sure that the practitioners are adequately trained. Stockbrokers, insurance agents, and other specialists are tested to see if they understand the rules governing their activities. Lawyers and physicians are tested in an effort to see that they meet reasonable levels of competence.

Enhance the ethical practices of the profession by assessing the applicant's knowledge of the ethical standards. Licensed or certified practitioners are responsible for meeting the ethical standards of their professions. At a minimum they should know the rules.

Congress amended Title VII in 1972 and 1991. The Age Discrimination in Employment Act was enacted in 1967 (ADEA 1967), and the Americans with

Disabilities Act in 1990 (ADA 1990). When President Bush signed ADA into law, he said that it was one of the most important pieces of legislation enacted during his tenure in office. The present discussion concentrates on Title VII. To administer ADEA the EEOC adopted the same standards for validity set for Title VII in the *Uniform Guidelines*. Nothing is said about adverse impact determination, but the EEOC does, in fact, not apply the same rules to these charges. ADA comes under a different set of rules, which are discussed separately in Chapter 17.

Myth: *Civil rights advocates viewed Title VII of the Civil Rights Act of 1964 as a victory.* On the contrary, it was considered a defeat because of the successful resistance of those whom the temper of the times forced to enact a law that they did not want. Proponents had to accept a series of limitations that led them to call Title VII "a toothless tiger." Perhaps it was toothless, but it learned how to use its claws.

Unlike its treatment of similar commissions, such as the Federal Trade Commission, the Nuclear Regulatory Commission, and countless others, Congress granted the EEOC limited powers. Under Title VII it can promulgate regulations only in the limited arena of record keeping. It does have rule-making authority under the ADEA (Section 9) and the ADA (Section 106). Since it cannot issue regulations with the binding force of those of the Internal Revenue Service, its position paper on selection procedures is called *Uniform Guidelines of Employee Selection Procedures*, although they are published in the *Federal Register* under the heading of *Rules and Regulations*. Title VII has changed the shape of employment in this country, and the *Uniform Guidelines* have been granted "great deference" by the courts, even though reluctant endorsers of Title VII intended the law to be impotent.

The EEOC has limited enforcement powers. To be sure, some of the more significant cases have been brought by EEOC, but there are severe limitations on the use of their ability to bring charges. The Department of Justice can initiate lawsuits under Title VII, but only against governmental practices. The intention of the opponents of fair employment was to make it virtually impossible for aggrieved minorities and women to sue. However, this idea backfired because of the activity of several legal defense funds, public interest law firms, and some of the more prestigious private law firms.

Part of the reason for the rise of these advocates was the provision in Title VII that the loser of the suit had to pay the legal expenses of the winner. Without some provision for financing lawsuits, the law would have been such a sham that even its fiercest opponents could have not sanctioned its inequity. The courts have interpreted this provision to mean that the employer pays the costs if it loses. Plaintiffs pay only if the suit is frivolous. Suits were initiated under the ancient doctrine of "private attorneys-general," which provides that, where government does not enforce the law, private parties can assume the role of the delinquent government and be compensated for their contribution. Despite the efforts to weaken it by its unenthusiastic sponsors, Title VII became a potent force.

Myth: *Title VII was originally directed at unintentional discrimination.* Section 703 (h), known as the Tower amendment in honor of Senator Tower, who introduced it, uses the terms *designed, intended,* and *used. Designed* and *intended* clearly express intention. *Used* could have been construed as an extension of the concept of intention. A case could be made that *use* is synonymous with *intention.* However, in *Griggs v. Duke Power Company,* the Court fastened onto that word, deciding that intention is not essential in establishing a prima facie case of discrimination. Whatever the original intention of Congress, the ban on systemic discrimination is now settled law. The Supreme Court said:

> The Court of Appeals held that the Company had adopted the diploma and test requirements without any "intention to discriminate against Negro employees." We do not suggest that either the District Court or the Court of Appeals erred in examining the employer's intent; but good intent or absence of discriminatory intent does not redeem employment procedures or testing mechanisms that operate as "built-in headwinds" for minority groups and are unrelated to measuring job capability.

Myth: *Title VII was a coordinated attack on employment discrimination against minorities and women.* The original drafts of Title VII did not include protection for women. Certain opponents of civil rights included women to discredit the law by inserting the (to them) preposterous notion that women could be as competent as men. The American Association of University Women recognized this point, urging (Legislative History, p. 3223) Congress not to include the word "sex" in Title VII:

> In our opinion, the word "sex" in this title on discrimination is redundant and could actually work to the disadvantage of this very important legislation. We urge you to speak against this and other amendments which could weaken or impede the passage of this vital legislation which you . . . know we in the association support.

The gambit was one of the all-time strategic blunders of the right wing. Not only did it fail to discredit the legislation, but also it opened the door to better employment opportunities for women.

Myth: *Title VII places an undue burden on the very small employer.* The original act covered employers engaged in interstate commerce with more than 25 employees. This number was later reduced to 15. Mom-and-pop operations do not have to be concerned with the law regarding systemic discrimination, which is rare and difficult to prove against a small employer. Small employers are nevertheless prohibited from exercising intentional discrimination.

Myth: *Only employers are covered by the act.* Unions and employment agencies are also covered. Unions have a mixed record; some are plaintiffs, some are defendants, and others stand on the sidelines. In recent years white-dominated unions have sued for reverse discrimination. Employment agencies are rarely challenged.

The Equal Employment Opportunity Commission, the Civil Service Commission, the Department of Justice, and Department of Labor promulgated the *Uniform Guidelines on Employee Selection Procedures* (1978) and *Questions and Answers to Clarify the Interpretation of the Uniform Guidelines on Employee Selection Procedures* (1979) to establish the principles for dealing with systemic discrimination. Systemic discrimination occurs when there is a disparity in the rates of hiring, promotion, layoffs, and any other employer actions that result in an adverse impact against protected classes. The Department of Transportation, in enforcing the department's responsibilities under the Railway Labor Act, also adopted the *Uniform Guidelines*. There are no guidelines relating to intentional discrimination.

UNIFORM GUIDELINES ON EMPLOYEE SELECTION PROCEDURES

Purpose

The *Uniform Guidelines on Employee Selection Procedures* were adopted on August 25, 1978, to replace the EEOC *Guidelines* (1965) and the *Federal Executive Agency Guidelines* used by the other federal agencies. The major shift in emphasis in the *Uniform Guidelines* was to spell out the standards for reporting the data generated in studies of the results of the use of the tests. Their purpose is stated in II ADVERSE IMPACT:

The fundamental principle underlying the guidelines is that employer policies or practices which have an adverse impact on employment opportunities of any race, sex, or ethnic group are illegal under title VII and the Executive order [11246] unless justified by business necessity.

The *Standards* and *Principles* apply to all selection procedures, but the *Uniform Guidelines* come into play only when there is an adverse impact.

Myth: *The Uniform Guidelines govern only written tests*. All procedures used for selection, promotion, layoff, and discharge are subject to the *Uniform Guidelines*. Although they are often informally called the "testing guidelines," the title and content refer to "Selection Procedure," which are defined in Section 16Q as:

[a]ny measure, combination of measures, or procedure used as a basis for any employment decision. Selection procedures include the full range of selection techniques from traditional paper and pencil tests, performance tests, training programs, or probationary periods, and physical, educational, and work experience requirements through informal and casual interviews and scored application blanks.

Myth: *The Uniform Guidelines are more stringent than accepted professional standards.* I can attest that this is not so. I served on the committee that wrote the *Uniform Guidelines* and on the Ad Hoc Committee on Testing for the Society of Industrial and Organizational Psychology. The ad hoc committee formulated and presented the society's position to the committee writing the *Standards for Educational and Psychological Testing* (APA 1985). Later the committee wrote the society's *Principles for the Validation and Use of Personnel Selection Procedures* (SIOP 1987). The clear instruction to those who wrote these professional standards was that they should not contradict the *Uniform Guidelines*. There was no difficulty in meeting this requirement. In fact, much of the comment from members of the APA and the ad hoc committee was that the proposed *Standards* were too stringent when compared with the *Uniform Guidelines* and professional practice.

At this writing, a proposed revision to the *Standards for Educational and Psychological Testing* is being circulated. It is even more detailed and more stringent than the existing *Standards* and the *Uniform Guidelines*.

Myth: *The APA Standards were made excessively stringent to increase the consulting fees of those who built tests for employers.* Associate Justice of the Supreme Court Clarence Thomas, while chair of EEOC, made this assertion repeatedly. To the contrary, psychologists, including the ad hoc committee, were concerned that the difficulty of adhering to unrealistic provisions of the proposed *Standards* would destroy testing and lobbied to remove unnecessary restrictions. For example, one reviewer of the draft standards, who was accustomed to educational testing involving millions of high school students, recommended an esoteric procedure that required "only 1,000 subjects." Even giant ATT has never had a selection study involving 1,000 applicants.

Myth: *The Uniform Guidelines were developed by pointy-headed bureaucrats working clandestinely without regard for professional opinion.* The final draft was published in the *Federal Register* on December 31, 1977. Interested parties responded to the invitation to participate in the development of the *Uniform Guidelines* by letter or by speaking at an open hearing on April 10, 1978. As a member of the interagency committee that was preparing to write the final version of the *Uniform Guidelines*, I, like my colleagues, attended the meeting and read the written comments. The meetings of the committee were private, but draft material was distributed routinely to interest groups that sprang up representing business, African-Americans, and unions. Their recommendations as well as comments from other groups and individuals were carefully considered. Some, but not all, of them were accepted. The American Psychological Association was kept abreast of developments and approved the final document. When the *Standards for Educational and Psychological Testing* were revised in 1985, well after the publication of the *Uniform Guidelines*, care was taken not to conflict with them.

Myth: *Employers condemned Title VII and the Uniform Guidelines.* On the contrary, many business executives and psychologists working for employers welcomed the *Uniform Guidelines* since they provided a set of rules that removed much of the uncertainty from their understanding of their responsibilities. Beyond that, many of them wanted to eliminate discrimination, and through Title VII and the *Uniform Guidelines*, they had the mechanism to do so. Many recognized that diversity in the workforce benefited the workers and the employers. Of course, there were, and still are, some who want to perpetuate discrimination, but their numbers and influence are waning. The reaction of many employers to the publication of the *Uniform Guidelines* was similar to that of the *Daily Worker* when reviewing the writings of left-leaning authors who were not members of the party. They praised with faint damns.

Myth: *The Uniform Guidelines require that validated tests be used.* Where there is no showing of an adverse impact, the *Uniform Guidelines* do not apply. They are guidelines on discrimination in employment, not guidelines on selection procedures in general. Employers are free to use any selection procedure that does not have an adverse impact (so long at it adheres to the provisions of the Americans with Disabilities Act). Some employers complain that the government is interested only in minorities and women and not with the validity of the selection procedures. As one psychologist put it, "You can be fairly stupid if you are stupid fairly." To impose standards for all employers would be an unwarranted intrusion into the conduct of business.

QUESTIONS AND ANSWERS

Purpose

The purpose of the *Questions and Answers to Clarify and Provide a Common Interpretation of the Uniform Guidelines on Employee Selection Procedures* (Q&As) is embodied in the title. The original 90 Q&As, augmented by two additional Q&As, cover purpose and scope, adverse impact, the bottom line, and affirmative action, validity, and technical standards. The Q&As provide illustrative examples of statistics and other explanatory material that were judged to be inappropriate in the body of the *Uniform Guidelines*.

Implications

The *Uniform Guidelines* embody the federal government's position regarding selection procedures that have an adverse impact against minorities or women. Of course, the basic interpretation is made by the courts. Although the *Guidelines* are not the law, they are accorded "great deference," the Q&As are often overlooked. This twelve-page document amplifies and illustrates issues discussed in the *Uniform Guidelines*. Several of them are cited in this text.

The Age Discrimination in Employment Act (ADEA) follows the same rules for validation of tests as does Title VII, including the wholesale adoption of the validation standards of the *Uniform Guidelines*. The Americans with Disabilities

Act (ADA) has different objectives and follows a different set of rules, discussed in Chapter 17.

The *Uniform Guidelines* have lasted for 20 years without revision. They have survived two hostile administrations. They even withstood the onslaught of Associate Justice Clarence Thomas while he was the chair of the EEOC. They have been supported by the American Psychological Association, the Society of Industrial and Organizational Psychology (Division 14 of the APA), and other professional groups.

At the time of this writing, the Joint Committee on the *Standards for Educational and Psychological Testing* is preparing a revision of the *Standards*. Since the proposed revision carries on each page the prohibition DRAFT—DO NOT CITE, I do not quote it here. The portions relating to employment testing are, if anything, more detailed and more rigorous than the present *Standards*.

The EEOC periodically provides information and interpretations of the law. Some of the more recent publications are referenced in Appendix 1.

Congress amended the Civil Rights Act in 1972 and 1991 to make it stronger. Fair employment is here to stay.

Chapter 2

Test Objectives and Job Analysis

BACKGROUND

Although this book is not a text on test construction, certain principles are relevant to my purpose of describing how an interested human resources manager or line executive can evaluate the selection procedures that are under consideration.

The first step in building and evaluating tests is consideration of the objectives. The *Principles* (p. 4) state the point clearly:

Before a selection procedure is considered, or a validation effort is planned, the researcher should be able to make a clear statement of the objective of the procedure. The statement of purpose must be based on an understanding of the work performed on the job and of the needs and rights of the organization and prospective employees. There should be clear objectives for the proposed selection procedure and the validation effort should be designed to determine how well they have been achieved. Objectives should be consistent with professional, ethical, and legal responsibilities.

Job analysis is the starting point for the development and validation of a selection procedure. A selection procedure is constructed on the basis of the knowledge gained about the work combined with knowledge of psychometrics. There are many excellent books on test construction. Two of the classics are Anastasi (1982), *Psychological Testing*, and Cronbach (1970), *Essentials of Psychological Testing*, which are recommended for those who are interested in building tests rather than assessing their worth.

Purpose

The purpose of job analysis is to record the duties of the job in a job description that can be used to develop and validate the selection procedure. Job analysis is used to develop statements of Knowledge, Skill, and Ability (KSAs) needed to perform the work. The *Principles* (Job Analysis, p. 5) point out:

One purpose of the job analysis is to assemble the information needed to understand the work performed on the job and the setting in which the work is accomplished. The written documentation of the results of the job analysis usually should include a job description. The job description should communicate what the job incumbents do, the resources and tools they use in performing their jobs, and any unusual or extreme characteristics of the job setting. The job description should identify the most important and complex duties and activities.

Population and Sample

Generally, the information is collected from a sample of Subject Matter Experts (SMEs), that is, incumbents and their immediate supervisors. Others, such as training officers and technicians, may contribute. It is politic and perhaps useful to make sure that minorities and women are included. Generally, however, the job descriptions are the same regardless of the composition of the group of SMEs. I once asked African-American firefighters how the job of African-Americans would differ from that of white firefighters. The only difference that they mentioned was that the sleeping arrangements may differ with race or socioeconomic status. They never specified how they would differ or how the difference would affect the job description.

Measurement

Panels of SMEs may make several different kinds of judgments relating to the relative importance of duties, the complexity of duties, and the need for the ability to perform immediately after being assigned to the position.

As a rule, existing job descriptions are inadequate and out-of-date. Some employers avoid writing job descriptions because they do not want to be bound by what the description says. Others refuse to have job descriptions to avoid jurisdictional and other disputes. One union found the ideal way to have a strike without violating the no-strike provisions of their contract. They announced that the members would do only what their job description required. With new equipment, methods, and technology, adherence to the outdated description would have crippled the operation. Management was forced to give in and then to revise the job descriptions.

Management misses the point by refusing to prepare and update adequate job descriptions. Job descriptions should report what the incumbents do, not what they should do and not what they will do when the job is revised with changing technology. When the duties change, the job description should change. The job description does not rule what the employees do, their work activity rules the job description.

Failure to conform to this principle puts management at a disadvantage. First, they do not have a clear picture of what they are paying people for. Second, if their selection procedures are challenged, they have placed themselves in a weak position to defend them if they cannot say with authority what their employees do.

Myth: *There is one best way to conduct a job analysis.* The *Uniform Guidelines* recognize that there is no fixed procedure for analyzing a job. Incumbents, their supervisors, and sometimes staff members with related duties, such as engineers and inspectors responsible for quality control, may be interviewed. The job analyst may supplement the information gained in the interview by direct observation of physical activities where they are central to the job. It may even be necessary for the analyst to receive training in the job to understand what information the incumbent must absorb and interpret to make decisions and to take complex actions.

For complex and important jobs, it may be necessary for the job analyst to be trained in the rudiments of the job. I once needed to learn the duties of operators of nuclear power plants. Interviewing them and their supervisors, observing them at work, and reading manuals did not help, even though I had the advantage of an engineering background. At my insistence, my colleagues and I had a week's crash course in power plant operation. Half the day was spent in the classroom; half, operating a simulator. Only then did I understand what they did, the pressures under which they worked, and what a selection procedure should include.

Myth: *Frequency and importance are the same.* Often, job analysts rely on the amount of time spent on a duty to be a measure of its importance. In most circumstances they are virtually identical, but there are many exceptions. A sales representative may drive 250 miles in a day to visit a half dozen customers. The sales representative is paid to sell; driving is a trivial nuisance. The extreme disjunction between time spent and importance is found in fire fighting. Firefighters spend about 3 to 5% of their time fighting fires, but the function of a fire department is to put out fires and save lives. The importance of these functions makes the public willing to pay them when more than 90% of their time is not productive.

Myth: *A complete task analysis is required by the Uniform Guidelines for content validation.*

Task and *task analysis* are not defined in the *Uniform Guidelines*. Cascio (1982, p. 50) defines task:

A TASK is a distinct work activity carried out for a distinct purpose. Sweeping a floor, typing a letter, or unloading a truckload of freight are examples of tasks.

A task is broader than an element:

An ELEMENT is the smallest unit into which work can be divided without analyzing separate motions, movements, and mental processes involved. Removing a saw from a tool chest prior to sawing wood for a project is an example of a job element.

A duty is broader than a task:

A DUTY includes a large segment of work performed by an individual and may include any number of tasks. Examples of job duties include conducting interviews, counseling personnel, and providing information to the public.

Section 15C(3), *Job analysis—Content of the job*, states: "A description of the method used to analyze the job should be provided. ... The work behaviors [and] the associated *tasks ... should be completely described*" (emphasis added). In this context, *behavior* is not limited to physical activities or to the production of physical objects. It includes less visible activities such as those involved in analyzing problems and making decisions. Literal reading of this sentence has led to the proliferation of task analyses that are sometimes more than an inch thick and consist of thousands of bits of information. Exhaustive, detailed lists of often trivial tasks are not required by the *Uniform Guidelines*. When the members of the committee that wrote the *Uniform Guidelines* saw the mischief this sentence caused, we tried to negate its effects with Q&A 77:

Q. Is task analysis necessary to support a selection procedure based on content validity?

A. A description of all tasks is not required by the *Guidelines*. However, the job analysis should describe all-important work behaviors and their relative importance and difficulty. ... The job analysis should focus on observable work behaviors and, to the extent appropriate, observable work products, and the *tasks associated with the important observable work behaviors and/or work products* (emphasis added). The job analysis should identify how critical or important work behaviors are used in the job, and should support the content of the selection procedure.

The *Principles for the Validation and Use of Personnel Selection Procedures* of the Society for Industrial and Organizational Psychology (1987) mention "important tasks" in connection with the job analysis required for the development of a content-valid test but do not require task analysis in which every minute task is listed and rated on several scales of importance and complexity or the requirement that the task be performed on the first day of the job.

The simple rule of thumb is that a reader who is sophisticated in the world of work should understand the basic duties of the job, their importance, and complexity. This information makes it possible to determine the degree to which the selection procedure assesses applicants' ability to perform the job. A balance must be struck between such generalities as, "The police officer patrols on foot,'' and page after page of trivia that cloud, rather than enhance, an understanding of the work.

Myth: *The standards for job analysis are the same for content-and criterion-related validity and for compliance with Americans with Disabilities Act.* A detailed understanding of the work performance and work products is required for content validity, since it is essential to show that the test adequately represents the job. Such detail is not needed in criterion-related validity. Under the criterion-related validity model, the test does not need to have a manifest relation to the work. All that counts is that scores on the test be adequately correlated with the scores on some measure of work performance. The description should be sufficiently detailed to identify the job and to make sure that the jobs that are included in the study are sufficiently homogeneous to be treated alike. The job description should provide enough information about the job so that it is possible to justify the selection of the criterion measure.

Myth: *Subject Matter Experts can define the Knowledge, Skill, and Abilities required by the job.* Psychologists have long tried to develop a list of psychological attributes that would help them to develop tests that would measure the most useful psychological constructs. They have had a hard time getting past measures of general intelligence.

An example is found in *Job Analysis of the Position of New York State Trooper* (1976), prepared as part of a project conducted under the guidance of the U.S. Civil Service Commission, predecessor to the Office of Personnel Management. More than 1,400 job element statements were collected from a representative group of 155 SMEs. Diverse groups such as troopers, supervisors, and traffic safety officers, including minority group members and female police, identified similar job elements as important in determining worker effectiveness. These 1,400 elements were rated on attributes on which superior and marginal workers differed. The following were listed as ''Job Element Statements Rated High in Total Value.'' Nowhere in the report are any of these job elements defined:

Possess good judgment

Ability to assume responsibility

Possess motivation for the job

Ability to make decisions under pressure

Possess dependability

Ability to work without supervision

Have common sense

Ability to make decisions

Ability to take orders

Enthusiasm toward the job

Thoroughness

This listing is useless for writing a test (or for any other purpose). The report does not define the constructs, presents no agreed-on way to measure the applicants' possession of the Knowledge, Skills, Abilities, and Other Characteristics (KSAOs), and cites no evidence that possession of these attributes is related to success. Section 16 of the *Uniform Guidelines* defines KSAs thus:

Knowledge. A body of information applied directly to the performance of a function.

Skill. A present, observable competence to perform a learned psychomotor act.

Ability. A present competence to perform an observable behavior or a behavior which results in an observable product.

There is no definition of *Other Characteristics.*

Section 14C(4), *Standards for demonstrating content validity*, says:

In the case of a selection procedure measuring a knowledge, skill, or ability, the knowledge, skill or ability being measured should be operationally defined. In the case of a selection procedure measuring a knowledge, the knowledge being measured should be operationally defined as that body of learned information which is used in and is a necessary prerequisite for observable aspects of work behavior on the job. In the case of skills or abilities, the skill or ability being measured should be operationally defined in terms of observable aspects of work behavior of the job.

The operational definition goes back to a seminal work by a Nobel laureate in physics, Percy Bridgeman's (1924) *The Logic of Modern Physics*. He said that "a concept is synonymous with a set of operations," which, in English, means that a concept is defined in the terms of how it is measured.

For example, I helped to develop an exercise for candidates for junior and senior high school principal. Job analysis showed what is obvious to anyone even without a job analysis. Principals need to be competent in pedagogy. Reliance on that one word could lead to multiple-choice tests, interviews, or other selection procedures. We chose to define *pedagogy* operationally as the ability of the principal to observe and evaluate the classroom practices of teachers. The candidates observed a filmed class of about one half hour in length. They then wrote the type of evaluative report that they would place in the teacher's file. With this procedure laid out as an operational definition of pedagogy, an external critic would have the information needed to comment on the adequacy of the measurement.

The best-known operational definition in psychology is, "IQ is what an IQ test measures." With this definition, one can examine an IQ test and the research evidence to decide whether or not it functions properly. If one said, "Intelligence is what an IQ test measures," critics would be able to argue that the operations that define intelligence are too limited to be useful, since there is no examination of problem definition, the accretion and analysis of complex data, the actions taken on long reflection and analysis, social intelligence, and many other concepts.

I once asked a test builder in the Department of Sanitation of New York City to define ''judgment,'' since it was a construct that the test attempted to measure. He replied, ''Judgment is the ability to make decisions in practical situations.'' I asked him how that definition distinguished between the judgment exercised by a garbageman who was throwing trash in the back of a truck and the Commissioner of Sanitation, who had to decide whether to spend millions of dollars to plow the streets on a snowy Sunday afternoon. He had no answer.

Years ago, an editor of *Fortune* asked 50 chief executives to define ''dependability.'' He identified more than 50 concepts in their replies, of which ''being thereness'' was typical. Operational definitions would have pointed out the virtues and weaknesses of these definitions and the tests that are designed to measure them.

Myth: *Common American work styles are used everywhere.* Work and the ways to succeed vary tremendously from culture to culture. Mainstream Americans value speed, but some Native Americans value thoughtful analysis so much that they hold back the answer so as not to appear rash. Manual work is looked down upon in India, so many office jobs are created to satisfy the need for status. Japanese workers cooperate within their *han* (work unit), but the *hans* compete with each other. Different selection procedures are needed for the different work styles.

Implications

Perhaps the most neglected aspect of test construction is the setting of objectives. If they are discussed at all, they are often dismissed as obvious, for example, ''We want to get the best people.'' But who are the best people? Where training costs are high, quick learning is important. Nuclear power plant operators require about 36 months of intensive, expensive training. Learning the job is obviously essential, but so is a sense of responsibility that motivates them to pay attention and to take care not to make costly errors, but not so strong that it drives them, literally, to drink.

On the other hand, machine operators may require a modest amount of mechanical understanding, and clerks must learn and apply rules that seem simpler than they really are. One organization that had a large number of low-level sales jobs staffed them with low-level people. They performed satisfactorily, but ten years later there was no one to promote.

An objective that has risen in importance since the civil rights movement is that of providing opportunities to those who have previously been the objects of discrimination. This list includes not only minorities and women, who are protected by Title VII, but older workers and the handicapped. This may motivate management to undertake affirmative action programs, especially where diversity in the workforce is also an objective. Long discussions involving top

management are essential to establish job-related, socially and legally acceptable, attainable objectives.

Job analysis is part of the setting of objectives but also permeates the sub-
sequent activities in developing, administering, and acting on the results of the
tests. Professionally sound job descriptions are needed to develop tests, particularly those that are designed to tap the content of the job. Eventually (see
Chapter 7), it will be necessary to demonstrate the linkage between the test,
item by item, and the major duties of the job.

Job descriptions are also an integral part of the development and evaluation
of tests that are validated by a criterion-related strategy. While the objectives
are being set, the policymakers will determine which jobs are to be covered.
For example, general clerical work in an office may be further classified in terms
of those who deal primarily with words and those who deal with figures. Some
may spend most of their time filing; others may provide answers to customer
queries. The tests and the measures of performance may be different for members of the subspecialties or clerical workers.

Professional test development is a complex task. However, those who are not
professional test developers can judge the adequacy of the tests, in part, by
following the steps taken in their development.

Chapter 3

Non-cognitive Selection Procedures

BACKGROUND

Non-cognitive selection procedures are tests and other measures that do not directly measure cognitive ability. They are designed to measure job-relevant characteristics of the applicants and to thus improve the accuracy of prediction that can be made by cognitive tests alone. There is no bright line separating cognitive from non-cognitive selection procedures. Some selection procedures, like multiple-choice tests of job knowledge and general ability, are clearly cognitive. Others, like personality tests and honesty tests, are clearly non-cognitive. In between are such procedures as ratings, interviews, and evaluations of education and work history. These measures are classified as non-cognitive because they depend not only on intellectual ability but also on motivation, work habits, personality, and other non-cognitive factors.

Purpose

Non-cognitive selection procedures improve selection success by evaluating aspects of the work other than the knowledge and intelligence needed to perform the job duties. A classic study by Gaudet and Caril (1957) underscores the importance of non-cognitive aspects of performance of executives. He found that about 10% failed because of lack of job knowledge, and 80% from a lack of other skills such as interpersonal relations, decision making, and leadership. The remaining 10% failed for a combination of reasons.

Most of the following procedures minimize the adverse impact against minorities and women. Even if they do not eliminate adverse impact, they fulfill the requirement of the *Uniform Guidelines*.

Measurement

Non-cognitive selection procedures include (but, as they say in governmentalese, are not limited to) unscored or scored application blanks, background surveys, structured and unstructured interviews, measures of person-environment congruence, personality tests, realistic job previews (used for self-selection), Assessment Centers, and drug tests.

Non-cognitive selection procedures are more general than cognitive tests, measuring many components of performance that are not directly tied to the cognitive processes. The score assigned to an applicant may depend on subjective impressions of observers or on a formal protocol. Some, like background surveys, are scored empirically by comparing the responses of successful and unsuccessful workers.

Non-cognitive selection procedures have improved because of the natural development of a professional field and the added stimulus from fair employment. The following are described in more detail in Barrett (1996):

Work samples (Reilly 1996) permit the direct assessment of skills of experienced workers in the most realistic setting, the job. The probationary period is a classic work sample. The incumbents are observed as they perform the work and are generally evaluated after a specified period. Work samples can be as short as a few weeks or months or extend for longer periods. The evaluation of professors for tenure, which may take seven years, is perhaps the longest work sample in our culture. Work samples are limited, of course, to applicants who are already trained, or who can be trained during the probationary period. Success depends on the adequacy of the evaluations by supervisors or trainers.

Simulations (Barrett 1996) are like work samples confined to only part of the job, or which replicate critical aspects of the work. The classic simulation is the typing test. It is not a work sample because the situation is artificial, the time span is only a few minutes, and the scoring procedure is more rigorous than in the usual work sample. Simulations have developed to a point where they can sometimes be more realistic than the work itself. For example, emergencies in nuclear power plants can be realistically simulated without danger to health or safety. No simulation is perfect. The applicant always knows that it is a simulation. If something goes wrong on a flight simulator, there may be a loud sound like a crash, but the pilot always walks away. Although only part of the job can be made into a test, work samples assess present skills better than written tests. However, they can be expensive to develop and administer.

Situational judgment tests (Hanson and Ramos 1996) present realistic problems to assess the decision-making capacity of the applicants. They differ from work samples and simulations in that the problem is generally presented orally or in writing. Their most common use is for selecting managers and supervisors, but they have been used for other types of jobs such as insurance agents and police officers. Their development and use require a sound knowledge of the kinds of issues that can arise and a well-developed scoring protocol.

Interviews (Latham and Sue-Chan 1996) have long been derided as invalid attempts to assess the chemistry that exists between two people. Recently, focused interviews have been shown to be more useful than the detractors thought. Like the situational judgment tests, they require careful preparation to get and evaluate relevant information. The questions focus on interpersonal or technical skills, as well as organizational fit.

Valid interviews are based on the results of a job analysis, often using the critical incident technique. Each question presents a dilemma that forces the applicants to state their intentions rather than merely respond to what they think the interviewer wants to hear. The scoring is based on the performance style that suits the employer's environment. An answer that may be given a good score in a highly competitive culture might earn a low score in an organization that emphasizes cooperation.

Assessment centers (Henry 1996) permit the evaluation of interactive styles. Sometimes a group is given a problem to solve, and its responses are evaluated by trained assessors. A common form of assessment is the *leaderless group discussion*, in which about half a dozen applicants attack a group problem posed by the assessor. Another exercise is the *in basket test*, which presents realistic problems for solution by the applicant. They can elicit revealing insights. I once read the responses to an emergency to find out why more than half the applicants earned the lowest score. They had planned no action until it was convenient to assemble an administrative group—which would take two weeks.

Assembling and training assessors can be time-consuming and administratively inconvenient. However, assessment centers can also be used as part of an executive development procedure.

Person–environment congruence measures (Barrett 1996) evaluate the degree of fit between the worker and the job. There are several different ways to measure person–environment congruence, including the situational interview described earlier. The rationale is that the "one size fits all" approach of many tests fails to take into account the differences in organizational mission and culture. Although there seem to be some consistently valid predictors, such as conscientiousness or willingness, organizations differ so widely that performance styles that work well in one fail in another.

As an example, I developed the *Performance Priority Survey*, which asks the applicants to rate the relative importance of certain work behaviors for the job they feel competent to fill. Firefighters who ranked "Know procedures for fighting fires" low were themselves ranked low. Company officers who thought that they should counsel firefighters on family problems, a task reserved for professionals, were also ranked low. Fundamental misunderstandings of the priorities in job duties is part of poor performance. Ratings and morale are high when the applicant's performance style is suited to the requirements of the position.

Peer evaluations. Employees have the clearest understanding of the performance of their co-workers. In a classic study of Air Force Cadets, student pilots were able to identify better than their instructors those who would earn their wings in the first ten of the thirteen weeks of flight training. Their predictions were more accurate than those of the instructors even though they knew virtually nothing about flying compared to the instructors, and the instructors decided at the end of the thirteenth week which students earned their wings.

Employers are uncomfortable about relying on peer ratings because of the obvious conflict of interest of raters who are seeking the same assignments or promotion. With a proper atmosphere and motivation, co-workers can make useful judgments, but certainly their judgments cannot be conclusive.

Self-assessments. Workers are more familiar with their own work than anyone else, but they are most likely to see themselves more positively than they deserve. The Lake Woebegone effect takes over; workers rarely rate themselves below average. Reilly (1996) reports that, although there is a reasonable level of validity in experimental settings, inflation destroys the validity when they are used operationally because there is so little variability.

Academic performance. Employers regularly look at academic performance, generally at the college level, but with little evidence that grades predict performance. The problem is the same as that with cognitive tests (see Chapter 4). So much preselection has taken place that the applicants for entry-level jobs are too homogeneous to permit the variation in predictor performance needed for a demonstration of validity. There is no question that engineering training is essential to engineering performance, but no psych majors apply for engineering jobs.

Personality tests (Hogan 1996) have long been considered too subjective to be useful. However, under the stimulus of modern research some "big five" personality traits have shown useful levels of validity. The big five are Surgency (Extroversion), Emotional Stability, Agreeableness, Conscientiousness, and Intellect. The greatest of these is conscientiousness. Scores on personality tests are relatively stable, and applicants appear either not to try to slant the results or to do it poorly. Meta-analysis has shown that well-constructed personality tests add to the validity of a test battery.

Background data (Stokes and Toth 1996) have a long history of success in those organizations that are large and sophisticated enough to conduct the research. They are objective measures to which a scoring key is applied. They are similar to scored application blanks, which require interpretation of trained personnel who follow a clearly specified protocol to evaluate specifics in the applicants' past histories. In both cases, the scoring key is empirically derived by comparing the backgrounds of successful and unsuccessful employees. The scoring key developed on one sample must be verified (cross-validated) by applying it to a hold-out sample. Otherwise, chance differences between the successful and unsuccessful subjects will be interpreted as reflecting reality.

The major drawback of biodata or scored application blanks is the need for a large enough sample to provide statistically stable results. Although some critics assert that the life experiences of minorities and women differ so much from those of the predominantly white male population that is likely to be used in the development process, these procedures have less adverse impact than the critics predict.

Performance ratings. Promotions and desired assignments, as well as demotions and discharge, are based primarily on the judgments of supervisors and higher management. When done systematically, they can be content-valid; when done carelessly, they are likely to be unfair and inaccurate.

A primary concern is top management's commitment to a comprehensive and effective rating procedure that emphasizes fair and accurate judgments. Adequate performance ratings depend on a clear statement of objectives and comprehensive, up-to-date job descriptions to determine what aspects of work behavior are rated. Raters should be trained to evaluate observed performance, not speculations about underlying personal characteristics. Ratings are more accurate when the raters must justify their judgments to higher management.

Background checks. Police applicants, for example, are screened on background checks, which they either pass or fail. Since there are no additional points added to the applicants' scores based on positive background checks, they are, strictly speaking, rejection, not selection, instruments.

Tests of physical ability are clearly related to performance on some jobs but not essential on many others where they may seem appropriate. Fire fighting is a prime example of a job that requires strength, since everyone in the company can be called upon to do heavy lifting and to exert strenuous effort for long periods. On the other hand, coal mining, which seems like the epitome of hard physical labor, has some jobs underground that are not especially demanding. Physical tests are relatively easy to construct and evaluate. The requirements for strength, agility, and endurance can be determined through job analysis, and reliable tests can be constructed to measure them.

The obvious problem with physical tests is their severe adverse impact against women and, to a lesser extent, against racial and ethnic groups with smaller stature, particularly Orientals. Job redesign can sometimes minimize the need for sheer strength, but when there is no way to limit the demands, there will be an adverse impact.

Integrity tests. Integrity, or honesty, tests are popular where employee theft can be a serious drain on inventory. Most ask the applicants about behavior that might be considered dishonest. They may be asked if they ever took any of the employer's office supplies home for their own use. Since almost everyone has taken at least a pencil or a pad, most feel that it would make them look foolish to answer, ''Never.'' The question asks the amount taken and offers a range from very little to a large amount. The theory is that the applicant will try to pick some acceptable amount. Since people's standards of what is acceptable are related to what they have actually done, those who admit to larger thefts are judged to be poorer risks.

Integrity tests are attacked as being invasions of privacy. Laws are pending in some states to forbid their use as employment procedures. Employers who contemplate the use of integrity tests are advised to check with counsel before proceeding.

Drug testing (Salyards and Normand 1996) is not in the same category as the other selection procedures. It is included because drug use and abuse reflect personality orientations of the users. It is used to reject those whose efficiency is likely to be impaired by drugs. It is controversial, but the most recent research shows that it predicts job performance. There is virtually no possibility that applicants will be falsely accused.

Myth: *The backgrounds of minorities are so different from those of whites that personality tests and background surveys discriminate unfairly against them.* Personality tests have not produced meaningful racial differences. Background surveys show some differences, many of which can be eliminated without reducing the validity of the scores (Stokes and Toth 1996).

Myth: *Background surveys, application blanks, and personality tests are so easy to fake that they are useless.* Faking is much less of a problem than it seems to the naked eye. Countermeasures are available that reduce the tendency to present oneself in the best light. Questions that emphasize verifiable information, even if checking is difficult, curb the applicants' tendency to exaggerate. Although background surveys and personality tests may seem transparent to the sophisticated human resource manager, they are not so obvious to the naive applicant.

Myth: *I can tell a good man by the cut of his jib.* Unstructured interviews have a long history of invalidity. Casual interviews are little better than the greasy palm test (some judge a weak, moist handshake to be a sign of nervousness that disqualifies the applicant). However, structured interviews and oral examinations help to identify the better applicants.

Myth: *Interviews are worthless.* The conventional wisdom in industrial psychology has, for a long time, asserted that the interviews relied on by so many executives do little more than make the employer comfortable with the decision. However, focused interviews, in which the interview questions and the protocol for evaluating the responses relate directly to the organizational needs and ethos, are valid. Hanson and Ramos (1996), and Latham and Sue-Chan (1996) describe effective interview procedures.

Myth: *Drug testing is so unreliable that the employer has no defense against a suit from disappointed applicants.* On the contrary, the standards for certified drug testing centers are so high that there is virtually no possibility that an applicant who is truly free of drugs would be disqualified (Salyards and Normand 1996).

Myth: *Analysis of handwriting reveals the inner psyche.* Perhaps so, but there is scant evidence that it helps to predict job success, despite enthusiasm in some European countries and among a few gullible executives in the United States. Handwriting analysis comes from an era when psychologists and laymen alike believed in phrenology. A phrenological bust (Fowler n.d.) bears this endorsement, for which there is no evidence:

For thirty years I have studied Crania and living heads from all parts of the world, and have found in every instance that there is a perfect correspondence between the conformation of the healthy skull of an individual and his known characteristics.

There is little more evidence for handwriting analysis. *Caveat emptor.*

Myth: *The validity of a personality test can be demonstrated by feeding back the results of an analysis to the person who took the test.* I demonstrated the fallacy of this approach in a seminar of human resources trainees. I had them complete a phony personality test in which they were asked to draw a worker and then to draw another worker of the opposite sex. I fed back the results with a checklist made up of statements like, "I haven't gotten as far as I expected to" and "Sometimes I drive too fast." When I handed back the results, some thought that I had hit the mark 20 out of 20 times. One skeptic said that it sounded like a horoscope. Of course, she was right. The feedback sheets were all the same.

Myth: *If you want to learn about the performance of an experienced applicant, just call the previous employer.* Some employers, fearing a law suit, do no more than verify the dates of employment. Others, motivated by the same fear or unwilling to jeopardize the career of even unsatisfactory employees, will report only positive information, avoiding harsh truths. As a result, getting unbiased information is difficult. If the recommendation is negative, you cannot be sure that it is not an expression of antipathy between the supervisor and the subordinate that results from the supervisor's deficiencies, not those of the applicant. For these and other reasons, most sophisticated employers do not seek information from previous employers beyond the basic dates of employment and position level.

One word of warning. One employer who gave a reference for a man who had been accused of rape did not tell the inquiring organization about the incident. Unknowingly, the new employer assigned him to work alone at night with a woman, whom he raped. She sued the previous employer successfully for placing her in jeopardy. Given the prohibition on using arrest records in selection on the grounds that a person is considered innocent until proven guilty, anyone in a similar situation would profit from the advice of competent counsel.

Myth: *Integrity testing reduces employee theft.* There is some evidence that integrity tests identify potentially dishonest employees. However, it is so difficult to collect information about thievery from those who are doing their best to hide their inappropriate behavior that the results are suspect. Further, organizations that are sufficiently concerned to conduct a research study relating to integrity tests generally take other measures, such as improving security and using other forms of screening, so that the criterion measures are contaminated.

There is also the nagging question, Is it acceptable for the potential employer to put applicants in a position of condemning themselves? The typical honesty test asks applicants if they ever participated in dishonest acts ranging from taking pencils home to substantial theft. The theory is that everyone will recognize some peccadilloes as trivial and admit to them rather than look foolishly goody-goody. Their problem arises when they are asked if they have committed greater transgressions. The threshold between minor, socially acceptable misconduct and serious wrongdoing is surprisingly variable. Those who admit to looser standards are expected to exhibit these standards on the job by converting the company's goods or assets to their own use. Some states are contemplating laws that would outlaw integrity tests, so it is best to check with counsel before using them.

Myth: *Objective measures are useful predictors.* Objective measures are appealing because they seem to provide a completely unbiased, valid measure of performance. The person who makes the most widgets should be promoted to the senior widget-maker position or to foreman. So runs the fiction. The first fiction is that dozens of people make widgets. Generally, when more than five persons use a machine to perform the same operations, someone either buys a more advanced machine or divides up the work assignments differently. Under union rules the senior workers may get the best machines and the easiest assignments. Of course, there are exceptions; there may be 50 clerks in a credit card company performing the same operations, but such examples are rare.

The business of the salesman is to sell, the reasoning goes; therefore, sales volume is a perfect measure of success. However, most sales personnel are assigned to districts that vary in potential and the effects of competition. House accounts negotiated at higher levels skim the cream, which may or may not be credited to the salesperson assigned to that area. One manufacturer of goods sold in supermarkets even contemplated doing away with the sales force by linking the supplier's computer to the customer's computer. Some sales departments have staffs whose entire task is to restructure sales territories to equalize them. Some sales personnel concentrate on today's sales, but others build customer relations to make for better market penetration five years later. There is some truth to the wheeze that by promoting the salesperson with the best sales record the company loses a good seller and gains a mediocre sales manager.

Myth: *Education is good; therefore, an employer should give credit for formal courses taken by employees or require them for promotion.* Education is a benefit to the student and to society, but not necessarily to the employer. Before giving credit for education, the employer should make sure three points are covered so that the credit granted for education is job-related:

1. The information taught must be directly useful to the employer. Courses in medieval needlework may enhance the applicant's appreciation of the arts, but if the training is not directly job-related, learning the material is of no real consequence to the employer.

2. The information imparted in the course must augment, not repeat, what was already in the individual's repertoire from experience or training.

3. The person seeking the credit must have demonstrated proficiency in what was taught. Simply sitting in the classroom is not enough.

Myth: *Low ratings of minorities, women, and older workers are evidence that the ratings are unfair.* Not necessarily. Black supervisors sometimes rate their black subordinates more severely than their white counterparts. Older workers may, in fact, be less effective than when they were younger. When ratings are based on observed behavior that is relevant to the job, and raters are motivated to give accurate ratings by having to explain them, with examples, to skeptical supervisors, they may be successfully defended against charges of discrimination. Focused ratings collected for a specific purpose, such as downsizing, provide the best and fairest information that is available. Routine administrative ratings are often worthless because of the complex pressures that impinge on the raters.

Myth: *Senior employees are the best candidates for promotion.* Most promotion procedures require some experience on the lower-level job, making a judgment of a lack of experience a rejection procedure. Sometimes points are added for seniority, in which case seniority becomes a combination selection and rejection procedure. Although no one would promote someone who did not have a chance even to learn the job duties, relying heavily on seniority to assign the worker to the more difficult job or to make promotions and automatically promoting workers with seniority is unwise. After a few months or years on the job, the incumbent does not learn any valuable new skills and may, in fact, become rigidly attached to antiquated methods. Furthermore, seniority unfairly penalizes minorities and women who have entered the workforce in large numbers too recently to have accumulated the necessary tenure.

Myth: *Projective tests provide useful insights not available through other means.* Projective tests, like the Rorschach ink blots or the Thematic Apperception Test, have been generally abandoned in personnel selection because of their dismal record as predictors of job performance. Much of the research was performed without the kind of exploration of job duties and requirements typified by the interviews and situational tests described earlier. As a result the protocols of the tests were evaluated on the basis of standards that did not relate to the work.

For example, according to the cliché, successful salesmen are outgoing extroverts who like people. Other observers believe that they are really introverts who get their pleasures from manipulating the customers, whom they really don't like. Which of these hypotheses, or more sophisticated hypotheses, would shed useful light on the selection process is typically not explored. An exception may be the Miner Sentence Completion Scale (Miner 1985), which was developed for use in selection.

Myth: *"There are no right or wrong answers to this personality test. What is right for you is right."* Nonsense. The first thing the psychometrist does is to apply a scoring key and look up the applicant's standing on the norm tables. It is better simply to advise applicants that they are asked to respond to a systematic procedure for describing themselves as part of the selection process.

The statement violates the spirit of Ethical Principle 6.15, Deception in Research (a), which says:

Psychologists do not conduct a study involving deception unless they have determined that the use of deceptive techniques is justified by its . . . value and that equally effective alternative procedures that do not use deception are not feasible.

Implications

Non-cognitive selection procedures have blossomed in recent years and are increasingly recognized as valid predictors of later performance. Most of them (tests of physical strength are an exception) have a lower adverse impact on minorities and women than do cognitive tests, particularly multiple-choice tests of aptitude or achievement. Their proper use requires more attention than the administration of an off-the-shelf intelligence test, but they provide insights that go beyond intelligence or job knowledge.

There some possible pitfalls to be avoided. The interview is a socially sensitive procedure that is subject to legal restraints on both the federal and state level. A manual, *The Legality of Pre-Employment Inquiries* (Ash 1989), contains lists of "permissible or legal and impermissible or illegal questions" under Title VII and ADEA. Some specific restraints on the interview and the application blank with respect to hiring disabled workers are discussed in Chapter 17.

Some interviews and questionnaires can be viewed as intrusive. Evidence that they work is not enough to satisfy disgruntled applicants. If the procedure does not have face validity, that is, if it doesn't give the superficial impression that it measures something important, it may meet with resistance. Lack of face validity is especially important in promotion tests because those who are passed over may feel that they have a legitimate complaint. Sticking to job-related issues not only is politic but can be expected to yield more useful information.

The "Ethical Principles of Psychologists and Code of Conduct" of the American Psychological Association (1992) addresses some issues relating to cognitive tests.

Chapter 4

Cognitive Tests

BACKGROUND

Cognitive tests are those tests most closely allied with intellectual functioning. They may measure intellectual functioning directly or may measure the results of applying intellect, such as job knowledge, rules of grammar, or electronics. They range from tests designed to be pure tests of intelligence to tests of specific knowledge, such as the subject matter of engineering specialties. The simplest measure that correlates with general intelligence is vocabulary.

Debates flourish about cognitive tests. It was once felt that intelligence was an innate, unchanging characteristic, but that view has suffered from evidence of changes resulting from nutrition, stimulation, and exposure to material similar to that included in the test. The most common theory is that there are a *g* factor of general intelligence and several specific aptitudes. It is not my purpose to debate this issue here; the controversy, although important theoretically, is of little relevance to employment testing.

Cognitive tests incorporate a scoring key applied in a systematic way to measure intellectual functioning. There are right and wrong answers based on the reality of the situation as perceived by the test writer. The tests are judged for a given population on how well they measure the applicants' intellectual ability, what they have learned, or how they solve real-world problems.

The lineage of aptitude tests goes back to the Army Alpha and Beta used in World War I and the Army General Classification Test (AGCT) used during World War II to assign recruits to the appropriate billets. The AGCT was a spiral omnibus test. It had successive sections testing verbal, numerical, and spatial aptitudes with progesssively harder questions. Despite complaints that cowboys were assigned to the motor pool, and mechanics were sent to the cavalry, they provided useful information for making assignment decisions.

Aptitude tests have been subject to meta-analytic studies, which combine the results of many smaller studies to permit the generalization that they are useful predictors of later performance. There remains some dispute of how valuable they are and how universal the adequacy of prediction is, but they generally contribute to the validity of any selection battery.

Purpose

The purpose of cognitive tests is to identify the applicants who have the knowledge necessary to do the work or have the intelligence to learn it. Most cognitive tests use the multiple-choice format, which is so pervasive that it is discussed separately in Chapter 5. In some simulations, the applicant performs some major job duties under test conditions.

Population

Employers use intelligence tests primarily for screening or selecting entry-level candidates for lower-level positions. The widely used General Aptitude Test Battery (referred to by its acronym, the GATB, pronounced GAT-BEE) was developed by the Department of Labor. It is administered by state employment offices, which submit the results to private employers, who use them to screen some applicants and to help in the selection decision. Measurements of specialized skills, such as clerical and mechanical aptitude tests, are also used with applicants who may not have any relevant experience.

The GATB was developed by the U.S. Employment Service, a branch of the Department of Labor, and is administered by state employment offices. The results are used by private employers as a screen when the high scorers are referred to them, and the scores may be used in a selection battery.

Tests of acquired knowledge are appropriate for entry-level selection only when the employer can expect the applicant to have had the education or training needed to take the test. High school graduates should know how to spell and can be appropriately tested for that knowledge if spelling is important to the job. Applicants for bookkeeping or other positions for which applicants claim that they have the appropriate training can be tested for their ability to make the appropriate entries and, of course, perform relevant arithmetic.

Civil service uses cognitive tests for promotion more than do private employers. Some promotion tests even contain a disclaimer guaranteeing that the promotions are determined only by test scores. Years of faithful and effective service do not count. Few private employers engage in this folly, but it has grown up in civil service because of the ever-present fear that promotion as well as selection decisions will be tainted by undue political influence.

Measurement

Most, but not all, cognitive tests are multiple-choice tests. Others use free answers to record the solutions to problems. Some performance tests are designed specifically to test the knowledge required by one job, such as bookkeeper or fire lieutenant.

No one can draw a clear line between cognitive and non-cognitive tests. All tests involve some cognition, and cognitive tests often have non-cognitive aspects. For example, speeded tests of cognition also involve the ability to react quickly without succumbing to test pressure and the ability to budget one's time.

Test theory calls the two basic types of cognitive measures, aptitude and achievement tests. They, too, are not as distinct as it might seem. Aptitude is considered an innate ability, but it generally cannot be tested without mastery of some material that must be learned or without controlling for the influence of cultural background that modifies the responses. Once upon a time psychometricians accepted the theory that everyone has had the same exposure, for example, to standard English vocabulary, so they assumed that the more rare or complex words the applicant could identify, the greater the level of native verbal ability. Evidence of the impact of inferior education, anti-intellectual social pressures, and foreign language background has led to the realization that all tests depend, to a large measure, on the cultural and education background of the test-taker. Of course, a large vocabulary depends largely on native ability, but there are too many extraneous influences to permit a vocabulary test to be the sole measure even of verbal aptitude. Besides, language skills involve more than the vocabulary needed for solving crossword puzzles.

Achievement tests are designed to measure how much the applicant has learned of what is required for performing the work as well as the ability to apply this knowledge on the job. The resulting performance depends both on the native ability supposed to be the province of aptitude tests and on the ability to perform adequately using the specific information. The difference between aptitude and achievement tests depends on the relation of the content of the test and the job.

There is more evidence regarding the validity of oral tests than there is for essay examinations. Both suffer from limited reliability, but with better structure, reliability improves. (See Hanson and Ramos 1996; Latham and Sue-Chan 1996.)

Simulations range from extraordinarily accurate electronic simulations, through paper-and-ink representation of problem situations, to multiple-choice problems stated in a sentence or two. *Work samples* are similar to simulations. Since there is always something artificial about work sample tests, even the traditional typing test, there is no point in trying to distinguish between simulations and work samples. What counts are the adequacy of the simulation and the validity of the measures taken from the applicant's performance.

The *purpose* of simulations is to decide whether or not the applicants can perform the duties required by some important aspect of the job. The effort is to reproduce as nearly as possible the stimuli that the incumbent would receive on the job and to make the response reflect how the applicant actually would respond on the job.

Population usually comprises applicants who have training and experience in the work. Simulations are therefore most useful in promotion or in the hiring of experienced applicants who have specific backgrounds.

Measurement is generally made by observing performance in response to a problem posed on either the actual equipment, simulated equipment, or a verbal or diagrammatic representation of it.

Reilly (1996) states that simulations are as valid as intelligence tests and have less adverse impact. Because of their face validity, they are easier for applicants and the courts to accept as reasonable selection procedures.

Myth: All intelligence tests are valid predictors in all circumstances. IQ tests have mixed results in practice (Schmitt 1996), and when they are valid, there is still much of the performance that is not predicted. There is no substitute for a brain, but brains are not everything. Every job involves cognition, some more than others, but every job requires non-cognitive behavior to use the cognition. It is a tribute to psychometricians who have developed the tests that they work as well as they do.

Intellectual power is so important that it is used to sort out people even before they start their formal education. Once in school, they soon learn which reading group they are in even if they are not given such transparent names as the "Smart Foxes" or the "Dumb Bunnies." Later, students are tracked in most educational systems. When they get to high school, they have course options that separate the talented from the poor learners. Some drop out of high school because the work is too intellectually demanding. After high school, college and graduate school further refine the status of those who later apply for work. The result is restriction of the range of abilities found in the applicants for any job.

A test is useful only when it contributes information that is not already available from another, more accessible, and, in many cases, less discriminatory source. In employment, preliminary decisions are made from academic achievement. Both extent and relevance of educational success determine, in large measure, the jobs for which one will apply, and academic achievement is used by employers to narrow the field. The Scholastic Aptitude Test (SAT) would seem to have the easiest job of prediction. It is an academic test used to predict academic performance. There is some method variance since most first-year students have had at least one course in which the major source of grades is multiple-choice tests. (Method variance refers to that part of the test score that depends on the testing method. People who are good at multiple-choice tests will perform better than those who are poor at them, even if they have the same information and skills.) Even so, the correlation between SAT scores and first-year students' grades varies around 0.40. To some extent the predictive power of the SAT is limited by restriction of range. The mix of students going to a community college is different from that of Ivy League schools, so the test scores of applicants to either kind of school do not cover the whole range. It is remarkable that intelligence tests work as well as they do when the effects of prior selection are taken into account.

Myth: *Tests measure what they appear to measure*. The classic example of a one-factor test, that is, a test that measures only one attribute, is the spatial relations test. One type requires that the test-taker visualize the three-dimensional object that is the stimulus of the test and recognize how it would look in another position. Some subjects who are weak in spatial relations compensate for their weakness at visualization by approaching the problem as a reasoning test.

Myth: *The major cause of failure is lack of job knowledge*. Gaudet and Caril's (1957) *Why Executives Fail* found that about 80% of failures came from deficiencies not related to job knowledge.

Myth: *If you can do it, you can verbalize it*. Sometimes. However, many skills depend on a nonverbal feel for the situation. The explanations by many artists of the meaning of their work are often opaque. Both mechanics and cardiologists can diagnose flaws in the function of the mechanism that they are studying through subtle differences in the sound, a skill that can be acquired only by practice. In attempting to computerize the reading of X-rays, physicians told the programmers what they looked for. Their procedures were programmed successfully for many types of problems. After several iterations, the procedure worked very well, but there were still cues used by the radiologists that they were never able to verbalize.

Myth: *People who know what to do will do it*. Every police officer knows that it is contrary to the rules to take bribes or cadge a drink at the local bar while in uniform, but some do. Knowing that the mission of the firefighter is to put out fires and save lives does not mean that some will not look for the safe assignment. The ethical requirements of the bar examination does not guarantee a nation of moral lawyers.

Myth: *Asking for reasons behind actions improves a test*. It is a canon of conventional wisdom and psychology that knowledge of how things work leads to better performance. Generally, but not always. Many excellent drivers do not understand the workings of the internal combustion engine, much less the automatic transmission. Mechanics and racing car drivers profit from this understanding more than the casual highway motorist. It is important to turn in the direction of a skid, but one does not necessarily have to know that the coefficient of static friction is greater than the coefficient of sliding friction to handle a car on a slippery pavement. Those with the feel for starting on an icy surface by applying as little power to the wheels as possible may never have heard of the coefficient of friction.

It is generally true that people do better when they understand what they are doing, but the depth of understanding that is tested must be appropriate to their tasks. The operators of nuclear power plants need to have deep understanding of the plants and a working knowledge of nuclear physics, but they are not nuclear scientists. Operators who work solely by rote can probably handle control functions and minor transients, but when several failures occur at once, valves stick, and meters give incorrect information or no information at all, a clear understanding of the plant is required. However, questions that ask about newly created elements with half-lives measured in microseconds do not help to identify the better power plant operators unless these elements impinge on the reactions they are monitoring.

Some jobs, particularly those at a higher level, require that the incumbent give an account of the reasons behind an action. A job-related test of understanding would be appropriate. The point of this discussion is that tests designed to tap the applicant's understanding of the work must be scrutinized carefully to make sure that understanding is necessary, that the level of understanding is appropriate, and that there is solid reason to believe that understanding is meas ured in a relevant way.

Scoring a test of understanding poses serious difficulties. How does one score a correct action if the applicant gives no reason or a faulty explanation for the action? In most situations employees are paid to do the work correctly. If there are enough questions that the applicants cannot score well by blind luck, they cannot keep getting right answers without having some understanding of what they are doing. It is difficult to justify penalizing applicants who give the right answers for the inability to articulate a reason. On the other hand, should one get credit for giving a correct reason but then doing the wrong thing?

Myth: *More intelligence is better.* Not necessarily. I once worked with a company that divided its sales force into two groups, career sales agents, who were expected to sell soap and syrup in supermarkets as long as they could drive from store to store, and development sales agents, who were expected to sell successfully for a few years and then move into management or marketing. Intelligence tests did not work for the development sales agents. They were highly selected college graduates who had the smarts that they needed; success came from other sources. The career sales agents, on the other hand, illustrated the significance of intelligence. Based on empirical evidence, both upper and lower limits were placed on the range of acceptable scores. If the score was too low, they could not master the job. If it was too high, they were overqualified. People with a tested intelligence of 120 who want to sell soap all their life have something wrong with them. The distinction between the two career paths is illustrated by the scored application blank. Interest in the arts—music, dance, and the like—was a positive indicator for the development sales agents and a negative indicator for the career sales agent.

Myth: *Oral responses are needed to overcome deficiencies in writing skills of minorities.* I conducted one study that showed that short-answers do not necessarily place blacks at a disadvantage. Because of administrative considerations, it was possible to compare oral responses to a simulation with the written notes on which the applicants relied while responding orally into a tape recorder. The results were essentially identical for all applicants in the sample.

Myth: *A passing score of 70% is about right.* We have all been educated in schools in which 70% was considered an acceptable score, even where 60% would earn a D. This has led to the practice of setting passing scores at 70% correct. By itself, this standard is meaningless, because test items can be made so hard that no one would achieve 70% correct or so easy that everyone would pass. Sometimes testers misjudge the difficulty of their test so badly that, when there are not enough who passed to fill the vacancy, they must shame-facedly lower the passing score.

The *Uniform Guidelines* is little help. Section 15C(9), *Uses and applications*, says: "If the selection procedure is used with a cutoff score, the user should describe the way in which normal expectations of proficiency in the work force were determined and the way in which the cutoff score was determined."

There is no standard, approved way to set a passing score. Passing scores that eliminate a large portion of minority applicants, keeping them from recouping their losses in later parts of the selection procedure, are worthy of close scrutiny.

Myth: *Face validity enhances the validity of the test.* Making a test look reasonable on its face does not make it valid. It should be unnecessary to mention this point, since face validity is the superficial appearance of validity rather than true validity. However, item writers try to enhance the validity of their tests by making them face-valid. For example, a question that asks, "Police officers are not allowed to accept gratuities. 'Gratuities' means . . ." is a vocabulary test, not a test of policing. One question asked police candidates how much a given quantity of bullets would cost if bullets cost $.06 each. The court noted that by changing the wording to ask about Bibles rather than bullets, the same question could be used to select nuns. Face validity may make the tests more acceptable and motivate the applicant, but it is not validity.

Implications

There is no doubt that aptitude and achievement make a positive contribution to the selection and assignment of applicants. The amount of contribution varies with circumstances such as the intellectual demands of the job, the homogeneity of the applicants, and the importance of personal characteristics other than intelligence. There is still enough doubt about the ability of the tests to predict success in a given situation to merit local validation when possible (Schmitt 1996).

Unfortunately, these tests, especially multiple-choice tests, have a severe adverse impact against minorities. Attempts have been made through internal analysis of the tests to eliminate the items that have the severest adverse impact, but there is always a residual impact. The topic is discussed in more detail in Chapters 12 and 13.

Chapter 5

Multiple-Choice Tests

BACKGROUND

Multiple-choice tests are pervasive in our culture. Many cognitive tests, discussed in Chapter 4, are multiple-choice tests. Multiple-choice tests are considered separately here because their format and other characteristics set them apart from essays, interviews, and other testing procedures.

They are used because they appear to measure important KSAs cheaply and efficiently. The typical multiple-choice test consists of a stem, which may be the first part of a sentence, that presents a situation or asks a question. Generally there are four or five response options. One, designed to finish the sentence or answer the question correctly, is called the wanted answer. The others are called distractors or misleads.

Some multiple-choice tests are speeded to determine how fast the applicants can respond. Most, however, have such generous time limits that almost everyone finishes with ample time to check the answers. Nevertheless, many applicants feel pressure from multiple-choice tests that causes them to blow questions to which they really know the answer.

Multiple-choice (often called by their detractors *multiple-guess*) tests are used more by civil service jurisdictions than by private employers as the primary selection procedure. They are often used for promotion decisions in fire and police departments and other sites where unions are strong enough to impose their will that no decisions may be made based on ratings of performance. In some jurisdictions, once a candidate for promotion has served long enough in the lower rank, the rank order list resulting from the multiple-choice test is the sole determiner of who is to be promoted. Quality of job performance does not count.

Part of the heavy use of multiple-choice tests is due to the tremendous volume of tests required in some jurisdictions, both in the number of separate jobs for which tests must be developed and in the number of applicants that may take one test. Furthermore, multiple-choice tests are cheap to write, administer, and score. Building a test costs little, especially when there is an item bank from which to draw. Multiple-choice tests are often cobbled together from item pools shared by different jurisdictions by an almost automatic procedure that relies on a computerized selection of the items. Test-scoring machines score tests for pennies apiece and can produce results in a few days even when the candidate pool exceeds 20,000 candidates.

A fundamental problem with multiple-choice tests is that the number of questions that can be asked is limited. Where promotion tests are given frequently, the supply of unique bits of information available begins to run dry. Repeating items is risky if old copies of the tests get out, or if the concerted efforts of a few good memorizers provide a reasonable approximation of a series of tests. The result is similar to the fraternity files of old exams in college courses. Savvy students have an advantage of knowing what the tests are likely to cover, so they study the test rather than the job.

Purpose

Generally the purpose of multiple-choice tests is to measure intelligence or aptitudes or the prior acquisition of knowledge, skills, and abilities in a convenient format that systematizes the testing process and makes scoring easy and accurate.

Population

Multiple-choice tests are used at the entry level for many government jobs and for promotion in some of them. They are more generally used for jobs populated mostly by high school graduates. Selection for professional civil service jobs is sometimes based, in part, on multiple-choice tests, but most are filled by unassembled tests, that is, examination of educational and other credentials, interviews, and references. Multiple-choice tests of job knowledge are also used by private employers and for licensing and credentialing. The highest-level widespread use of multiple-choice tests is the Multi-State Bar Examination.

Measurement and Data Collection

For administrative convenience and to foster security, civil service tests are generally administered simultaneously to all of the applicants for hiring or for promotion. Where the number of applicants is small, as in many private organizations, tests may be administered individually. Interactive testing using computers also uses the multiple-choice test format. There is increasing use of computerized testing in which applicants are tested at their convenience. Often these tests are interactive in that, if the applicant gets several correct in a row, the test skips to a higher level of questioning.

Analysis

Once a multiple-choice test has been administered and scored, the results can be analyzed statistically to identify possible flaws. One such analysis, item difficulty, is discussed later. There are other indicators available in most commercial statistical packages. There is little agreement on the satisfactory level of these statistics, but examination of a whole set of data on a test can help to identify problem items.

They include:

Reliability. Well made multiple-choice tests are reliable. When one-half of the test is compared with the other, the reliability is likely to fall between .85 and .95, a more than satisfactory level.

Item–test correlation. There should be a modest positive correlation between the test and the item. Very low or negative correlations indicate that the item is not contributing to the total score.

Item response rate. Sometimes the distractors attract more responses than the wanted answer, suggesting that there is something wrong with the item.

Differential item response rate. Rarely, there is so much difference between the responses of minorities and non-minority applicants to suggest that there is some flaw in the item.

Difficulty. Some items are so easy that they attract too many responses, as many as 90%. Such items just take up space, since they do not differentiate between candidates. Easy items are sometimes placed early in a test booklet to remove the pressure that would come from a series of items that an applicant could not answer. Some items are too hard.

What follows is a somewhat cynical description of steps followed by countless multiple-choice test writers over the years:

1. Write a brief description of the job and the KSAs presumed to be important for job performance. Collect information on the relative importance of the job duties and the KSAs.

2. Find training manuals, rules, personnel policies, and other documents relating to the aspects of the job to be tested.

3. Find a sentence that discusses something that seems relevant. The first part, called the stem, states the problem. The rest of the sentence is the wanted answer. When the stem is read with the wanted answer, the original sentence is manifestly correct because it came from a formal document. Alternatively, pose a question to form the stem and follow it with the wanted answer, which is designed to be the correct response.

4. Conjure up some distractors, that is, incorrect answers. They should be wrong, but close enough to being correct to mislead the uninformed.

5. Edit the items to make sure that they meet item-writing standards and apply a reading difficulty formula to make sure that the language is not too complex for the applicants.

6. Assemble the test.

7. Administer the test.

8. Score the test.

9. Conduct an item analysis.

10. Conduct other internal analyses.

Let us examine these steps one by one.

1. It is relatively easy to describe the job duties, their relative importance, and level of complexity, but it is difficult to identify and define the KSAs.

2. Manuals, policies, regulations, and so on are slender reeds on which to depend. Generally, they deal with specialized vocabulary, basic concepts, and other classroom-oriented information. What is generally lacking in tests is the measurement of hands-on, practical experience that goes beyond the basic material to its application in the real world.

3. Finding relevant material is harder than it sounds. Much covered is so basic that it becomes second nature with training and experience and is not difficult enough to distinguish among test-takers. More obscure information is appealing to the item writer because it is certain that some will not have the information, but if it is so obscure, there may not be a good reason to test for it. Training manuals quite properly provide explanatory material and information that are nice to know but are not about the applicant's performance on the job. It may be nice to know who appoints the commissioner, but possession of that information does not affect the applicant's job performance. Testing should be confined to information where there is a need to know, not just where it is nice to know.

4. Distractors are difficult to prepare because, typically, the item writers are not trained in the job for which they are writing items, and they do not know what kinds of mistakes applicants are likely to make. It is hard to find three attractive distractors. Only about 5% of the applicants pick the most unpopular alternative in a four-option test.

5. Items are edited, and sometimes measures of reading difficulty are computed.

6. Assembling the test requires matching of the test to the job so that the coverage on the test matches the importance of the job duties. One seaport, which has only one fireboat in action at one time, devoted almost 25% of the test to the operation of the boat. The rationale for using the questions about the boat is simple. The questions were specific, and there would obviously be a spread of scores since many did not know what the test items were talking about because they did not have to. The test was judged to be invalid.

7. Administering tests should be routine but often isn't. Unclear instructions or clear

instructions that are misread cause questions that monitors may answer incorrectly. If the test is given is several rooms or at different times, the same questions may be answered differently.

8. Tests given to large numbers of applicants are scored by specialized computers. However, disgruntled applicants who challenge answers they believe to be incorrect may prevail, requiring a wholesale rescoring.

9. There are several programs for analyzing item responses. They generally record the number and percentage of responses to each item, item–test correlation, and sometimes differences between racial or ethnic groups. When the percentage of correct responses is too low, the item may be difficult or scored incorrectly. If the item does not correlate with the total score, it may be that it is not related to the rest of the test.

10. Two other analyses are sometimes used but are of real interest only to psychometricians. The first is an internal analysis designed to identify the items that have the most adverse impact in a test. The second, more esoteric, is the analysis of item response curves. To compute and interpret these statistics, the person who is not a professional psychometrician will need the help of a professional.

To explain some problems with multiple-choice tests, I illustrate some myths by quoting items taken from tests that have been the subject of litigation and have been found wanting by the courts or by defendants who settled. Since it is not my purpose in this chapter to point the finger at anyone, the sources are not identified unless the opinion of the court is cited.

Myth: *Multiple-choice tests adequately represent real-life situations.* Consider this item prepared by the U.S. Civil Service Commission for a test developed for a state police force. It does not come from the test, since the test is secure. It was published in the report submitted to the court to illustrate the kinds of questions used in the test. The item was defended as job-related because it represented a real incident:

You are a Trooper working on the Thruway and stop a car for speeding. As you are obtaining the license and registration from the motorist, another car, containing six occupants, two of whom are children, pulls up behind the first car and stops. Three of the adults from this car run from the car and assault you, knocking you to the ground. They take your revolver and begin to kick you repeatedly.

1. When a passing motorist stops, ask him to come to your rescue. [Assuming, of course, that a passing motorist will stop and would come to your rescue.]

2. Yell at passing motorists to call the station for help. [The test was used before cellular phones were common, so calling for help might have to wait while the motorist found a telephone miles down the road. The applicant must assume that at 55+ miles per hour they can hear you even with windows closed because the heaters or air conditioners are in operation.]

3. Remain silent on the ground and pretend you are unconscious. [While three psychopaths are kicking you.]

4. Ask the motorist whom you originally stopped to help you to fight them. [Even if she is a 95-pound grandmother on the way to a christening.]

5. Yell at passing motorists to stop and help. [See # 2 and 4.]

6. When a passing motorist stops, ask him to call for help. [See #1 and 2.]

7. When a passing motorist stops, yell at him to go on because they have your gun. [See #1.]

The court (*U.S. v. New York State*, 1978) noted:

The examination for the position of Trooper was a situation test which, in essence, sought "will do" response to situations that normally do not occur behind a desk. The fact that someone selects a particular course of action as appropriate in such an examination does not mean that the same course of action would be followed by that individual under different circumstances in a real life situation. . . . The situations on the written examination are simulated situations that bear little resemblance, marginal at best, to the actual situation in which the behavior might occur. Sitting at a desk selecting the best alternative in response to a written situation, I find, is quite different from being in the real situation deciding what to do and doing it effectively.

Myth: *We can learn about what a person will do by asking what he should not do.* One test had 75 questions in a row that asked, "Which of the following is a false statement about . . ." The instructions in the test for state trooper also asked for the worst thing the trooper could do while being kicked. As the court wrote, "Certainly, in such situations, no one would consider and determine what would be the worst action to follow."

Myth: *Tests give applicants all the information that they need to know to answer a question.* The question cited before requires the applicants to make many, often unrealistic assumptions to answer the question. An item in the same test started by saying that a man who was walking into a park with a young girl was "acting suspiciously" but never said what he was doing. It is part of the craft of the police officer to notice people acting suspiciously. There is no homunculus telling him not only that the man was suspicious but also (in the case on which the question was based) that he would murder her.

Myth: *The wanted answer is the single correct answer.* Despite references to published sources and successive editing, it is common for some questions to be rekeyed or thrown out because the wanted answer is not correct or is not the only correct answer. One expert, 13% of whose items were thrown out after protests were evaluated, was not embarrassed, saying that routinely 10–15% of the items were incorrect. Even the Educational Testing Service, which has one of the most elaborate item-editing procedures, has to admit every few years that one of its items is incorrectly scored.

Test-takers are in a quandary when they think they may know more than the item writer. One test asked whether "Octane is determined by establishing the knock characteristics of the equivalent proportion of heptane to octane." As a graduate engineer I knew that the statement was a quote from an obsolete text-book. This definition does not take into account the development of gasoline with greater than 100 octane. I had to assume that the item writer did not know that and would mark it *true*. Another question asked whether automobile batteries were six-volt or twelve-volt. I checked the copyright date on the test. It was so old that I chose "six-volt" with confidence.

A more serious problem is the tacit belief that life has but one acceptable answer to its serious questions. Norman Frederiksen (1986) of the Educational Testing Service wrote in an article based on his presentation as a recipient of the Distinguished Contributions Award of the American Psychological Association:

[T]he expectation is that the examiner should strive for as many "right" answers as possible, following the standardized procedures and time limits. In real life, one might decide to settle for an approximation or a probability that satisfied one's needs, rather than strive for an optimal solution; or one might postpone the problem, hire a consultant, or even decide that the problem is not worth solving. The strict, monitored setting of a test is likely to frustrate any effort to reformulate the problem or develop an original solution.

The correctness of items is so often challenged successfully that New York City attempted briefly to get around the problem by using the "E-Choice," which read, "Select (E) as your choice if *none* of the preceding choices is correct OR if *two or more* of the choices (A), (B), (C), or (D) are correct." It was dropped when the test makers realized that if an applicant selected (A), which was intended to be correct, and (B) had to be allowed because of a successful protest, the applicant who chose (A) lost credit, though the answer was the one that the item writer originally had in mind because the only accepted answer is (E).

Myth: *Test-takers would respond in real life as they do in the test*. The question about the attack on a state trooper cited earlier describes a situation that is extremely stressful. There are other reasons that performance may not follow the chosen response. Firefighters, for example, know that the rule requires that they wear seat belts while their vehicle is in motion, but in that macho line of work, few comply. It is not a new idea to note that people often do not practice what they preach.

Myth: *The choices always include a correct answer*. During the development of assessment centers, a consulting firm (Byham n.d.) tried to shortcut the scoring process by using a multiple-choice format to record what they had previously written in short-answer essay form. The procedure was abandoned because the applicants could not match their freely created responses with the choices supplied by the test writers. People divide up real-world experience in ways that differ from those of test writers.

One witness justified a response regarding the procedures for determining the value of stolen property by quoting a sentence from a manual. The judge remarked that he had been on the bench for seventeen years and still didn't know how to place a fair value on stolen property.

Myth: *The distractors (also called misleads) are incorrect.* The classic way to develop a multiple-choice test in mathematics, where there is clearly one right answer, and all other answers are wrong, is to administer the test to a sample who respond freely. The most common incorrect answers are then used as the distractors. Applying this procedure in human relations or supervision does not work because there are many acceptable ways to approach some problems.

Myth: *Recognition of the correct response is an adequate measure of understanding.* Rarely does life provide the answers to the problems it poses. That homunculus is not sitting on your shoulder saying, "Here is a list of things you can do; pick the winner." For any important real-life problem, we have to dig for information, develop solutions, evaluate them, and take action.

Sometimes the test provides an answer that the test-taker would not have thought of. One question asked how to take fingerprints from a corpse that has been in the water so long that the fingers have wrinkled. No one that I have tried the item on, including me, knew the right answer. But they all recognized that one alternative, injecting water in the fingers to plump them up so that the prints could be taken, made sense.

Myth: *Test-takers can do what the item calls for.* Knowing what to do and being able to do it are two different things. According to one question, the first thing a social worker should do when counseling a pregnant teenager is to win her confidence. True enough, but what the agency really wants to know is whether or not the applicant knows how to win the confidence of a scared, hostile teenager. Stressful jobs, like those of police officers and firefighters, are especially prone to this problem. An old, politically incorrect adage points out, "No man can tell in cold blood what he would do in a passion."

A Federal Court (*Boston Chapter NAACP v. Beecher*) summarized the issue succinctly:

[T]here is a difference between memorizing (or absorbing through past experience) the fire fighter terminology and being a good fire fighter. If the Boston Red Sox recruited players on the basis of their knowledge of baseball history and vocabulary, the team might acquire authorities . . . who could not bat, pitch, or catch.

Myth: *Test wiseness has little influence on test results.* For years the Educational Testing Service claimed that the cram courses advertised when a new round of SATs is in the offing do not improve scores. The overwhelming evidence has finally convinced them that such programs produce a meaningful improvement in scores, sometimes more than 100 points. The paradox is that the time spent in these courses is wasted, except for the marginal benefit to those who need to take similar tests later. The time spent on learning to take tests is of no benefit to the employer. One researcher using testwise subjects found that they could answer many questions about reading passages without reading them. They relied on general knowledge and knowledge of the thought processes of the test writers.

Savvy test-takers know when to guess. They weed out the obvious distractors and guess at the rest, although guessing is a bad policy on most jobs. They scour the test to find items that give them clues to answering other items. They give special attention to the longest answer, knowing that it is often necessary to give more detail in the wanted answer. (I could almost have passed an Illinois driver's test by choosing the longest alternative every time.)

An egregious example of telegraphing answers came from the Multi-State Bar Examination. In answering one item, I guessed that certain evidence was inadmissible but changed my answer when the next question mentioned cross-examination on the same evidence. One does not need a law degree to know that attorneys do not cross-examine witnesses on inadmissible evidence.

Myth: *The multiple-choice format is so simple that it presents no special difficulty to the test-taker.* The following from a police entrance test covers an issue that is complex in its own right and presents it in a way that challenges test-taking skills beyond the understanding of adolescent behavior.

Below are four examples of behavior that might be considered "normal".

1. Masturbation

2. Sodomy

3. Vocal abuse of police officials

4. Claiming to hate their parents

Which one of the following choices lists all of the above that are considered [by whom?] normal behavior and which are not?

A. 1, 2, 3, and 4 are all normal adolescent behavior.

B. 1 and 3 are normal and 2 and 4 are not.

C. 1, 2, and 4 are considered normal adolescent behavior, but 3 is not.

D. 3 and 4 are considered normal adolescent behavior but 1 and 2 are not.

Untangling the options is difficult even if the applicant understands the issues and sees them the same way as the item writer. Besides, what does a police officer do with this information?

One item and the wanted answer read, "Which of the following is *not* a good rule for maintaining discipline? Do not withhold needed reprimands because of fear that you will be disliked for giving them." Counting "fear" and "being disliked," there are five negations that applicants would have to disentangle.

Myth: *Word counts are good indexes of the difficulty of reading passages.* Test writers routinely apply the Flesch count or a similar index to measure the reading difficulty of the test. They ignore the obvious point that such indexes are designed to measure the difficulty of written material for little kids, hence the reporting of scores in grade-level terms. Second, items are honed until the writer is satisfied that the item says precisely what is intended. Some items hinge on subtle differences in wording that are beyond the experience of applicants, who are often average graduates from average high schools, where they have not been taught to read for the nuances that are often critical in interpreting a multiple-choice item.

Myth: *Multiple-choice tests present no special problems to minorities.* Over a period of more than 40 years, researchers have studied the effects of stress on the performance on multiple-choice tests of whites and African-Americans. When told that the tests were important measures of intellectual functioning, whites did about as well as when they were told that the test was being tried out and that the scores were meaningless. Not so the African-Americans. Their performance was markedly poorer under the conditions of stress. There can be few situations in which test taking is more stressful than when it is the sole determiner of whether or not the applicant gets the job or the promotion.

Myth: *The typical multiple-choice test gets at important information.* Generally, important information and the situation to which it is applied are too complex for the multiple-choice format. The result is a test that relies heavily on trivia. Lawyers are asked the meaning of arcane Latin phrases; supervisors are expected to remember obscure personnel policies. The big failure of multiple-choice tests is that the possession of specific information, which they can measure, is not the same as understanding. It is easy to see if a person knows the dates of Columbus' voyages, but multiple-choice tests cannot reflect the complexity of the times, the decisions that were made, and the pressures that led to his downfall.

Myth: *The response to the pressure of multiple-choice tests predicts the response to job pressures.* The pressures are not alike. Test pressure can cause panic in otherwise stable persons, and there are those who remain calm while taking a test but crack under threat of physical harm.

Myth: *An average score of 25% correct is the sign of a difficult test.* On the contrary, it is the sign of an impossible test, because blind guessing would give 25% correct answers, and if one obvious distractor can be eliminated, the average would be 33.33% correct. Table 5.1 shows the effects of guessing blindly or guessing blindly after eliminating one obvious distractor. It oversimplifies the situation because the many guesses are not truly random, but it gives a start to understanding the difficulty of a test based on the number of correct responses.

Myth: *Multiple-choice tests cover a wide range of issues and approaches to problems.* Much of the limitation of multiple-choice tests can be summed up by the term *surface processing.* They are characterized by superficial information that is discrete and trivial. They do not reward—in fact, they punish—the applicant who carefully considers problems before acting.

Myth: *Multiple-choice cognitive tests predict the most important aspects of human performance.* Sternberg and Williams (1997) tested the efficacy of the

Table 5.1
Percent Answering Correctly for Percent Who Know the Correct Answer, with the Rest Guessing Randomly

Percent Who Know	Four Options	Three Remaining Options
0	25	33
20	40	47
40	55	60
60	70	73
80	85	87
100	100	100

Graduate Record Examination (GRE) for predicting success of 170 Yale graduate students in psychology. They employed a triarchic theory, which:

Distinguishes among academic-analytical, synthetic-creative, and practical-contextual aspects of human abilities. Academic-analytical abilities are used when one analyzes, compares and contrasts, evaluates, judges, or critiques. Creative abilities are used when one invents, discovers, supposes, hypothesizes, or theorizes. Practical abilities are used when one applies, uses or implements. (p. 633)

They conclude (p. 636):

First . . . the GRE scores did have some modest value for predicting grades, at least in the first year of graduate study. The median correlation . . . for men and women combined was .17.

Second . . . none of the correlations for the second year was statistically significant (with a median . . . of just .02).

Third, the Advanced test in psychology correlated with Year 1 GPA (r = .37). To the extent that one wishes to predict grade-based achievement, test-measured achievement was, perhaps unsurprisingly, a strong predictor.

Fourth, with one exception . . . the GRE scores were not useful as predictors of other aspects of graduate performance: ratings of analytical, creative, practical, research, and teaching abilities.

Translating these results into an employee selection context, the general cognitive test was only moderately successful in predicting learning ability of the type measured by grades but was unsuccessful in predicting what the employer wants, the synthetic-creative, and practical-contextual aspects of human abilities. The best results were obtained from a test designed to measure earlier success in learning the subject matter.

To facilitate the development and evaluation of the validity of multiple-choice tests, I have developed the *Content Validation Form II*, which is described in Appendix 2.

Myth: *Cheating is virtually impossible*. Cheating is always a problem, particularly in civil service testing because the stakes are so high. Multiple-choice tests are especially vulnerable because all that the test-taker must do is check the right box. Many tests and their scoring keys are easily obtained from publishers by writing for them with some false identification. The *New York Times* (''Giant of Exam Business'' 1997) details how the Scholastic Aptitude Test and tests used to assess the literacy of aliens seeking citizenship have been compromised. It is essential to be constantly vigilant to avoid disclosure of the tests in advance.

Implications

Multiple-choice tests are high-stakes tests. Employment and, in many government jobs, promotion depend on the scores earned by the applicants. Promotions in big-city police and fire departments sometimes are determined entirely by the scores on multiple-choice tests of those who are eligible for promotion. The GATB is a multiple-choice test, as is the Multi-State Bar Examination. Of the most commonly used selection procedures, they have consistently had the greatest adverse impact.

The adequacy with which they are effective gatekeepers had been repeatedly challenged in court, and the employers have repeatedly failed to demonstrate that they are sufficiently useful to be acceptable when they are challenged under Title VII. They are seldom justified on the basis of their demonstrated ability to predict success. Meta-analysis demonstrates that, in general, they modestly predict job success, but there are enough exceptions to cast doubt on any specific application, particularly when they are built by the same kinds of item writers following the same rules and sometimes even drawing on the same item banks.

Attempts to justify them on the basis of content validity are often unsuccessful. Rigorous use of the principles behind *Content Validation Form II* can help. In one attempt to validate a multiple-choice test against a performance measure, a test in which half of the items had been screened out showed moderate validity.

It is time that test users and the public recognized that the ease and low cost in developing and administering multiple-choice tests are an illusion when compared with the difficulties and costs resulting from selecting and promoting the wrong people and defending the action. More weight should be given to the cognitive and non-cognitive measures described in the two preceding chapters.

Chapter 6

Job Relatedness

BACKGROUND

Job relatedness is a general term for what psychologists call validity. Validity is the subject of *Uniform Guidelines*, Section 14, *Technical standards for validity studies*, and Section 15, *Documentation of validity evidence*. It is not my purpose here to repeat the standards as described in the *Uniform Guidelines* but to highlight some basic principles over which there is some confusion.

Validity is defined by the *Standards* (1985, p. 9):

> Validity . . . refers to the appropriateness, meaningfulness, and usefulness of the specific inferences made from test scores. Test validation is the process of accumulating evidence in support of such inferences. A variety of inferences may be made from scores produced by a given test, and there are many ways of accumulating evidence to support any particular inference.
>
> Validity, however, is a unitary concept. Although evidence may be accumulated in many ways, validity always refers to the degree to which that evidence supports the inferences that are made from the scores. It is the inferences regarding specific uses of a test that are validated, not the test itself.

The *Uniform Guidelines* and the profession in general recognize three kinds of validity, content, criterion-related, and construct. They are defined in Section 16:

D. *Content validity*. Demonstrated by data showing that the content of a selection procedure is representative of important aspects of performance on the job. . . .

E. *Criterion-related validity*. Demonstrated by data showing that the selection procedure is predictive of or significantly correlated with important elements of work behavior.

F. *Construct validity*. Demonstrated by data showing that the selection procedure measures the degree to which candidates have identifiable characteristics which have been
determined to be important for successful job performance. . . .

Content validity is the most direct procedure for demonstrating the job relatedness of a selection procedure. The more the behavior on the selection instrument resembles the behavior required by the job, the stronger the claim for
content validity. In recognition of the importance of knowledge, skill, and abilities, the *Uniform Guidelines* cautiously admit these attributes as eligible for
being demonstrated by content validation when they are "necessary prerequisites" to performance.

Criterion-related validity is the most defensible way to show job relatedness,
but also the most difficult. If scores on the selection procedure predict a meaningful measure of job success, the value of the prediction is clear. Selection
procedures validated by criterion-related validity may be more distant from the
work. The test does not have to look like the job. All that counts is that higher
scores on the test are associated with better performance.

Construct validity forms the basis for construct validity. To avoid the trouble
and expense of validating every test for every use, the *Uniform Guidelines*
14C(1) provide for the demonstration of the validity of a construct, which is
defined in the *Standards* as:

A psychological characteristic (e.g., numerical ability, spatial ability, introversion, anxiety) considered to vary or differ across individuals. A construct . . . is not directly observable; rather it is a theoretical concept derived from research and other experience
that has been constructed to explain observable behavior patterns. When test scores are
interpreted by using a construct, the scores are placed in a conceptual framework.

Construct validity is defined in the *Standards* as "Evidence that supports a
proposed construct interpretation of scores on a test based on theoretical implications associated with the construct label."

The best-known, best-researched construct is intelligence. There is no such
thing as intelligence, which is defined as the source of intelligent behavior. It
is hypothesized to pull together behaviors that have a common thread running
through them. Different researchers include different kinds of behavior depending on the milieu in which they are operating and their own proclivities.

A recurring issue in personnel selection is deciding which tests are subject to
content validity and which require either criterion-related or construct validity.
The extremes are obvious. Tests of intelligence, mathematical ability, and the
ability to visualize spatial relations measure constructs. Ratings of probationary
performance and work sample tests are evaluated under the rules of content
validity. To help to clarify the distinction, I present the Content-Construct Scale,
which runs from tests that are amenable to content validity to those justified by
construct strategies.

Content

Performance on all or part of the job

Simulations

Prerequisite knowledge, skill, and ability

Peripheral knowledge, skill, and ability

Classical constructs

Construct

Performance on all or part of the job. Evaluation of performance on the job is, by definition, subject to content validation. Ratings of job performance are used as criteria for the empirical validation of tests because, if well done, they are direct measurers of relevant performance. They are also used, formally or informally, in determining salary levels in a job category. They are most eligible for consideration under the standards of content validity when they are used to terminate employees through layoffs, downsizing, or discharge. When used for this purpose, they are more realistic measures than even the best simulations.

When used for promotion and transfer, the appropriateness of job performance ratings depends on how many elements of the job for which the incumbents are rated are consistent with the new job. It is a cliché that when the best sales agent is promoted, the company loses a good sales agent and gains a mediocre sales manager. In any event, performance measures, when adequately developed and administered, qualify under the heading of job relatedness of that portion of the job that they measure. Performance ratings are of limited value when they are poor measures of job performance.

Simulations. Simulations are sometimes more useful than measures of job performance. Electronic simulators used for testing the ability to handle emergencies in flying an airplane or operating a nuclear power plant can be more thorough and even more realistic than flying a plane or operating a reactor because it is possible to have a simulated disaster strike without destroying the equipment or risking anyone's life. In this sense they are more real than real life. Even so, they are not perfect replicas of operations because nuclear plant operators know that there is no core to melt down, and pilots know that they will not crash. These devices are designed to test acquired skills. No one yet knows how to produce the adrenaline rush that perceived danger can generate. Simulations of important functions can be job-related if they do it well enough, even if the emotional response is not adequately aroused.

Some paper-and-pencil simulations can adequately test the applicant's ability to appraise complex situations and select the appropriate responses. Although they are more remote from the work than the electronic simulators, video presentations or photographs can pose realistic problems and provide for realistic solutions. The wide variation in the quality of responses in such tests supports their usefulness in differentiating between those who know what to do and those who do not.

Prerequisite knowledge, skill, or ability. Before discussing this point, repeating the definitions of knowledge, skill, and ability from the *Uniform Guidelines* may be helpful. *Knowledge* is a body of information applied directly to the performance of a function. *Skill* is a present, observable competence to perform a learned psychomotor act. *Ability* is a present competence to perform a behavior or a behavior that results in an observable work product.

The central issue here is whether the test qualifies under the standard of "need to know" rather than "nice to know." Many jobs, particularly those governed by rules and regulations like bookkeeping or selling stock, are most amenable to content-valid tests. At the other extreme some tests measure such peripheral information that, even if they are well constructed and indubitably correct, they do not qualify. It might be nice for the police officer to know who appoints the commissioner or for the social worker to know who is the father of social work, but such information is not subject to content validation.

Peripheral knowledge, skill, or ability. It takes more than faith to demonstrate that knowledge of the history of the typewriter is an adequate measure of the skills needed by a typist. The question is whether the information can be considered nice to know rather than need to know. Though the topic may deal with the subject matter of the test, it does not qualify for content validity if it is too far removed from performance.

Classical constructs. Intellectual functioning measured in the abstract is a valid predictor for most kinds of work, but it is not content-valid. Vague similarities do not count. The only way that classical constructs can be shown to be job-related is by an empirical investigation.

An aspect of selection procedures that is associated with job relatedness is reliability, a statistical measure of consistency. Reliability is a measure that is sometimes confused with validity, partially because of the infelicitous choice of words. In the vernacular, when we say that people are reliable, we mean that we have confidence in them based on our experience. Statistics borrowed the word and endowed it with a more narrow meaning, that is, consistency. In statistics, a reliable measure is consistent but not necessarily job-related. It may be consistently wrong, as with a thermometer that always registers 5.0 degrees too high, or may be inconsistently wrong, like a rubber ruler. There is no measurement without error, but in the ordinary course of life one depends on measurements made with a well-made foot rule to be as consistent and as accurate as a carpenter needs. In this case, careful measurements are both reliable and valid for the purpose for which they are intended. The reliability of a test sets a limit on its validity, because the unreliable measure contains random error, which cannot consistently relate to anything.

Myth: *The Uniform Guidelines require measures of reliability for every test.* Section 14C(5), *Reliability*, says:

The reliability of selection procedures justified on the basis of content validity should be a matter of concern to the user. When feasible, appropriate statistical estimates should be made of the reliability of the selection procedure.

The reason that reliability is recommended but not required for tests that are justified based on content validity is that sometimes reliability measures are impractical. It may be possible to get only one rating of the probationary employee. Interviews cannot be repeated to get two contrasting evaluations that could be compared because the second interview will be modified by the experience of the first.

However, the requirement that reliability should be a matter of concern is not taken lightly. For example, I once worked with a team that evaluated a standard background information form for high-level government applicants. Since there were four professionals familiar with the use of the application form, we started with two pairs of raters working independently on a sample of the applications. The results were not sufficiently reliable, so we used all four as a committee to make the judgments. Since they consulted with each other before agreeing on an evaluation, there were no independent judgments with which to measure reliability. However, we exhibited our concern by developing the most sensible procedure that was practical under the circumstances.

Reliability measures are not required for criterion-related validity studies because unreliability leads to an automatic diminution of the correlation between the test and the criterion measures to a level that can be expected in operational use. The test is already penalized for its lack of perfect reliability because the randomness in the unreliable measure detracts from the observed validity.

Myth: *It is appropriate to correct both the test and the criterion for unreliability.* Penalizing the test for the failure of the raters to agree on the quality of the performance of the experimental subjects is unfair to a test. Corrections for unreliability in the criterion are reasonable and proper. However, it is not appropriate to correct for unreliability of the test because it is an inherent attribute of the test. It might be theoretically interesting to know how well a perfectly reliable test of the construct would correlate with a perfectly reliable criterion, but the information does not establish the validity of the test.

Myth: *Correlations of pairs of ratings, as of observers of an assessment center, are an acceptable measure of reliability.* Correlations between the scores assigned by the observers is called "interrater agreement." It is not reliability, but it sets an upper limit on reliability, because the testing procedure itself is not completely reliable. Two test-scoring machines scoring the same papers would produce an "intermachine" reliability coefficient of 1.00, but the tests would still have less than perfect reliability.

Myth: *Testing is too expensive to be worthwhile.* Most organizations do not conduct a cost–benefit analysis. If they did, they would generally find that money and effort spent on selection procedures would pay off over the career of the employee. For this reason the *Uniform Guidelines* Section 3B refers to both "the user's legitimate interest in efficient and trustworthy workmanship" and not just "valid for a given purpose."

I once calculated that a police department would easily spend $250,000 on a police officer, including pay, training, and supervision. At that time many police departments used a popular test that cost $.35. No one would dream of investing $250,000 in a piece of property or equipment based on a $.35 investigation. There should be a reasonable balance between the cost of the selection process and the benefits derived from using valid assessment of potential.

In the next two chapters, Chapters 7 and 8, I discuss content validity and the *Content Validation Form II*. In Chapter 9, I cover criterion-related validity, and in Chapter 10, construct validity and validity generalization.

Implications

Some demonstration of the validity of selection procedures—or any other procedure, for that matter—is necessary to protect the users from procedures that are, at best, worthless and, at worst, harmful to their operations. The evidence is overwhelming that there are many ideas in psychology, as well as other lines of work, that sound good and win acceptance but simply do not work. The only way for the test user to proceed with confidence is to demonstrate that it predicts success or is so closely related to the work that a prudent person would endorse its use.

Validation is looked on by some as an unnecessary frill added to the *Uniform Guidelines* by pointy-headed bureaucrats. The test validation procedures required by the *Uniform Guidelines* are lineal descendants of a series of standards adopted by the American Psychological Association for generations. These professional standards are explicit about the responsibilities of psychologists. For example, Ethical Standard 1.06, *Basis for scientific and professional judgments*, says: "Psychologists rely on scientifically and professionally derived knowledge when making scientific or professional judgments."

Ethical Standard 2.03, *Test construction*, elaborates the same point:

Psychologists who develop and conduct research with tests and other assessment techniques use scientific procedures and current professional knowledge for design, standardization, validation, reduction or elimination of bias, and recommendations for use.

Section 15 of the *Uniform Guidelines*, *Documentation of impact and validity evidence*, is devoted entirely to a specification of what should be in a report so that an outside observer can judge its merits. Psychologists appropriately document their professional and scientific work in order to facilitate provision of services later by other professionals to ensure accountability, and to meet other requirement of institutions or the law.

SIOP's *Principles for the Validation and Use of Personnel Selection Proce-*

dures specify that validity is important but recognize that a full-blown study is not always possible when they say: ''There should be at least presumptive evidence for the validity of a predictor prior to its operational use'' (SIOP 1987, p. 14).

Chapter 7

Content Validity

BACKGROUND

Content validity is defined in the *Standards* (p. 90) as:

Evidence that shows the extent to which the content domain of a test is appropriate relative to its intended purpose. Such evidence is used to establish that the test includes a representative or critical sample of the relevant content domain and that it excludes content outside that domain. In employment selection testing the content domain consists of tasks, knowledge, skills, and abilities associated with a job.

Standard 10.6 and the comment elaborate the concept:

When content-related evidence of validity is presented, the rationale for defining and describing a specific job content domain in a particular way (e.g., in terms of tasks to be performed or knowledge, skills and abilities, or other personal characteristics) should be stated clearly. The rationale should establish that the knowledge, skills, and abilities said to define the domain are the major determinants of proficiency in that domain. (Primary)

The comment adds:

When content-related evidence of validity is presented for a job or class of jobs, the evidence should include a description of the major job characteristics that a test is meant to sample, including the relative frequency or criticality of the elements. The supporting argument might be provided by additional construct-related evidence of validity or by appropriate kinds of job analysis data.

Content-based testing is confined to those situations in which the applicants have had education, training, or experience that makes it possible for them to perform on the test and on the job. Applicants can be expected to spell and do high school arithmetic even if they have never been employed. There are few other exceptions, such as tests of strength and endurance, to the rule that content-based tests are useful only with experienced applicants.

A content-valid test has two major virtues. The first is that it can be used where empirical evidence of validity is difficult to generate. The second is that, if it adequately measures the KSAs or the work itself, it gives direct evidence of the competence of the applicant to perform on those KSAs.

Purpose

The purpose of content validation is to determine whether the selection instrument adequately replicates one or more important aspects of the job duties or measures the necessary prerequisite knowledge, skill, or ability required to perform the job.

Population

Content validation is appropriate only when the applicants can be expected to have had an opportunity to learn how to perform on the job or develop the KSAs required for adequate performance after a brief orientation. Thus, for a selection procedure to be used, the applicants should have had training through their basic education (e.g., spelling ability), specialized training (e.g., engineering drawing), or job-related experience (e.g., work activities).

Not all selection procedures are amenable to content validity. Many measure constructs, which are more general functions. Section 14C(1) of the *Uniform Guidelines, Appropriateness of content validity studies*, states:

Users choosing to validate a selection procedure by a content validation strategy should determine whether it is appropriate to conduct such a study in the particular employment context. A selection procedure can be supported by a content validity study to the extent that it is a representative sample of the content of the job. Selection procedures which purport to measure knowledges, skills, or abilities may in certain circumstances be justified by content validity, although they may not be representative samples, if the knowledge, skill or ability measured by the selection procedure can be operationally defined ... and if that knowledge, skill or ability is a necessary prerequisite to successful job performance.

A selection procedure based on inferences about mental processes [constructs] cannot be supported solely on the basis of content validity. Thus, a content strategy is not appropriate for demonstrating the validity of selection procedures which purport to measure traits or constructs such as intelligence, aptitude, personality, common sense, judgment, leadership, and spatial ability. Content validity is also not an appropriate strategy when the selection procedure involves knowledges, skills, or abilities which an employee will be expected to learn on the job.

(The *Uniform Guidelines* use the neologism *knowledges* because performance on a job may require more than one kind of knowledge.)

Content validation depends on a detailed job description, discussed in Chapter 2. The standard for job descriptions is more stringent for content validity than for criterion or construct validity. Section 14C(2), *Job analysis for content validity*, states:

There should be a job analysis which includes an analysis of the important work behavior(s) required for successful performance and their relative importance. . . . Any job analysis should focus on the work behavior(s) and tasks associated with them. . . . The work behavior(s) selected for measurement should be critical work behavior(s) and/or important work behavior(s).

The standards for demonstrating content validity are rigorous because less stringent standards lead to the endorsement of selection procedures that do not reflect the requirements of the job. Section 14C (4), *Standards for demonstrating content validity*, states:

To demonstrate the content validity of a selection procedure, a user should show that the behavior(s) demonstrated in the selection procedure are a representative sample of the behavior(s) of the job in question or that the selection procedure provides a representative sample of the work product of the job. In the case of a selection procedure measuring a knowledge, skill, or ability, the knowledge, skill, or ability being measured should be operationally defined. In the case of a selection procedure measuring a knowledge, the knowledge being measured should be operationally defined as that body of learned information which is used in and is a necessary prerequisite for observable aspects of work behavior of the job. In the case of skills or abilities, the skill or ability being measured should be operationally defined in terms of observable aspects of work behavior of the job. For any selection procedure measuring a knowledge, skill, or ability the user should show that (a) the selection procedure measures and is a representative sample of that knowledge, skill, or ability; and (b) that the knowledge, skill, or ability is used in and is a necessary prerequisite to performance of critical or important work behavior(s). In addition, to be content valid, a selection procedure measuring a skill or ability should either closely approximate an observable work behavior, or its product should closely approximate an observable work product. If a test purports to sample a work behavior or to provide a sample of a work product, the manner and setting of the selection procedure and its level of complexity should closely approximate the work situation. The closer the content and context of the selection procedure are to work samples or work behaviors, the stronger is the basis for showing content validity. As the content of the selection procedure less resembles a work behavior, or the setting and manner of the administration of the selection procedure less resemble the work situation, or the result less resembles a work product, the less likely the selection procedure is to be content valid, and the greater the need for other evidence of validity.

Measurement

Content validation is used with a wide range of procedures from direct observation of the incumbent's performance, to written tests and interviews. Section 16D says that content validity is "demonstrated by data showing that the content of a selection procedure is representative of important aspects of performance on the job." This definition would appear to confine the use of content validity to work performance or simulations, but such a limitation would be too restrictive. Accordingly, Section 14C(1) opens the door to knowledge, skill, and ability when it says:

Selection procedures which purport to measure knowledges, skills, or abilities may in certain circumstances be justified by content validity, although they may not be representative samples, if the knowledge, skill or ability measured by the selection procedure can be operationally defined.

Myth: *If there is a rational relationship between a test and the job, the test is content-valid.* During the writing of the *Uniform Guidelines*, the Civil Service Commission proposed rational validity, which would require only that the test user show that there is some rational relationship between the selection procedure and the job. This standard was rejected because it is too loose. Anyone can propose a rational relationship between almost any test item or test with practically any job if the test is couched in the phrases recognized as part of the jargon of the trade. The Board of Examiners of the City of New York defended this question for selecting elementary school principals:

Of the following characters in the nursery rhyme, "The Burial of Poor Cock Robin," the one who kills Cock Robin is the:

1. Lark
2. Thrush
3. Bull
4. Sparrow

The rationale went like this. At that time—and it is still largely true—elementary school teachers were women, and principals were men. Almost the only men available for promotion were physical education teachers, who were not expected to have read much children's literature. This question was designed to test whether or not they were familiar with elementary school subjects. Under the principle of rational validity, this argument might stand up, since it makes superficial sense. The item and the rationale do not meet the standard of business necessity, and are unacceptable under the *Uniform Guidelines*.

Another example may clarify the issue. To answer one question on a test for junior high school principals, applicants had to know (or guess) that Kublai Kahn built his pleasure dome in Xanadu. This question was justified as measuring the content of three KSAs. The first called for knowledge of junior high school poetry. Although the knowledge asked for was not profound, it did measure some degree of exposure to poetry and is, I would judge, marginally acceptable.

The second was the ability to select appropriate poetry for a junior high school class. The question did not relate to that KSA. There could be an objective test that measured that ability. It would require that the applicants identify which poems, presented in a list ranging from nursery rhymes to *The Wasteland*, were appropriate. The scoring key would be developed by experts in the field.

The third was the ability to instill a liking for poetry in the students. Merely knowing where Kublai Kahn built the pleasure dome has nothing to do with this objective.

The Supreme Court in *Washington v. Davis* (1976) ruled that the constitutional standard of "rational relationship" did not apply to Title VII cases but let stand the principles set forth in *Griggs*. The Court pointed out that the appropriate standard would still be the affirmative demonstration of a relationship between scores on the selection procedure and measures of job performance.

Myth: *Content validity is a process, not a product.* Misreading of the *Uniform Guidelines* has led some practitioners to conclude that content validity is a process; that is, if one goes through the prescribed steps, the result is a content-valid selection procedure. Citing Section 14C(2), they note that there must be a job analysis and that certain procedures must be followed. However, they neglect Section 14C(4), *Standards for demonstrating content validity*, which says that "to demonstrate the content validity of a selection procedure, a user should show that the behavior(s) demonstrated in the selection procedure are a representative sample of the behaviors(s) of the job in question." Being able to demonstrate that the test was developed according to a sensible plan is not enough. The resulting test and its use must be shown to be job-related.

Myth: *Face validity is sufficient evidence of validity.* Face validity is the appearance of validity. It helps to sell the instrument to applicants because the test uses familiar jargon and asks about familiar concepts. However, unless more convincing evidence can be produced that the test measures prerequisite KSAs or replicates important work behavior, it is not valid.

To systematize the development selection procedures and the evaluation of their content validity, I have developed and used the *Content Validation Form II*, which is reproduced in Appendix 2 and discussed in Chapter 8.

Implications

Content validation has the potential for providing solid evidence that the selection is a representative sample of the content of the job or that the knowledge, skill, or ability measured by the selection procedure is a necessary prerequisite to successful job performance. The evidence depends on showing that there is a close link between the selection procedure and the work duties.

Content validity must not be confused with face validity, which is the superficial appearance of validity. It is always good for public relations to have a test look sensible, but that is not enough. Asking the definitions of words that are part of the jargon of the trade does not necessarily make the question content-valid. Applicants can memorize the definitions of words that appear in the glossary of a training manual and not really know what they mean when applied to the job. Nor is content validity the same as rational validity, which was considered and rejected by the profession. There must be more than some logical connection between the selection procedure and the job duties.

Tests of content differ from cognitive and non-cognitive tests. Cognitive tests measure what applicants have learned in their general education or during employment, or their capacity for learning what is needed to perform the work. Non-cognitive tests are more concerned with how the applicants can be expected to perform once they are hired. Both are concerned more with potential than with prior accomplishment. Tests of content focus on what the applicants have learned or have done that could be transferred directly to the job.

The report of the development and use of the content study should meet the standards of Section 15C, *Content validity studies* of the *Uniform Guidelines*.

In the following chapter, I discuss *Content Validation Form II*, a procedure that I have developed to systematize the evaluation of the content validity of a selection procedure.

Chapter 8

Content Validation Form II

BACKGROUND

Content Validation Form II is a guide for analyzing the content validity and appropriateness of employment tests, particularly multiple-choice tests. It comprises questions for showing that the test or an item is acceptable or for showing the way in which it is deficient. An earlier version is discussed in *Fair Employment Strategies in Human Resource Management* (Barrett 1996) with emphasis on more general concepts. A copy of Content Validation Form II is presented in Appendix 2.

Purpose

Content Validation Form II is a systematic procedure for judging the content validity of a selection procedure. It focuses on multiple-choice tests, but, with some adaptation, many questions can be directed at any procedure expected to replicate a significant portion of the job or measure "necessary prerequisites" to performance. Its use can support the use of the selection procedure as described in Section 14C(4), *Standards for demonstrating content validity*. It can provide the raw material for compliance with Section 15C(5), *Relationship between the selection procedure and the job*, which says:

The evidence demonstrating that the selection procedure is a representative work sample, a representative sample of work behavior(s), or a representative sample of a knowledge, skill, or ability as used as a part of a work behavior and necessary for that behavior should be provided (essential). The user should identify the work behavior(s) which each item or part of the selection procedure is intended to sample or measure (essential). Where the selection procedure purports to sample a work behavior or to provide a sample of a work product, a comparison should be provided of the manner, setting, and the level of complexity of the selection procedure with those of the work situation (essential).

The form is divided into *Test as a Whole, Item-by-Item Analysis*, and *Supplementary Indications of Content Validity*. *Test as a Whole* is concerned with the relevance of the test to the employer's needs, appropriateness of content validation, the adequacy of the job description, the proportion of the job covered by the test, the passing score, and empirical standards. These issues are discussed in detail in *Fair Employment Strategies* (Barrett 1996).

Item-by-Item Analysis is used to evaluate the linkage of each item to job duties. It raises questions about each item, including correctness of the scoring key, linkage with the job, need for the knowledge called for by the item, preparation of the applicants, and other points. Its use can help you to develop better multiple-choice tests and head off criticism if the test is challenged.

Supplementary Indications of Content Validity raises questions that are not dispositive of the issue of content validity but that support the reasonableness of the claim of content validity.

Content Validation Form II is best used by Subject Matter Experts (SMEs) working under the guidance of a test expert. The group should be large enough, about six to eight articulate, competent incumbents, supervisors, or specialists, such as trainers, to assure diversity of opinion. The test expert should probe each proposed decision to make sure that the standards are met and that they are not too stringently applied.

Test as a Whole

Are the objectives of the selection procedure articulated?

> Are objectives described in the report?

> Are objectives relevant to employer's needs?

> Is the procedure planned to conform to Title VII of the Civil Rights Act of 1964, Americans with Disabilities Act, and Age Discrimination in Employment Act?

> Is the procedure planned to conform to professional and ethical standards?

Too often scant attention is paid to the objectives of the testing. Management wants better people, but it is essential to define what makes for better employees. Top management can provide information about the problems that they have seen that might be alleviated by testing. Do people have trouble mastering the work? Is there a dearth of candidates for promotion? Are drugs interfering with the work? Is morale low, and is turnover high? Only by a searching examination of work performance can an adequate set of objectives be articulated.

It should go without saying that the selection procedure should conform to fair employment laws and professional and ethical standards. Examining each step of the procedure can help the user to avoid pitfalls such as inappropriate interview questions, especially in the employment of the disabled.

Is the selection procedure subject to content validation?

Does the procedure measure content, not a construct?

Is the procedure designed to measure prerequisite work behavior or KSAs?

Content and construct validity are discussed in Chapters 7 and 10. The difference between them is central to the appropriateness of content validity studies. Q&A 75, 78, and 79 address this issue:

75. Q. Can a measure of a trait or construct be validated on the basis of content validity?

A. No. Traits or constructs are by definition underlying characteristics which are intangible and are not directly observable. They are therefore not appropriate for the sampling approach of content validity. Some selection procedures, while labeled as construct measures, may actually be samples of observable work behaviors. Whatever the label, if the operational definitions are in fact based on observable work behaviors, a selection procedure measuring those behaviors may be appropriately supported by a content validity strategy. . . .

78. Q. What is required to show the content validity of a paper-and-pencil test that is intended to approximate work behaviors?

A. Where a test is intended to replicate a work behavior, content validity is established by a demonstration of the similarities between the test and the job with respect to behaviors, products, and the surrounding environmental conditions. Paper-and-pencil tests which are intended to replicate a work behavior are most likely to be appropriate where work behaviors are performed in a paper and pencil form (e.g., editing and bookkeeping). Paper-and-pencil tests of effectiveness in interpersonal relations (e.g., sales or supervision), or physical activities (e.g., automotive repair) or ability to function properly under danger (e.g., firefighters) generally are not close enough approximations of work behaviors to show content validity.

79. Q. What is required to show the content validity of a test of job knowledge?

A. There must be a defined, well recognized body of information, and a knowledge of the information must be a prerequisite to performance of the required work behaviors. The work behavior(s) to which each knowledge is related should be identified on an item by item basis. The test should fairly sample the information that is actually used by the employee on the job, so that the level of difficulty of the test items should correspond to the level of difficulty of the knowledge as used in the work behavior.

Is the job description adequate?

Does the job description cover job duties, their importance and complexity?

Is the job description up to date?

Does the position description (relative to hiring disabled applicants) comply with ADA?

The job description (Chapter 2) must provide the necessary information, and the test, in combination with other selection procedures, covers a substantial portion of the job. Many job descriptions are out-of-date, limiting their usefulness. The special requirements of ADA are discussed in Chapter 17.

I have said it before, but it bears repeating: task analysis is *not* required by the *Uniform Guidelines*. It is not necessary to list hundreds of minute tasks, rate each one on several scales, and produce thousands of ratings that are incomprehensible until the related tasks are organized into major job duties. The result gives essentially the same information as a standard job analysis. See Q&A 77 (page 15 of this book).

Is an adequate portion of the job covered by the selection procedure?

    Does it, combined with other procedures, measure the most important content of the job?

Part of the function of the job description is to establish the relative importance of the job behaviors. There should be a reasonable match between the content of the test and the more important behaviors. If a test battery includes other procedures that can be linked to the important job duties, the report should indicate how thoroughly each is evaluated.

Is the selection procedure administered and scored properly?

    Is the administration adequately monitored?

    Are the tests secure?

    Is the scoring procedure verified as accurate?

    Is adequate accommodation made for disabled applicants in the content of the selection procedure, its scoring, and administration?

Candidates have won costly suits because they could prove that tests were administered under unsatisfactory conditions. Lawsuits aside, the user should make sure that the test atmosphere permits the applicants to do their best. Careless administration in poorly appointed surroundings cast a bad image for the employer.

Security of tests is a continuing problem. The Educational Testing Service, despite its elaborate procedures, is plagued by leaks. Many commercial tests are readily available to anyone with a little ingenuity or an unethical friend who has the proper credentials. One psychologist, suspicious of the uniformly high scores on intelligence tests of applicants with little education, administered an obscure test of the same construct to the same applicants. They did not do as well as they had on the earlier administrations.

Computerized testing administered at the individual's convenience makes it difficult to keep items from applicants. Conspirators agree to memorize a few questions each and later reassemble the test to transmit to their friends. Tests that are transmitted in computer networks are especially vulnerable to hackers.

Making sure that the scoring is accurate seems too obvious to mention, but I have seen Form B being scored with the key for Form A. One psychologist made a realistic typing test in which the rough draft, with corrections and additions, was to be typed in final form. The applicants were to be graded, in part, on the quality of their formatting of the revised text. The psychometrist, lazy or ignorant or both, did not want to go to the trouble of grading the quality of the typists' finished product. She told the applicants to simply type line by line, producing a letter no one would sign.

The special requirements of applicants under ADA are discussed in Chapter 17.

Is the passing score set at the appropriate level?

(No passing score.)

Does the passing score conform to reasonable expectations of proficiency?

Is the passing score modified for disabled applicants?

Setting an accurate passing score is critical when candidates are rejected completely on the basis of the score. Unfortunately, there is no way to establish the reasonableness of a passing score. Inspection of the results of the test makes it obvious that some applicants perform well enough to be acceptable, and others fail to meet any reasonable standards. The problem comes in setting that absolute cut score that divides the passers from the failures. In some settings it is more reasonable to pass everyone and then make the selections on the basis of their total performance. For a description of some current methods of setting the passing score, see Barrett (1996, p. 63).

Using an otherwise reasonable cut score for disabled applicants can lead to unfair rejection of qualified persons who could succeed with more reasonable standards. The most reasonable solution is to ignore the passing score and evaluate the applicant for the job on a case-by-case basis.

Does the selection procedure meet empirical standards?

Is it reliable?

Does it discriminate between levels of performance?

Is its weight in the battery appropriate?

Does internal statistical analysis support the use of the selection procedure?

Reliability is rarely a problem with multiple-choice tests but is a serious consideration with procedures in which scoring is based on judgment. Reliability should not be confused with interrater agreement. It is important that those who assign scores agree relatively well, but their agreement is not the same as reliability, since what they are agreeing on may itself not be reliable. Ten observers' agreement in their reading of a broken thermometer does not help you decide whether or not to wear an overcoat.

Most measures spread out the scores in a useful way, unless they are so easy that many applicants get nearly the top score, indicating that the test is too easy for the applicant pool. An exception is to be found in administrative ratings when they are used as part of a promotion program. Too often the pressures lead to inflation, as must have occurred when an irate marine commandant was miffed that ratings in the other services were higher than those of the marines. He set about a program "to get those ratings up." Another option is to rate everyone as "meeting requirements." One solution is to require rankings, but they can be used only when there are enough (generally five or more) with comparable jobs.

Weights assigned to different parts of a selection procedure are often reported to two decimals. Calculating weights beyond the first digit does not improve the accuracy of prediction. Some authorities go so far as to assert that unit weights, in which all instruments are given the same weight, are all that can be justified by the current state of the art.

There are many internal measures of tests, particularly multiple-choice tests. They include item–test correlation, difficulty, and more esoteric analyses based on item response theory. These measures are helpful for the builder of tests but are of little value in evaluating the end product because there are no agreed upon standards for these statistics.

Item-by-Item Analysis

Each item can be evaluated by answering the questions in Content Validation Form II. Where the reasons for judgments are not obvious, the rationale should be recorded for later use in evaluating a proposed test in connection with other selection procedures, reviewing the work of the SMEs, training item writers, or supporting litigation. Each question is followed by questions that direct the SMEs' attention to the more significant issues. These supporting questions do not cover all possibilities, and some items may have more than one flaw. Without an affirmative answer to each of the following questions, the item is, to some extent, deficient. Whether the deficiency is fatal or not depends on the circumstances; no test is expected to be perfect, but some imperfections are more serious than others.

Is the wanted answer correct?

    Is the source up-to-date?

    Does the wanted answer conform to accepted practice?

    Is the correct answer supplied?

Multiple-choice tests depend on there being a correct answer for the applicant to choose. The items should be scored based on correct, up-to-date information. All too often item writers use obsolete texts or rely on manuals that reflect bygone policies or principles. Many answers are simply wrong. At times it may be necessary to supplement the opinions of the SMEs by calling on a consultant, such as an engineer or lawyer, to verify the correctness of the wanted answer.

Reality should rule. Knowledge of a policy that is routinely ignored is not job-relevant.

Test writers sometimes hedge for their lack of knowledge by instructing the applicants to choose the correct answer or the answer that is most nearly correct. Such a practice can be a hardship for the knowledgeable test-taker who has a right to expect the right answer to be an option. Applicants for promotion to police sergeant were expected to know that "To a large extent, 'probable cause' is a question of common sense." Countless perpetrators are released because the arresting officer did not understand the voluminous law on probable cause. They need to be quizzed on what constitutes probable cause to greater specificity than the application of common sense.

With a professor of law and a former assistant district attorney, I once examined an item from a police promotion examination that was based on a 5–4 Supreme Court decision in which the nine justices wrote seven separate opinions. At issue was the First Amendment rights of a group that was picketing the home of a judge who had rendered an unpopular opinion. The inherently complex issue was so distorted in the question that the attorneys believed that the Supreme Court would probably have disagreed with the wanted answer. Since there was no emergency, the obviously correct action was to call the district attorney for advice. This option was not presented.

> Is each distractor acceptable?
>> Is the behavior or knowledge presented incorrect under all reasonable circumstances?
>> Is there a clear distinction between the distractor and the wanted answer?
>> Is the distractor likely to attract responses?

The distractors are designed to attract the uninformed. They are more complex than the true-and-false tests that are sometimes used. Writing them is difficult when the item writers are not themselves experts in the job, and experts in the job are seldom experts in writing test items.

We now come to one fundamental difficulty in the writing of multiple-choice items. Almost anyone can eliminate distractors that are wildly incorrect and based on general, not job-related, knowledge and thus improve the chances of guessing correctly. To avoid the use of this strategy by testwise applicants, item writers sometimes write distractors so subtly different from the wanted answer that they may be as correct as the wanted answer under some reasonable circumstances.

A classic procedure for writing multiple-choice questions in a field where there are definitely right and wrong answers, such as mathematics, is to base the distractors on the free responses of a sample similar to the expected applicants. The distractors thus developed are attractive and demonstrably wrong. However, this procedure works poorly in complex judgment or interpersonal relations where there may be several satisfactory ways of handling a difficult situation. Take, for example, this item from a promotion test:

Assume that a supervisor has several important reports, and a work schedule to prepare which will require considerable thought and concentration. If possible when should he try to get his work done?

A. After his regular working hours.

B. During the early part of his shift.

C. When possible during his shift.

D. During the latter part of his shift.

E. On his relief period.

The right answer depends on the situation and on personal taste. Besides, what bad things happen if he does his planning at the less than optimal time if the plan is timely and sound?

To make an item of reasonable difficulty, some item writers capitalize on trivial distinctions. For example, building maintenance workers were asked whether a ladder should extend one and one-half feet or two feet above the bottom of a roof. A manual must have given a figure, but no one can tell from the ground whether the overhang is six inches more or less than the prescribed amount. Firefighters are asked whether a ladder should be set at an angle of 30, 40, or 50 degrees. Estimating the angle a ladder makes with the vertical is difficult. Firefighters learn from experience and training that the ladder is about right if, when they set their feet by the base of the ladder, they can comfortably grasp the rung in front of them.

Is there a clear link between the wanted answer and work performance?

Does correct behavior follow from the wanted answer?

Is the response relevant to important work behavior?

It is central to the concept of content validity to test for knowledge that applies to the job. Nurses should know the appropriate dosages of dangerous drugs so they can apply the knowledge to avoid serious errors. A bookkeeper should keep the books according to accepted accounting procedures so that the statements reflect the true state of the finances of the organization.

Asking irrelevant questions about information that appears to be rationally related to the job is easy but does not relate to action. Firefighters are endlessly quizzed about the fire triangle, which symbolizes the three requirements of a fire: oxygen, heat, and fuel. Unless there is some special hazard not covered in the question, they generally pour water on the flames until they go out.

My favorite comes from a test for fire lieutenants. Applicants were asked where to put the flags after the parade. Somewhere a manual tells where the flags should go, but the implied action is totally irrelevant to putting out fires and saving lives.

> Would the applicant be expected to act in conformity with the response?
>> Does the answer show that the applicant would be able to perform adequately?
>> Would applicants be motivated to act in congruity to the response?

In many circumstances, the desired performance flows from knowledge. I am concerned with tests that make it easy to get credit for paying lip service to some cliché from a text when there is a reasonable likelihood that candidates may be unable to perform in accordance with their answers on a test.

Teachers know that they should make the subject interesting, but many are inherently boring or poorly informed. Aspiring social workers were asked, "Of the following abilities, which one is most important for an interviewer to possess?" Checking the wanted answer, "the ability to ask the right questions and to listen and understand what is said," is no guarantee that the interviewer can perform this difficult and subtle task.

Most supervisors know that they should organize their workday, but many never learn how. Unless there is reason to believe that a person will act according to knowledge, testing the knowledge is probably useless.

> Would the applicant need to apply the knowledge immediately on appointment?
>> Would the applicant be required to perform adequately without further training?
>> Would the knowledge be used by incumbents at this organizational level?
>> Would the new incumbent work without benefit of close supervision?

If the applicants will be trained in the material on the test after appointment, or if they are closely supervised so that they can learn while the organization is protected from their errors or inefficiency, the questions are inappropriate.

Much information in a given line of work is not directly relevant to an incumbent at a given level because the work is someone else's responsibility. Arson investigations are important to fire departments, but many of the techniques are needed only by specially trained members of the arson squad. There is no point in asking those in fire suppression about work they do not perform. Police officers are asked about the admissibility of hearsay evidence, and their supervisors are asked about the proper disposition of papers after they turn them in. These questions are in the province of lawyers and office managers, not police sergeants. A favorite form of testing is to ask for detailed information on personnel policies or other rules that can be easily looked up or obtained from a specialist without interfering with the flow of work.

First-line supervisors are asked about purchasing decisions made at the level of the chief. Applicants are asked about disciplinary procedures in which they are the recipients of discipline, not the disciplining authority. Police officers are asked to determine the degree of felony, a decision that is the province of the district attorney. Machine operators need to know the speed and feeds for cutting certain materials, but design engineers do not. Salesmen need to know delivery schedules, but sales managers probably do not.

Keeping detailed information about little-used procedures is taxing and can lead to mistakes. The conscientious physician is not embarrassed to look up the dosage of a rarely used drug, and the patient is protected from lapses in memory. Tax laws are so complex that many questions should be researched rather than evaluated by a fallible memory. Often, the right answer to technical questions should be to identify the source of information, not the information itself.

How important would the ability to respond be to successful job performance?

Would there be serious consequences for safety or efficiency if the applicant does not have the information or skills needed to respond?

This is the crucial question. If information or skills are unimportant, there can be no reason to ask the applicant for the information or to demonstrate the skills. SMEs tend to accept questions that appear to be in the proper area as being relevant. It is necessary at this point for the test expert to ask for a justification of any evaluation made. SMEs can be asked to give examples from their experience or to compare the importance of information with other information that is clearly relevant.

The ideas of the SMEs are critical at this point. They must be supplied with a standard that sets a threshold on the importance of the information. The issue requires a reasonable set of reference points for importance, which is developed by the test expert and the SMEs. When they have agreed on the threshold, they may need to go back to the early decisions and reevaluate them to make sure that the same standard is applied.

The knowledge of how to fight fires is basic to the work of fire lieutenants. No matter how knowledgeable or effective the lieutenants are in other areas, such as filling out forms, if they do not know how to lead a crew to attack fires, citizens and their property are placed at an unacceptable risk. A simulation that taps this knowledge in a realistic way and meets other standards gets at important information.

Some information that is superficially job-related is really trivial. The test then becomes a measure of whether or not applicants have read and remembered minutiae taken from the books on an assigned list, not whether or not they have the information and skills needed to perform on the job. There is no simple way to determine whether or not the consequences of ignorance are important, but often, it is obvious that the loss of performance because of ignorance would be inconsequential.

Some questions are obviously not intended to measure potential job performance. Item writers sometimes fail to distinguish between "need to know" and "nice to know." Social workers are asked in one jurisdiction to reorder a randomly organized set of sentences about robots into a well-organized paragraph. They should be able to write clear reports, but constructing a paragraph about robots is not part of the job.

Does the selection procedure provide adequate background information?

Does the stem or introduction correctly provide all the needed information?

If the question is a simulation, does it communicate the information?

Many questions ask the applicant what to do in a situation described in a few words in the stem. If the issue is not trivial, it is likely that all the relevant information cannot be presented, requiring the applicant to fill in the missing detail with assumptions that may not coincide with the assumptions that the item writer had in mind.

Firefighters may be asked how to attack a fire in a garage that is "fully involved" without any information about whether or not it is a one-car garage near a house or a repair shop, whether or not there are inflammables nearby, and so on.

Some questions use terms that properly are the subject of substantial training. Without more specification, no one knows whether or not the applicant who chooses the wanted answer really understands the principle.

For example, in one test, candidates for promotion to police sergeant were given this question:
In making an arrest, the officer may use:

a. Only the force which the suspect deserves.
b. Only the force which the officer believes would be fair.
c. Only that force which is necessary, including extreme force.*
d. Only that force which is necessary short of deadly force.
* Wanted answer.

This emotionally charged, possibly dangerous confrontation is not described, nor are the alternatives spelled out clearly.

In this context, simulations include the hypothetical situations found in many multiple-choice tests as well as the more elaborate simulations of assessment centers. Item writers often try to bring the realities of the job to the test by describing a situation and asking the applicants how they would respond. Unfortunately, complex situations cannot be described in the few lines available for a multiple-choice test. Consequently, applicants must guess at relevant details before they frame their answers. If they guess wrong, they may miss or distort the point of the question as perceived by its author.

Since there is always some slippage between the job and its simulation, professional judgment based on knowledge of both the situation being simulated and the exercise is needed to determine whether or not performance on the simulated activity is an adequate representation of reality.

Do applicants have adequate backgrounds to respond?

Can applicants be expected to have the necessary education?

Can applicants be expected to have the necessary training or experience?

Section 14C(1) states: "Content validity is also not an appropriate strategy when the selection procedure involves knowledges, skills, or abilities which an employee will be expected to learn on the job."

Content-valid tests are useful only when the applicant has had an opportunity to learn the material and absorb the behaviors that are integral to the test. Generally, it is not suitable for use where it would be most helpful: initial entry. There are some exceptions. Applicants are not expected to arrive at the employment office totally ignorant. All people should have acquired some relevant information and skills that are available to them in public education, such as language usage and arithmetic, by the time they apply. Specialists, such as typists, engineers, and bookkeepers, who present themselves as trained can be tested fairly with content-valid tests. Promotion involves the application of some skills of the lower-level job to the next level. Journeymen pipe fitters or first-line supervisors could reasonably be tested to determine the level of their possession of the relevant information and abilities that they claim.

A content-valid test is appropriate when applicants can be expected to have acquired the necessary KSAs on the current job. Some applicants for promotion work so closely with their supervisors that they have ample opportunity to observe performance on many important supervisory functions; others do not. Sometimes, they even take over in an acting capacity or receive training relevant to the job they are seeking. For them, it is reasonable to test for KSAs they have observed or have been trained to use.

Sometimes applicants may never observe or participate in a function that is an important part of the job for which they are applying and may receive all their training, if any, after their promotions. For example, no one in the schools in one major city deals with the teachers' union except the principal. Although dealing with the union is important at that level, it is not a fit subject for testing applicants because the applicants have no experience in these matters, and, besides, the Board of Education employs labor lawyers who are trained in negotiations.

If there is a readily available source of information, such as a coworker, training manual, or supervisor, the KSAs may not be suitable for preemployment testing. Information imparted during an orientation period or break-in is not appropriate. Material that is quickly learned, such as the location of the various offices or workplaces, is inappropriate for testing.

Supplemental Indications of Content Validity

Would the test distinguish between those who have appropriate training and experience and those who do not?

>Would competent journeymen probably respond correctly?

>Would persons with inadequate training or experience be likely to answer incorrectly?

If a test is content-valid and deals with important information specific to performance on the job in question, those who know the subject matter should pass, and those who are not knowledgeable about the job should fail. It is possible to make items so hard that no one can answer them or so easy that anyone can answer based on general knowledge or shrewd guessing.

An acid test would be to administer the test to a sample of experienced workers who are acknowledged by their peers to be competent and see how they perform. If they fail, the test should be examined to see if it relies on trivia from textbooks and training manuals that are never used. Similarly, if a person who is not trained can answer the test on the basis of general knowledge and testwise guessing, the information measured is probably not job-related.

Is the test free from the effect of extraneous influences?

>Would applicants who are not testwise be likely to do well as well as they should?

>Are the language and mathematics demands of the test commensurate with those required by the job?

Extraneous aspects of tests interfere with their measuring what they are intended to measure. Each of these features of the selection procedure would be evaluated to make sure that it meets professional standards.

Test wiseness is the art of selecting the wanted answer without knowing the material. Careless item writers give away the answer by clues such as agreement between the plural subject and plural verb in the wanted answer, but not in the others. Sometimes the statement in the stem of one item provides the answer to another item in a different part of the test. When in doubt, some choose the longer alternative because there are sometimes more qualifiers in the wanted answer than in the distractors. And so on.

Length and difficulty of reading and writing passages. Items that are too long or too difficult convert a test of knowledge into a test of reading. The items should be carefully edited. When a test calls for written responses but is not a test of writing ability, care should be taken to avoid measuring written expression.

Multiple-choice tests are often evaluated with reading formulas, such as the Flesch count, that report the reading level in grade equivalents. The theory behind most counts is that short sentences and short, common words make the item easier to read. Whether or not this is true of children's books is a matter of considerable professional debate among educators, but it is clearly not true of multiple-choice tests. In an effort to keep the items short, they are worked and reworked to a level of subtlety and precision that is beyond the skills of the typical high school graduate who is taking the test. Qualifiers such as "may" or "generally" complicate the meaning of otherwise simple concepts.

Is the selection procedure free of bias?

Are selection procedures of this kind free of a history of discrimination against minorities and women?

Would the content of the selection procedure be acceptable to minorities and women?

Some employers continue to use selection procedures with known bias despite the availability of tests that have less adverse impact. Sometimes, this persistent use borders on intentional discrimination. Employers who want to reduce adverse impact may successfully explore some of the alternatives mentioned in this book and by Reilly (1996).

Blatant racism and sexism have been eliminated from most tests, but subtle problems remain. Constant use of *he, his*, and *him* and reference to male-oriented activities and interests in reading passages make tests more difficult and offensive for women. Unnecessary use of abstractions for selection for a concrete, physical, or interpersonal job makes the tests more difficult for those with deficient language skills and for those who never had an opportunity for quality education or for whom English is a second language. Physical tests can be biased against women by overemphasizing upper-body strength or against women and some minorities by emphasizing height.

Would the employer benefit from teaching the applicants how to take the test?

Are the skills that would be taught related to work behavior?

Test-taking strategies have no relevance to the work. The time spent on them does not improve the applicants' performance. On the other hand, if an employer is upgrading typists to make them able to use the word processor, training them to perform well on a job-relevant test is in the employer's best interest.

Does the item require a constructed response?

Is it sufficient that the applicant recognize, rather than construct, a response?

Generally, multiple-choice tests require only that the applicant recognize the wanted answer. To be sure, some questions require calculations or interpretation of a chart before the answer is chosen, but they are the exceptions. Although there is a relation between constructed response and recognition, the two abilities are different. Recognition is passive, but creating a response is an active process. It is difficult to think of situations in which recognition alone is enough.

Implications

In this chapter I have focused attention on multiple-choice tests because they are so pervasive, and the problems that can arise are so clear. However, many of the same principles apply to any measure of competence on the job or to the KSAs needed to perform the job duties. Simulations, work samples, situational judgment tests, assessment centers, reference checks, and measures of strength and abilities can all be evaluated on some of the same standards. The fundamental standard is a demonstration of the linkage between the test and the job duties or the KSAs needed to perform them.

Content Validity Form II is appended to show how it is organized with a checklist format for ease in summarizing the data from the test. You may obtain permission to use this copyright material from Fair Test, 342 Broadway, Cambridge, MA 02139.

Chapter 9

Criterion-Related Validity

BACKGROUND

The *Standards* define criterion-related evidence of validity succinctly as "Evidence that shows the extent to which scores on a test are related to a criterion measure."

Criterion-related validity provides the clearest evidence of the job relatedness of a selection procedure by comparing, with a correlation coefficient, the scores on the test with a measure of performance on the job. This simple paradigm has many subtleties, discussed in more detail in texts on the subject. See Schmitt, Borman and Associates (1993) and Schneider and Schmitt (1986). Rather than repeat all that they say, I emphasize those issues that are relevant to fair employment.

There are two major variants on criterion-related validity, *predictive validity* and *concurrent validity*. In a predictive study, the tests are administered to applicants, and their test scores are later correlated with the measures of their performance. The virtue of this approach is that the applicants are generally similar to the next cohort of applicants. They are motivated to perform well, so their scores are comparable to those of later applicants. There are, unfortunately, two major problems with predictive validity. First, if the tests are used to screen out any of the applicants, there is a restriction of range in the sample. The sample of minorities and women will be small, and if there is an adverse impact, it will be smaller yet. There are statistical corrections for restriction of range, but, particularly with the small samples that are typical in this field, they give unstable results. Second, except for very large employers, the collection of a suitable sample can take years.

Concurrent validity studies use present employees as the research sample. The tests are administered, and the performance measures could, in principle, be collected in one day. The major problem is that the sample includes long-term employees who are not typical of the applicants. If there was an adverse impact, the sample of women and minorities will be small. Many are older and have had different educational and work experiences. Some may refuse to participate. The more talented members of the cohort have been moved to higher-level positions, and some of the less talented have been eliminated. Others have simply changed jobs. They are not motivated in the same way as applicants and may not do their best. Further, some skills have eroded, and others have been enhanced with the passage of time.

Purpose

The purpose of criterion-related validity is to estimate the job relatedness of a selection procedure by measuring the degree to which the scores on the procedure are related to measures of job performance.

Population and Sample

Different populations are used for the two kinds of studies. The later performance of applicants who took the test as part of the employment process is used to measure *predictive validity*. The present performance of current employees who took the test as part of the research program is used to measure *concurrent validity*. The samples taken from these populations are selected with the conflicting aims of getting a large sample to maximize the statistical stability of the data and studying only those subjects who are representative of the applicants who will be selected using the validated test.

Measurement and Data Collection Procedure

Two measures are critical to the determination of criterion-related validity. The first, of course, is the scores on the selection procedures, which should be administered under circumstances that are as similar to operational conditions as possible. The second is the criterion measure of job performance that is to be predicted, generally supervisory ratings but also other measures such as training time and tenure.

The criterion is crucial to the validity study and is often given too little attention. One pioneer in the field, Edwin Henry, said that the criterion should require three-quarters of the effort in a validation study. The task is strange and sometimes threatening to the raters because they may feel that they are harming someone's career or that they are being put on the spot themselves if they report that they have not developed an adequate workforce. This threat and unfamiliarity can be reduced by administering the criterion measure personally. I explain to each rater that the purpose of the project is to help the organization hire more people like the ones they want, and fewer like the ones they do not want. They are being asked to tell me the kinds of people that the organization should hire to get the work done. Their ratings will be used to develop a system to identify the more promising applicants, not to make personnel decisions about the ratees. I guarantee that no one's career, their own or those of the employees whom they are rating, will be affected by their ratings. It is useful to dramatize the confidentiality of the ratings by locking them up as soon as they are collected.

By the nature of the problem, the criterion measure must be convertible into numbers. There are two basic ways to do this, graphic ratings and ranking. Rating scales generally consist of descriptions of several types of job perform-ance to be measured, generallly including quality and quantity of work, appli-cation to the work, and whatever else is considered important. The ratings are made on a scale, generally of five points, ranging from superior through satis-factory to unsatisfactory.

Ranking is easier to administer and is better understood by supervisors, who are asked only to place the names of their subordinates in order from best to worst. The judgments are converted to numbers that reflect the relative position of each. Rankings are more meaningful when there are more people being ranked. Rankings are rarely used when there are fewer than five subjects.

Although some issues require an extensive background in testing and statis-tics, much of what is done can be understood and evaluated by anyone who perseveres. Of the ten basic steps in a criterion-related validity study, nine re-quire no mathematics, but they are crucial to interpreting the results and deciding the action that is to be taken. The following discussion describes how a thought-ful reader without training in statistics can understand and evaluate what was done to demonstrate the validity of a selection procedure. The following steps are typical.

1. Establish the objectives of the selection procedures.
2. Identify the population of jobs.
3. Select the sample to be studied.
4. Determine what selection procedures are used.
5. Administer the tests.
6. Collect criterion measures.
7. Analyze the results.
8. Draw conclusions.
9. Use results.
10. Report.

You and your expert should be able to address each of these questions sat-isfactorily.

What are the objectives of the selection procedure? The purposes of the selection procedure should be clearly defined. It is not enough to state that the test is designed to get better people without defining what ''better'' means. Generally, it is defined as performance on the job after orientation, training, and experience have given the new employees enough time to settle into a stable work style. However, some tests are designed to select applicants who will achieve adequate tenure or who will move after a reasonable time to higher-level positions. Rarely can a test meet more than one objective, so it is important to decide just what the test is to accomplish.

What jobs are included? Covering too few related jobs decreases the size of the research sample. A small sample increases the likelihood of failing to find validity when it really exists. Including unrelated jobs leads to the dilution of the validity of the test when jobs for which the test is unlikely to be predictive are included. For example, are all craft jobs considered part of the same population, or are the crafts broken down in more detail? Carpentry requires more understanding of arithmetic principles than does painting. Electricians need to understand the basic principles of electricity; plumbers do not. Machinists need manual skills that are different from those of paperhangers.

The job description does not need to be as detailed as the description used in a content validation study. All that is required is information to support the use of the criterion measure and to classify the jobs.

On what sample is the study based? Generalizations based on inferential statistics are, according to theory, based on random samples drawn from a defined population. In selection research, identifying the population of interest is not possible. When the study is performed to predict the performance of future applicants, it is necessary to consider its use with those who might apply for the same job in the indefinite future, an impossibly vague condition. At one time, applicants for secretarial positions with a large employer were older, experienced, but minimally educated women. Then, younger, better-educated women began to apply as women entered the workforce in greater numbers. Even later, many of those who would have been stuck on secretarial jobs moved into the professions. Selection tests that were valid for one group or at one time might not predict success for the other groups or other times.

The interpretation of the results should take into account how the sample differs from the ideal random sample drawn from a defined population of interest because a biased sample can lead to biased results. If there is any distorting effect in the recruiting of applicants, the elimination of some at a prior stage in the selection process, or other influence on the representativeness of the sample, the report should describe the issues, and the interpretation should be appropriately modified. For example, the use of volunteers may distort the study because volunteers are generally different from those who do not volunteer. If there is substantial reliance on volunteers, the researcher should try to minimize the effect or compensate for it.

A recent study examined the effect of drugs detected during the employment process on later performance. Applicants who had successfully passed through the initial stages of a long selection process were told that urine, collected as part of the routine physical examination, would also be tested for drugs. Despite the assurance that the results would be kept confidential and would not affect their employment, about 30% dropped out. The conclusions of the study cannot be generalized without qualifications to all applicants, since the sample is biased.

What selection procedures are used? It is essential that the same selection procedures be used in the study as are used in the research. Printed tests are no problem if care is taken to guarantee that the same editions and forms are used. However, it is difficult to standardize performance ratings and interviews in an assessment center.

How are the selection procedures administered? It is essential that the tests be administered, as nearly as possible, as they are routinely in the selection process. If the research subjects are not currently candidates for selection or promotion, their response patterns may differ from what their responses would be if they knew that their future employment depended on the test results.

How is performance measured? Special criterion measures should be developed and used solely for the validation study. Administrative ratings are generally subject to too many pressures to be useful. Supervisors sometimes give consistently high ratings or "satisfactory" ratings to avoid conflict with disgruntled subordinates. There is creeping inflation because tough raters see their subordinates denied promotions or raises that they deserve.

The criterion measure is subject to two major concerns. The first, contamination, occurs when the raters' judgments are influenced by extraneous considerations that should not be rated. Models should be rated high on their beauty; secretaries often are but shouldn't be. Long-term employees are rated higher than they deserve, while new, more competent employees are likely to be rated too low.

The second problem is deficiency, which occurs when important matters are not addressed. Some sales managers who have their eyes on today's net sales fail to give credit to the salesperson who services customer accounts and builds goodwill toward later market penetration.

How were the data analyzed? This is the only portion of the study that requires a knowledge of statistical computation. Without formal training, few people can compute and interpret statistics. At this point, it is essential to rely on a statistician, but the statistician should be selected carefully; statisticians are not all alike. Mathematical statisticians know more statistics than almost anyone, but many do not understand the problems of the real world such as small, biased samples and unreliable measures. Business statisticians understand index numbers, but they are irrelevant to employment issues. Get someone who is trained in statistics in the social sciences who can explain what is being done, why, what alternatives were rejected, and what actions are warranted.

What conclusions are drawn? Conclusions often go beyond the data. Each conclusion should be clearly related to the data on which it is based, and recommendations should follow from the conclusions.

How is the selection procedure used? Tests are used generally in two ways, to eliminate unsatisfactory applicants from further consideration or to make a selection from the remaining pool of applicants. The top-down selection procedure is discussed in Chapter 13. The test must fit with other selection procedures. Is the test part of a multiple-hurdles system, in which it is used to eliminate some candidates so that more attention can be paid to the applicants with the most promise? Is it part of a battery in which the final score is the sum of the weighted scores? If so, how much weight does it get compared to the others?

What information is included in the report? The requirements for a report are spelled out in Section 15B of the *Uniform Guidelines*, which prescribes the details required to report the results of the study. Much of what is covered by Section 15B is discussed in this book. Section 15B makes a convenient checklist to determine whether all the bases are covered.

Myth: *Graphic ratings permit fine distinctions between ratees. Graphic rating* describes any rating procedure in which the rater evaluates the performance of a subject. Originally, such ratings were literally graphic; that is, the rating was made by placing an *X* on a line, the end points of which were labeled to indicate that the right end represented good performance, and the left end unsatisfactory performance. The number to be assigned to the rating was determined by measuring the distance from the lowest rating to the *X*. Graphic ratings make it possible to recognize the differences between ratees that are more refined than is possible with rankings. The argument runs that rating Einstein first in a college class of typical physics students does not permit the rater to show just how far above the others Einstein really is. In practice, raters are governed more by response set than they are by the subtleties of the fine distinctions between levels of performance. Some like to rate everyone nearer to the top than do others. Even when the raters know that their ratings are confidential, some are reluctant to give anyone low ratings.

To focus the raters' attention on different aspects of performance, several scales that are conceptually different from the point of view of the psychologist are used before the summary or overall rating. Unfortunately, halo, the tendency to rate a person all high or all low based on some global perception, washes out the attempts to measure important differences in performance. However, not all intercorrelations among the ratings are unwarranted, because positive traits correlate positively. The ambitious are generally harder working but also work more intelligently and are likely to be punctual and not take days off to go fishing. The net result is that rankings, which are easy to understand, give just as good results, if, of course, there are enough ratees to make the ranks meaningful.

Myth: *Ratings of minorities by white supervisors lead to a downgrading of their performance.* The evidence is not clear on this issue. Often, minorities and white employees are rated about the same. In fact, there are instances where the black supervisors are harder on members of their own race than on the whites.

Each situation should be evaluated on its own merits. A proper rating procedure, in which the raters are trained and supervised, and the ratings are based on observed performance and rated on a meaningful scale, can help to reduce any such biases, which would lead to a misunderstanding of the research results.

Myth: *If the scores on a test correlate with measures of training, the test is valid*. Not necessarily. Section 14B(3) of the *Uniform Guidelines* states in part:

Where performance in training is used as a criterion, success in training should be properly measured and the relevance of the training should be shown either through a comparison of the content of the training program with the critical or important work behavior(s) of the job(s), or through a demonstration of the relationship between measures of performance in training and measures of job performance. Measurers of relative success in training include but are not limited to instructor evaluations, performance samples, or tests. Criterion measures consisting of paper and pencil tests will be closely reviewed for job relevance.

Justice Brennan joined Justice Marshall in a dissenting opinion in *Washington v. Davis* regarding the assertion of the U.S. Civil Service Commission that its test was valid because it correlated significantly with scores in training:

Sound policy considerations support the view that at a minimum, petitioners should have been required to prove that the police training examinations either measure job related skills or predict job performance. Where employers try to validate written qualification tests by proving a correlation with written examinations in a training course, there is a substantial danger that people who have good verbal skills will achieve high scores on both tests due to verbal ability, rather than "job-specific ability." As a result employers could validate any entrance examination that measures only verbal ability by giving another written test that measures verbal ability at the end of the training course. Any contention that the resulting correlation between examination scores would be evidence that the initial test is "job-related" is plainly erroneous.

People are not hired to be perpetual trainees; they are hired to produce. Unless there is convincing evidence that the scores in the training program predict success on the job, or training is so expensive that failures are prohibitive, performance in training is a poor criterion.

Myth: *Performance measures used as criteria must be free of extraneous influences*. They can't be. A fundamental problem in criterion measures is contamination that occurs when knowledge about the performance on the selection procedure influences the performance ratings. Sound practice demands that the raters be ignorant of the subjects' performance on the selection instruments. In principle, supervisors can be denied access to personnel records, but in reality secrecy may not be possible. When applicants are selected from civil service lists in rank order, all the supervisors know is that those hired first had higher scores than those in successive cohorts.

Performance measures are subject to all kinds of contamination, including personal friendship or antipathy. Some people rate the better performers below their true worth so that they will not be lured away by someone else. The problem was acute in the Navy in World War II, where the more talented members of a crew were needed to commission new ships. To avoid losing their best officers, some captains rated their losers high and their winners low. Eventually, the Navy had to resort to random selection using orders cut in Washington without knowledge of the ratings.

Myth: *Administrative ratings, being formal documents of the employer, are suitable as criterion measures.* Rarely. People are not used to giving thoughtful, meaningful, and accurate ratings for administrative purposes. They have been conditioned to be suspicious and to avoid controversy, which means that sometimes there is pressure to rate everyone as ''satisfactory'' or ''superior.'' Management often does not take routine ratings seriously, and the lack of purpose translates itself into sloppy ratings. A better procedure is to collect ratings for experimental purposes, guaranteeing that the ratings will not affect the careers of either the raters or the ratees.

Myth: *Targeted performance measures give more valid results.* One senior psychologist facetiously told me how to get good validities for a selection program for secretaries. He recommended that I correlate the typing test with ratings of typing, and an intelligence test with ratings on intelligence, and so on. The validity coefficients would be satisfactory, but the sample subjects would not be evaluated on many important functions of secretaries. By tailoring the criterion to the test, having a spurious appearance of validity is possible because the test measures only a superficial part of the job.

Myth: *Only positive, significant results need to be reported.* One psychologist testified that he did not present a complete table of results because he was hired to find significant results, and when he did, he reported them. Never mind that most of the table was blank. To interpret results of a complex study, one needs all the data so that patterns can be detected. When statistics are corrected for restriction of range or for unreliability, all of the corrected and uncorrected data should be reported. People, not statistics, prove things, and they need all the help they can get from a complete set of data.

Myth: *The use of four significant figures enhances the accuracy of prediction.* Correlation coefficients and weights carried out to four significant figures (e.g., .4232) give a spurious picture of the accuracy of the prediction. One significant figure—or perhaps with large samples two—is meaningful; the rest are random. Some civil service test scores are reported to five significant figures, suggesting an accuracy of about three inches in a mile. Performance ratings are used both as the criteria for the validation of other tests and to determine who is to be promoted or downsized or where the employees fit in the salary range for their jobs.

Getting accurate measures of performance is extremely difficult. Under the best of circumstances raters who know the work of the subordinate they are rating disagree. They open the door to conscious and unconscious biases of all kinds, including those based on race, ethnic background, religion, and sex. They should be examined carefully to make sure that they are not themselves a source of unfair discrimination.

Myth: *Validity studies are prohibitively expensive.* Seberhagen (1996a) in "How Much Does a Test Validation Study Cost?" points out:

Most discussions of testing fail to note that good testing is normally an investment, not an expense, because the selection of better employees will result in higher efficiency and productivity for the organization. Even a small improvement in productivity because of test validation can have a large payoff. For example, assume that a new employment test improved the production value of each new hire by only $1000 per year and the employer used the same test to hire 50 new employees per year for five years. If these 250 new hires stayed with the employer for an average of ten years, the dollar gain in productivity would be $2,500,000 from using the new test, which is probably 50–100 times the cost of test validation.

Implications

Employers who have the required number of employees to populate a reasonable sample would be well served to commission validity studies. If the selection procedures can be shown to predict success at an adequate level, they will be assured that they are on the right track and that they can rebut any charges that they are discriminating against members of protected classes. If there is no relation between the scores on the selection procedures and success on the job, they are not taking advantage of the modern technology that could improve the quality of their workforce.

Validity studies are not as expensive as they seem, and the payoff can be substantial. As shown in Chapter 14, there is a direct relationship between the validity of the test and its value to the employer. The costs of hiring at random from a pool of applicants and of defending—and perhaps losing—fair employment suits can be minimized. Although criterion-related validity studies require expertise in psychometrics, they are not especially costly or time-consuming when compared with the costs of hiring and retaining the incompetent.

The report should meet the standards of Section 15B, *Criterion related validity studies*, of the *Uniform Guidelines*.

Chapter 10

Construct Validity and Validity Generalization

BACKGROUND

Construct validation is the process of generalizing the validity of tests of a *construct* from collected research studies. Validity generalization is the process of generalizing about the validity of a *test* from a collection of research studies. The difference is subtle but important.

Construct validity is used to develop generally true statements about the validity of a construct by meta-analysis, that is, by combining data from different studies that bear on the validity of the construct. A construct is defined in *Standards* (p. 90):

Construct. A psychological characteristic (e.g., numerical ability, spatial ability, introversion, anxiety) considered to vary or differ across individuals. A construct . . . is not directly observable; rather it is a theoretical concept derived from research and other experience that has been constructed to explain observable behavior patterns. When test scores are interpreted by using a construct, the scores are placed in a conceptual framework.

Construct-related evidence of validity is defined in *Standards* (p. 90) as "Evidence that supports a proposed construct interpretation of scores on a test based on theoretical implications associated with the construct label."

The definition in the *Uniform Guidelines* is similar. *Construct validity* is defined in Section 16E:

Construct validity. Demonstrated by data showing that the selection procedure measures the degree to which candidates have identifiable characteristics which have been determined to be important for successful job performance.

A frequently overlooked requirement of construct validity is that it does not measure extraneous constructs. For example, an early personality measure distinguished between unsociability and introversion. Research data showed that the two scales were measuring the same construct. Applying the principles of construct validity to contaminated constructs would lead to spurious conclusions about the validity of the construct.

Validity generalization allows an employer to use, for example, the same clerical aptitude test in each of its locations. When the validity has been established, the employer does not have to repeat the same studies, which could be expected to have the same outcome because the situations are so similar. It runs counter to the earlier held belief that the same test may be valid in a shipyard in Norfolk but not in Seattle.

Validity generalization is defined in the *Standards* (p. 90): "Applying validity evidence obtained in one or more situations to other similar situations on the basis of simultaneous estimation, meta-analysis, or synthetic validation arguments."

Purpose

The purpose of both validity generalization and construct validity is to spare test users the trouble and expense of repeatedly validating tests when sufficient evidence has been accumulated that they are valid.

Population and Sample

In meta-analysis, the population of interest comprises all the validity studies that relate to the same or similar tests. The sample includes the available reports, including published and unpublished reports. The standards for the studies are the same as for criterion-related validity studies in general.

Measurement and Data Collection Procedure

Data for construct validity studies are collected from the literature and from unpublished reports. Data for validity generalization are collected on the same test within the organization or from cooperating organizations with similar jobs and similar labor pools.

Analysis and Conclusions

Meta-analysis is a specialized statistical technique for combining the data from different studies to permit generalization. The standards set forth in Sections 14D and 15D, *Construct validity*, generally apply to validity generalization. Meta-analysis has been used with mixed results to establish the generalized validity of cognitive tests (see Schmitt 1996).

Myth: *The meta-analyses are conducted on a representative sample of the research results.* Most studies are never published. Many studies conducted internally are not even formally reported. Pilot studies in which several tests are tried out to identify those suitable for more thorough analysis are less likely to be described than the results on the survivors.

The results of construct validity studies benefit from the "file-drawer" phenomenon. People do not advertise their failures. For several years, *Personnel Psychology* published a *Validity Information Exchange*, which consisted of short reports on the results of validity studies. The feature was eventually dropped for many reasons, one of which was that the editor could not persuade researchers to submit reports of negative findings.

Implications

Both validity generalization and construct validity require sophisticated statistical analysis. Schmitt (1996, p. 104) characterizes the state of the art:

In assessing the possibility of generalization to a particular set of job applicants, one must be concerned that the same construct is measured and that the job behaviors (or required knowledge, skills, and abilities) are the same as those that were the focus of the studies summarized in the validity generalization data base. If appropriately conducted, a validity generalization study should be of greater value than any single criterion-related validity study.

The same is true of construct validity studies.

Before relying wholly on either validity generalization or construct validity to select and defend tests, users would benefit from the advice of experts who are up-to-date in the field.

Chapter 11

Intentional Discrimination

BACKGROUND

Intentional discrimination in employment based on race, ethnicity, sex, disability, and age is prohibited. The original focus of Title VII was on intentional discrimination, while prohibition of systemic discrimination had to be clarified by the Supreme Court in *Griggs v. Duke Power Company*. It has not received the formal attention accorded to systemic discrimination by the *Uniform Guidelines*. Consequently, there is no comparable set of formal standards or codified procedures for determining whether or not the results of any personnel action, hiring, promotion, demotion, firing, layoff, pay, or work assignment were intentional.

The intent to discriminate against protected minorities is seldom advertised, but there are exceptions. One insurance company distributed a directive advising its managers that agents should be hired whose ages ranged from 25 to 40, a clear violation of ADEA. In another setting, a background survey used different scoring keys for applications of different ages. The testing agency maintained that the differences were justified because the same level of accomplishment that would be exceptional for a young applicant would signify little success for an older one. One stockbrokerage firm told the woman at the employment agency not to send over any "Number twos," a code word for African-Americans. They judged correctly from her accent that she was white, but they could not tell that her husband was black. She was happy to testify.

More subtle forms of discrimination are more common. One police department cut off the promotion list repeatedly just before a black activist was due to be promoted. One union not only used an invalid test with an adverse impact but also went out of rank order in the hiring hall to favor whites. Minorities and women are simply told that a more qualified person was hired. A large utility company refused to promote an African-American despite performance reviews that extolled his performance in saving more than $1 million per year. The office in one state police barracks where applicants picked up their application forms was decorated with Confederate battle flags. Unless there is a smoking gun, proving intentional discrimination is difficult; most people who consciously want to discriminate cover their tracks. Some who respond to barely conscious urges to keep an all-white, all-male workforce do not display their feelings.

Intentional discrimination and unintentional discrimination are clearly separated in the text of the law, but not in practice. A suit based primarily on adverse impact can be strengthened by evidence that seems to show a pattern of decisions that disfavor members of the protected classes. Plaintiffs' attorneys will cite both the systemic issues and impact data to develop a preponderance of evidence in their cases.

Section 11 of the *Uniform Guidelines*, *Disparate treatment*, refers to the use of validated tests in a discriminatory way when it states:

The principles of disparate or unequal treatment must be distinguished from the concepts of validation. A selection procedure, though validated against job performance following the Guidelines, cannot be imposed upon members of a race, sex, or ethnic group where other employees, applicants, or members have not been subjected to that standard. Disparate treatment occurs where members of a race, sex, or ethnic group have been denied the same employment, promotion, or membership, or other employment opportunities as have been available to other employees or applicants.

The standards of proof are very different from those relating to systemic discrimination. Statistical imbalance is not an issue. Charges of disparate treatment can be brought by one person without regard to how others of like race, sex, or ethnic group membership are treated. Intention to discriminate is difficult to prove or disprove. For example, when Title VII was enacted in 1964, one could assume that employers used discriminatory tests naively, without any intention to discriminate. Now, more than 30 years later, there is a history that some kinds of tests, built according to the same time-honored procedures, have regularly been found discriminatory and rarely to be valid. Meta-analysis has been used to support the position that tests are generally valid. No one has bothered doing a meta-analysis to prove that multiple-choice tests have an adverse impact against minorities because the impact is so obvious. Is an employer who continues to use such tests discriminating intentionally? It is hard to prove either way.

Myth: *All intentional discrimination is outlawed.* Section 702 of Title VII exempts certain employers:

This title shall not apply to an employer with respect to the employment of aliens outside any State, or to a religious corporation, association, or society with respect to the employment of individuals of a particular religion to perform work connected with the carrying on by such corporation, association, or society of its religious activities or to an educational institution with respect to the employment of individuals to perform work connected with educational activities of such institution.

Another exception is the Bona Fide Occupational Qualification (BFOQ), which permits purposeful discrimination based on sex (but not of race) where society agrees that there is a rationale for the discrimination. BFOQ has been interpreted narrowly. It is lawful to insist that an actor or singer be of the appropriate sex, but not a cellist or sculptor. Persons of the opposite sex can be excluded where mores require a separation of the sexes, such as in locker rooms, but female reporters fight to get into at least the outer reaches of the locker rooms of professional athletes. There is no BFOQ for race, but this provision is rarely invoked where race is clearly relevant, for example, when casting a play. Shades of the Cold War: another exception permits the deliberate exclusion of members of the Communist Party.

Myth: *Employers are free to describe jobs as they see fit.* One of management's cherished prerogatives is defining the job. Such job descriptions are sometimes part of a Realistic Job Preview (RJP), which is designed to describe the duties in enough detail so that interested and qualified applicants are encouraged to apply. Those who cannot perform the duties or do not want to are encouraged to look elsewhere. An accurate Realistic Job Preview that clearly describes both the pluses and minuses of the job is a benefit to both applicants and employers. However, some employers try to discourage unwanted applicants by overstating the requirements. For example, poorly educated applicants can be discouraged from a job they can do when it is described as requiring verbal and mathematical skills at an unrealistic level. Similarly, women have been unfairly treated by employers who exaggerate the strength required.

Myth: *Background checks are fair and impartial.* One police department hired a white applicant despite the knowledge that he was a convicted felon, a knockout factor in any police department. Black candidates were eliminated by the same department for such youthful indiscretions as throwing a brick through a window. Incidentally, the mayor of that city showed his dedication to civil service tests by naming his brother Fire Commissioner after he had failed the fire captain's examination.

Myth: *Sexual harassment must involve persons of the opposite sex.* In a unanimous decision, the Supreme Court ruled that it was the conduct that controlled, and not the sex or motivation of those involved. Justice Scalia wrote for the court, "We see no justification in the statutory language nor our precedents for a categorical rule excluding same-sex harassment claims from the coverage of Title VII."

He added,

Whatever evidentiary route the plaintiff chooses to follow, he or she must always prove that the conduct at issue was not merely tinged with offensive sexual connotations, but actually constituted discrimination because of sex. . . . The prohibition of harassment on the basis of sex requires neither asexuality not androgyny in the workplace; it forbids only behavior so objectively offensive as to alter the conditions of the victim's employment.

This ruling is the latest step by the court to outlaw discrimination in the workplace on the basis of sex. It leaves open milder forms of interplay between workers and supervisor.

Implications

Yes, Virginia, there is still intentional employment discrimination. Fair employment laws and changing times have reduced unfair practices and have sent some of them underground. It is the responsibility of senior management to educate and supervise those in charge of personnel decisions to eliminate or at least minimize the effect of practices that work against the interests of the protected classes and, when such practices are discovered, to rectify the situation.

Chapter 12

Adverse Impact

BACKGROUND

Adverse impact is any substantial disparity in hiring, promotion, layoff, or other personnel action between members of protected groups and the most favored race or sex. A demonstration of adverse impact is the trigger that places in motion the enforcement of systemic discrimination under Title VII of the Civil Rights Act, and the *Uniform Guidelines* should be invoked. Where there is an adverse impact, the user must show that the procedures used to make the decision are job-related for the job or a family of jobs in question. If there is no showing of job relatedness, the test user faces the penalties prescribed by law.

Q&A 10 defines adverse impact:

Q. What is adverse impact?

A. Under the Guidelines adverse impact is a substantially different rate of selection in hiring, promotion, or other employment decision that works to the disadvantage of members of a race, sex, or ethnic group.

Statistical information is used to identify adverse impact based on a substantially different rate of selection as defined in Q&A 11:

Q. What is a substantially different rate of selection?

A. The agencies have adopted a rule of thumb under which they will generally consider a selection rate for any race, sex, or ethnic group which is less than four-fifths (4/5ths) or eighty percent (80%) of the group with the highest selection rate as a substantially different rate of selection.... This "4/5ths" or "80%" rule of thumb is not intended as a legal definition, but as a practical means of keeping the attention of the enforcement agencies on serious discrepancies in rates of hiring, promotion and other selection decisions.

Despite this disclaimer, the 80% rule has been virtually enshrined as the standard for determining whether or not there is adverse impact.

Q&A 22 requires that statistical significance be computed only in rare circumstances, saying: ''Where large numbers of selections are made, relatively small differences may nevertheless constitute adverse impact if they are both statistically and practically significant.''

This provision has been generally ignored, and most courts entertain testimony about the statistical significance of the differences in hiring rates, while recognizing the lack of stability when there are few cases. The use of statistical significance in establishing adverse impact is discussed in Chapter 14.

Population

Generally, the population of interest is all applicants, but where promotion, layoff, or other personnel actions are at issue, the population is the affected incumbents. Applicants are those who have shown an interest in employment or promotion. *Applicant* is not defined in Q&A 15, which leaves the definition up to the employer:

Q. What is meant by the term ''applicant''?

A. The precise definition of the term ''applicant'' depends upon the user's recruitment and selection procedures. The concept of an applicant is that of a person who has indicated an interest in being considered for hiring, promotion, or other employment opportunities. This interest might be expressed by completing an application form, or orally, depending on the employer's practice.

Q&A 15 distinguishes between applicants and candidates. The latter are present employees who may be considered for training, promotion, or other treatment. The distinction is made to protect current employees who may be deliberately kept in the dark about opportunities so that they do not apply and would therefore not be included in the impact statistics. The problem seldom comes up, possibly because those who would keep their best openings secret know that they would be open to charges of intentional discrimination.

Q&A 15 continues:

A person who voluntarily withdraws whether formally or informally at any stage in the selection process is no longer an applicant . . . for purposes of computing adverse impact. Employment standards imposed by the user that discourage disproportionally applicants of a race, sex, or ethnic group, however, may require justification.

This means that the data on applicants who go through the entire process and then turn down a bona fide job offer are not counted anywhere in the statistics that determine adverse impact. Even this simple-appearing rule has its complexities. Applicants who turn down offers of civil service jobs soon after a list is promulgated are treated in the analysis as if they had never been interested in the job and therefore are not bona fide applicants. However, civil service lists can last four years or more. Applicants who turn down an offer three years after the test was administered might be appropriately included in the statistics regarding adverse impact because they might really have wanted the job if it had been offered when they were available.

Information on the applicants and the disposition of their applications should be available from the employer's records. If the information is not available, the *Uniform Guidelines* permit the use of demographic data that describe the appropriate labor pool. The Supreme Court, in *Wards Cove Packing v. Antonio* (1989), identified the population to which the hiring rates were to be compared to be those who were qualified, not all those who were in the local labor market. Qualifications are defined here primarily as relevant academic training, such as a degree in accounting for financial officers.

The idea of *applicant* implies the identification of the job that the applicant is seeking. In civil service this is not a problem when all applicants for a given job take the same test battery. Sometimes the same tests are used for different jobs. For example, in some fire departments the tests are geared toward fire suppression, but applicants for fire prevention, an entirely different kind of work, may be required to take a test of knowledge of fire fighting. Showing the job relatedness of the test would depend on acceptance of the organizational decision that everyone needs to know fire suppression, and appointment to fire prevention is a lateral transfer.

On the other hand, there may be problems in establishing job groups when skilled craftsmen apply, as I mentioned earlier. Different standards and different results may obtain when electricians, plumbers, painters, and welders are being hired. A job knowledge test that is valid for identifying journeymen electricians would be useless for selecting plumbers. However, a general ability test may cut across crafts and could be used on a wider basis. Again, judgment is required to determine how the boundaries between jobs are established.

Job classifications can be manipulated. One railroad, under threat of litigation, noted that almost all of its ticket agents were white. In one month, the number of employees listed as being in the sales force exploded, as did the number of African-Americans. The railroad had changed the designation of the work group from "ticket agent" to "sales force" and then counted the janitors who cleaned the ticket offices. The subterfuge did not convince anyone.

Breaking down the job categories to discrete jobs with small populations leads to statistical instability. Too-broad job classifications lead to the inclusion of jobs that should be considered separately. Like all statistics, the numbers used to establish adverse impact require close scrutiny to assure that they reflect the reality of the situation.

Measurement and Data Collection Procedure

Two types of data are collected: the race, ethnicity, and sex of the applicants and the results of the hiring or promotion process. Despite a spate of interest in testing female athletes to be sure that they are, indeed, female, the categorization by sex is straightforward. Identification of race seems simple, but borderline cases of mixed race and ethnicity require careful adjudication. On October 29, 1997, the federal government adopted a rule that people may identify themselves as members of more than one race. The effect of this rule on the calculation of adverse impact is unpredictable, except that it will lead to endless litigation.

It is not my purpose here to debate the definition of race. The employer is expected to apply a good-faith procedure for placing individuals in racial categories for the determination of adverse impact.

The data on hiring decisions are generally, but not always, straightforward. Applicants and those who were hired are easily counted. However, it is not always clear whether a change in job duties accompanied by a modest increase in salary is a transfer or a promotion. Each such situation must be evaluated on its own merits.

The trigger that initiates an inquiry into systemic discrimination is disparity in the hiring or promotion rates of two different groups, divided on lines of race ethnicity or sex. The law was written with the expectation that the higher-scoring racial/ethnic group would be whites and the higher-scoring sex would be male, but the wording is neutral. In the rare instance when the minority group scores higher, as happens sometimes with Asians, there are likely to be too few to provide a stable basis of comparison.

Comparing a protected group against all others is incorrect, for example, comparing Hispanics with all other applicants. When this comparison includes other protected minorities who may themselves be underrepresented, their inclusion would understate the impact that would have been observed if the Hispanics were compared with non-Hispanic whites. The inappropriateness of this analysis is more obvious if another minority is bringing charges of unfair discrimination separately.

Sometimes specific subgroups complain of discrimination. For example, African-American men may charge that they are hired at a lower rate than white men, ignoring both African-American and white women. It is the position of the *Uniform Guidelines* that discrimination based on race or ethnic group membership and discrimination based on sex are two distinct issues. Although both groups are covered in the same text by Title VII and the *Uniform Guidelines*, they should be treated separately. The employer might object that the categories are contrived by troublemakers who search through the data for numbers that fit their objectives. Using a grouping in which the plaintiffs simply capitalized on chance relations would be inappropriate. Q&A 17 states:

Q. In determining adverse impact, do you compare the selection rates for males and females, and blacks and whites, or do you compare selection rates for white males, white females, black males, and black females?

A. The selection rates for males and females are compared, and the selection rates for the race and ethnic groups are compared with the selection rate of the race or ethnic group with the highest selection rate. . . . There is no obligation to make separate comparisons for subgroups (e.g., white male, white female, black male, black female).

Analysis

An example of computation of adverse impact is presented in Table 12.1.

Myth: *Applicants can be required to identify their race or ethnic group membership.* The method of classification favored by EEOC is self-identification, but if for any reason that method is unworkable, the identification may be made by a member of the test user's staff. The alternative procedure of identifying race or ethnicity is provided to respect the sensitivity of the applicants while permitting the collection of necessary data.

Myth: *The only basis for determining adverse impact is the five racial/ethnic categories listed in the Uniform Guidelines and the two sexes.* The *Uniform Guidelines* list the five major racial/ethnic groups in Section 4B, *Applicable race, sex, and ethnic groups for record keeping.* Almost all litigation by minorities has focused on these five racial and ethnic groups. However, persons of other racial or ethnic groups are protected by the same statutes, although they do not have the same ready access to the data routinely provided in EEO-1, a quarterly report of hires, as do members of the five main groups. Generally, there are too few applicants from other protected groups to permit statistical analysis.

Section 4B of the *Uniform Guidelines* defines the groups:

Blacks (Negroes), American Indians (including Alaskan natives), Asians (including Pacific Islanders), Hispanic (including persons of Mexican, Puerto Rican, Cuban, Central or South American, or other Spanish origin or culture regardless of race), whites (Caucasians) other than Hispanic . . .

The complexity of the definition of a protected class is illustrated by a case brought by Hispanics in San Francisco. Many applicants with Hispanic surnames and therefore classified as Hispanics came from the Philippines, where they had attended schools taught in their native tongue, English. Since the adverse impact was too small to support litigation, the case was refiled in Los Angeles in the expectation that there would probably be an adverse impact because Spanish was the native tongue of most Angelenos with Hispanic surnames.

Table 12.1
Computation of Adverse Impact

	Hispanic	White
Hired	12	41
Not Hired	130	160
Total	142	201
Percent Hired	8.5	20.4

Adverse Impact = 41.4% [100(8.5 /20.4)]

The racial and ethnic mixture in Hawaii is so complex that the basic categories do not apply.

Myth: *Using the EEO-1 report schedule for determining adverse impact is adequate.* EEO-1 provides quarterly data, which are generally aggregated annually. The data may not reflect reality. Hiring patterns vary, particularly in cyclical industries. An oil refinery in boom times may hire a large staff, starting in November and ending the following March. Annual figures do not represent the situation adequately, particularly if the boom is followed by a bust with virtually no hiring a few years later while excess staff is downsized by attrition. Judgment is required to establish the appropriate interval to be covered. Lengthening the period provides more stable data but may include results from times when different policies or economic conditions prevailed.

Civil service testing presents both unique problems and unique solutions. The appropriate interval might seem to be the life span of a test, since the applicants are seeking the same job, and only when the list expires can its results be known. However, since some lists last four years or even longer, it would be an injustice to the plaintiffs to make them wait until the last employment decision is made for the data to be complete. The unique solution is provided by rank-order lists. By projecting retirements, deaths and disabilities, promotions, and transfers, the employer can project the number to be hired from the list. By counting down from the top of the list, a reasonably accurate estimate of the impact ratio of the test under this policy is possible. Experience with these projections shows that they are accurate and that minor deviations from the result make little difference.

Myth: *The EEO-1 categorization of jobs is adequate for determining which are covered.* The EEO-1 covers only broad categories that may not be appropriate for determining the impact ratio. Applicants for entry-level production line jobs in an automobile plant generally do not know or care whether they will be assigned to press operations, hand or robotic assembly, the paint shop, or anywhere else in the plant. After being hired, they may be transferred or promoted to different work. There is no reason to break down the jobs into more refined categories.

Myth: *Employers must keep a complete record of applications.* Section 4A, *Information on impact*, states:

Each user should maintain records and have available for inspection records and other information which will disclose the impact which its tests and other selection procedures have on employment opportunities of persons of identifiable race, sex, or ethnic group.

However, several exceptions to the rule are set forth in Section 15A(1), *Simplified record keeping for employers with less than 100 employees*, which reduces the record keeping requirements, a section too long to be quoted here. It requires only that such employers should keep employment statistics by race, ethnic group membership, and sex and that they should also keep a record of the selection procedures used. Further, no records need to be kept on groups that constitute less than 2% or more than 98% of the labor force in the area.

Employers with more than 100 employees are required to keep data on each of the five major racial and ethnic groups listed in Section 4B only if that group constitutes more than 2% of the workforce. Employers with fewer than 100 employees come under Section 15A(1).

Myth: *Records must be kept on everyone who expresses an interest in employment.* Section 15A, *Documentation of impact and validity evidence*, hinges on the term "applicant," but the *Uniform Guidelines* do not define the term in Section 16, *Definitions*. The committee that wrote the *Uniform Guidelines* was unable to define *applicant* operationally because the term covers so many situations. Many college graduates broadcast dozens of résumés, and colleges may receive hundreds of applications from new Ph.D.'s in English literature. Employers cannot track everyone who might show some interest in a job, particularly if interest is expressed by mail on a "to whom it may concern" basis. Instead of trying to prepare a definition that can be applied in all circumstances, employers are granted freedom under the sentence in Q&A 15 quoted earlier, "This interest might be expressed by completing an application form, or orally, depending on the employer's practice."

Failure to keep such data does not protect the testing practices from scrutiny. In the early days of enforcement of Title VII some employers invoked state laws that prohibited the keeping of racial and ethnic data on applicants. The federal government quickly invoked the doctrine of federal supremacy, and the courts ordered the recalcitrant employers to comply with the record-keeping provisions of the *Uniform Guidelines*.

Myth: *Plaintiffs may demonstrate adverse impact by comparing the number of employees of the minority and non-minority groups with the population in the labor market.* This provision depends on the definition of *labor market*. Section 4D, *Adverse impact and the "four-fifths rule,"* states:

[T]he Federal enforcement agencies may draw an inference of adverse impact of the selection process from the failure of the user to maintain such data if the user has an underutilization of a group in the job category, as compared to the group's representation in the relevant labor market . . .

The key word in this provision is *relevant*. In *Wards Cove Packing v. Antonio* (1989) the Supreme Court defined the relevant labor market to include only those who were qualified for the work in question by virtue of training or experience. For example, in hiring engineers, the relevant labor market is those who have the necessary training and experience to be engineers, not merely all those who lived within commuting distance of the workplace. Reliance on demographics may distort the impact data for entry-level jobs when a disproportionally large number of minorities apply.

Civil service testers often label those who pass their test as "qualified." Accepting this definition of *qualified* begs the question when the test itself is under scrutiny. There must be more convincing evidence of qualifications than a test score.

Myth: *If minorities and women pass the preemployment or promotion test at the same rate as non-minorities and males, there is no adverse impact.* No. Passing or failing a test in itself is not relevant to the issue of adverse impact. Title VII is concerned with employment decisions, and if no action is taken on the pass–fail status of an individual, Title VII does not apply. On the other hand, if there is any action, such as eliminating some applicants from further consideration or placing them in some subordinate or conditional status, the *Uniform Guidelines* apply. This provision negates the ploy of some employers who set such a low passing score that there can be no adverse impact under the 80% rule but who then select from the top of the list, resulting in adverse impact.

Myth: *If there is no adverse impact in the whole process, there is no need to establish the validity of any individual procedure.* Section 4C, *Evaluation of selection rates*, clearly states that if there is no adverse impact for the entire selection process, there is no need to show the job relatedness of any portion of the test, even if it has an adverse impact. This is the so-called bottom line provision. However, the Supreme Court, in *Teal v. Connecticut* (1982), ruled otherwise, and it is necessary to justify any portion of the selection procedure that has an adverse impact.

The notion of the bottom line is not entirely dead. If three successive hurdles exactly meet the 80% rule, the user is not home free, because the overall effect is a severe adverse impact ($80\% \times 80\% \times 80\% = 51.2\%$).

Pinpointing the offending procedure is difficult when test scores, data from the application blank, and the result of interviews are assembled into one overall score. It is even more difficult when no score is derived from some or all of the selection procedures, and the employment decision is made by informal judgments.

Myth: *A passing score of 70% is about right; 75% is too hard; 65% is too easy.* Passing scores of 70, 65, or even 60 are enshrined in the minds of most of us because we have been subjected to a grading system in which 100% is the highest possible score, and some score around 70 is passing. This scoring system is totally arbitrary. In some tests, the score is determined directly by counting the percentage of questions answered correctly. The test builder sometimes has to adjust the difficulty of the test to make the scores come out so that enough applicants pass to fill the employer's needs and reduces the number of applicants who go on to a later step in the selection process to a manageable size. When the test builders miss the mark, and so few pass that the vacancies cannot be filled, the passing score is likely to be adjusted downward.

Setting a passing score is a complex art. In one popular method Subject Matter Experts are asked to estimate the percentage of successful employees who would be expected to choose the right answer for each question. The results are collated, and a passing score is computed. However, there is no evidence that the resulting passing score is more appropriate than any other. As far as I know, no one has successfully applied an empirical standard to the setting of a passing score.

Myth: *If the hiring or promotion rate of minorities is greater than 80% of the rate for whites, or for women is more than 80% of that of the men, there is no adverse impact under the* Uniform Guidelines. Not necessarily. Q&A 20 says, in part:

Q. Why is the 4/5ths rule called a rule of thumb?

A. Because it is not intended to be controlling in all circumstances. If for the sake of illustration, we assume that nationwide statistics show that use of an arrest record [see later] would disqualify 10% of all Hispanic persons but only 4% of all whites other than Hispanics (hereafter non-Hispanics), the selection rate for that selection procedure is 90% for Hispanics and 96% for non-Hispanics. Therefore, the 4/5 rule of thumb would not indicate the presence of adverse impact (90% is approximately 94% of 96%). But in this example, the information is based upon nationwide statistics, and the sample is large enough to yield statistically significant results, and the difference (Hispanics are 2½ times as likely to be disqualified as non-Hispanics) is large enough to be practically significant.

[Under the principle that a person is presumed to be innocent until proved to be guilty, arrest records can no longer be used.]

The point is underscored in Q&A 19, which states:

Q. Does the 4/5ths rule of thumb mean that the Guidelines will tolerate 20% discrimination?

A. . . . the differences in selection rates of less than 20% may still amount to adverse impact if the differences are significant in both statistical and practical terms.

Despite the efforts of the committee that wrote the *Uniform Guidelines* to produce a flexible standard, few cases are brought where the impact ratio is greater than 80%.

Myth: *The 80% (4/5ths) rule is scientifically based.* The 80% rule was developed in the living room of William C. Burns (Burns 1996), who chaired the group writing the California Technical Standards. After a debate, the limit was set at 80% because 85% seemed too high, and 75% seemed too low. There is no empirical basis for setting the dividing point at a selection ratio of 80%.

Myth: *Practices that lead to the rejection of no minority applicants insulate the employer from charges of adverse impact*. During the depression one employer adopted a policy of employing only applicants who were sponsored by present employees. By the time Title VII took effect, all of the employees were white, and, not surprisingly, all of their nominees were white. Since minorities knew that there was no point in applying, none tried. The employer's claim that there was no adverse impact because no minorities had been turned down did not stand up under scrutiny.

This is an extreme example of the basic principle that discouraging minority or female applicants can be linked to a determination of adverse impact when it suggests deliberate discrimination. Plaintiffs' attorneys will bring in any evidence that even hints at intent, and the courts give the evidence whatever weight it deserves.

Myth: *The organization-wide impact ratio gives an accurate picture of the effects of its selection procedures*. It may not. The administration of a large university, dedicated to equal treatment of men and women, was disturbed to learn that women seeking admission were being rejected at a higher rate than men. They called in a statistician, who found an explanation in the eponymous Simpson's paradox. The overall adverse impact against women was the result of variations in the application and acceptance rates of different departments. Few applicants and even fewer women sought majors in mathematics and the hard sciences. Many were accepted, and men and women were accepted at the same rate. On the other hand, more applicants and a higher proportion of women sought admission to the humanities. With men and women rejected at the same rate, many more women were rejected than men. When the data were combined, the large number of women rejected by the humanities department overwhelmed the statistics, creating a false impression of an adverse impact against women.

Implications

Adverse impact is fundamental to the *Uniform Guidelines* and the enforcement of Title VII. As is the case with all statistics, the seemingly simple 80% rule is more complex than it appears, particularly when considerations of statistical significance are introduced (see Chapter 14).

Some critics have asserted that the 80% rule means that Title VII endorses an adverse impact of up to 80%. Section 4D, *Evaluation of selection rates*, notes that: ''smaller differences in selection rate may nevertheless constitute adverse impact, where they are significant in both statistical and practical terms.''

Chapter 13

Reducing Adverse Impact

BACKGROUND

Reducing adverse impact against qualified minorities and women without violating the rights of the employer or other workers is the primary goal of Title VII. There are two major means toward this objective. The first is to use alternative selection procedures that have less adverse impact than those traditionally used to identify the better applicants. Section 3B, *Consideration of suitable alternative selection procedures*, says:

Where two or more selection procedures are available which serve the user's legitimate interest in efficient and trustworthy workmanship, and which are substantially equally valid for a given purpose, the user should use the procedure which has been demonstrated to have the lesser adverse impact. Accordingly, whenever a validity study is called for by these guidelines, the user should include, as part of the validity study, an investigation of suitable alternative selection procedures and suitable alternative methods of using the selection procedure which have as little adverse impact as possible, to determine the appropriateness of using or validating them in accordance with these guidelines. If a user has made a reasonable effort to become aware of such alternative procedures and validity has been demonstrated in accord with these guidelines, the use of the test or other selection procedure may continue until such time as it should be reasonably reviewed for currency. Whenever the user is shown an alternative selection procedure with evidence of less adverse impact and substantial evidence of validity for the same job in similar circumstances, the user should investigate it to determine the appropriateness of using or validating it in accord with these guidelines.

Since much of this book has been devoted to the development and use of valid, nondiscriminatory procedures, I refer the reader to the preceding chapters. A second means of reducing adverse impact is through affirmative action.

Purpose

The purpose of affirmative action is to remove barriers to the employment of members of the protected classes and to redress the balance where discrimination has been shown. Affirmative action is the major strategy for reducing adverse impact and the most misunderstood and reviled issue in fair employment. Hypocritical politicians continue to equate affirmative action with quotas, although Title VII of the Civil Rights Act clearly states:

Nothing contained in this title shall be interpreted to require any employer . . . to grant preferential treatment to any individual or to any group . . . on account of an imbalance which may exist with respect to the total number or percentage of persons of any race, color, religion, sex, or national origin employed by an employer . . . or in the available work force.

The EEOC Office of Communication and Legislative Affairs (n.d.) spells out the limitations of permissible affirmative action (p. 1):

It is important to clarify that the extent of permissible affirmative action is strictly limited under law. Affirmative action is lawful *only when it is designed to respond to a demonstrated and serious imbalance in the work force, is flexible, time-limited, applies only to qualified workers, and respects the rights of non minorities and men.*

Policy Statement on Affirmative Action. The Equal Employment Opportunity Coordinating Council (Appendix 1, *Uniform Guidelines*, Section 17) points out:

Equal employment opportunity is the law of the land. In the public sector of our society this means that all persons, regardless of race, color, religion, or national origin shall have equal access to positions in public service.

Section 17 of the *Uniform Guidelines* sets forth the position of the Equal Opportunity Coordinating Council regarding voluntary programs in private employment:

When an employer has reason to believe that its selection procedures have an exclusionary effect, it should initiate affirmative steps to remedy the situation. Listed are the following steps:

1. The establishment of . . . goals . . . which should take into account the availability of basically qualified persons.

2. A recruitment program . . .

3. A systematic effort to organize jobs in ways that provide opportunities for persons lacking "journeyman" level knowledge or skills.

4. Revamping selection procedures . . .

5. The initiation of measures designed to assure members of the affected group . . . are included in the [applicant] pool . . .

6. . . . career advancement training.

Section 17 continues:

[T]he Council has not attempted to set forth here either the minimum or maximum voluntary steps that employers may take to deal with their respective situations. Rather, the Council recognizes that under applicable authorities, State and local employers have flexibility to formulate affirmative action plans that are best suited to their particular situations.

Myth: *The Office of Federal Contract Compliance (OFCCP) of the Department of Labor, in enforcing Executive Order 11246, imposes quotas on employers.* OFCCP (1995) ''reaffirms its longstanding policy that affirmative action program goals . . . are used as a tool for breaking down barriers to equal employment opportunity for women and minorities without impinging upon the rights and expectations of other members of the workforce.'' It states, ''The essence of affirmative action programs [is] contractor self-evaluation and self-correction,'' and ''Goals and timetables are neither set-asides nor a device to achieve proportional representation or equal results.''

It makes the point more explicit:

In seeking to achieve its goals, an employer is never required to: 1) hire a person who does not have the qualifications needed to perform the job successfully; 2) hire an unqualified person in preference to another applicant who is qualified; or 3) hire a less qualified person in preference to a more qualified person. Unlike preferences and quotas, numerical goals recognize that persons are judged on individual ability, and are, therefore, consistent with the principles of merit hiring and promotion. . . . Failure to meet goals is not a violation of the Executive Order. Therefore, a contractor that has not met its goals will be found in compliance if it has made good faith efforts.

The purpose of affirmative action is to foster fairness, but the *Uniform Guidelines* recognize that fairness is hard to define and to establish. The definition and measurement of fairness are still a subject to debate, largely because it is a social, not psychometric, concept. Fairness is defined by its antonym, unfairness, in Section 14B(8)(a), *Unfairness defined*:

When members of one race, sex, or ethnic group characteristically obtain lower scores on a selection procedure than members of another group, and the differences in scores are not reflected in differences in a measure of performance, the use of the selection procedure may unfairly deny opportunities to members of the group that obtains the lower scores.

Section 14B(8) also discusses at length *(b) Investigations of fairness, (c) General considerations in fairness investigations,* what to do *(d) When unfair-*

ness is shown, (e) Technical feasibility of fairness studies, and *(f) Continued use of selection procedures when fairness studies are not feasible.* Few opportunities to conduct fairness studies exist, and they require the application of sophisticated statistics. Your attention is referred to the previously mentioned sections of the *Uniform Guidelines* and to more technical works.

FAIRNESS

Figures 13.1–13.7 give a simplified introduction to the issues involved in defining and measuring the fairness of a selection procedure. Since fairness is a social-political concept that reflects the point of view of the beholder, no statistical standard has won universal acceptance. The debate over fairness has been with the profession for at least 20 years and will probably continue indefinitely.

I first produced these figures in 1968. In the intervening years, there have been many formulations of the way to define and measure fairness. The spring 1976 issue of the *Journal of Educational Measurement* was devoted entirely to articles on bias in selection. I do not try to resolve the many complex issues or to anticipate the direction the debate may take in the future. If you are seriously concerned with the problem, I recommend that you consult psychometricians and current journals about the ongoing debate.

Figures 13.1–13.7 are schematic representations of the outer limits of the scatter plot. Each dot represents simultaneously the scores on the test and on the measure of work performance for a single individual. The ovals and circles trace the outer limits of the swarm of dots. They give a misleading impression of the distribution of the data, because they suggest that there are more cases farther from the mean than there are. In the later diagrams, the dots representing the test scores and performance measures are eliminated for the sake of clarity. The scores cluster around the regression line, as shown in Figure 14.1–14.11 in the following chapter. These correlation diagrams give a more mathematically and perceptually accurate representation of the relationship between test scores and performance measures than do the ovals.

Figure 13.1 shows the ideal situation, a test that is valid and fair to both groups. If the test scores and performance measures of the two groups are distributed similarly throughout the scatter plot, the test is valid and fair. Its use would benefit the employer by improving the quality of the workforce while fostering fair employment. It would benefit members of both groups because they would be hired on the basis of their potential performance. There would be no room for charges of unfair discrimination because there is no adverse impact.

Figure 13.2 illustrates a test that is fair but invalid. If the test scores of the two groups are distributed as shown, the test is fair to both groups. It, too, can be used without fear of repercussions under Title VII because there is no adverse

Figure 13.1
Fair, Valid for Both Groups

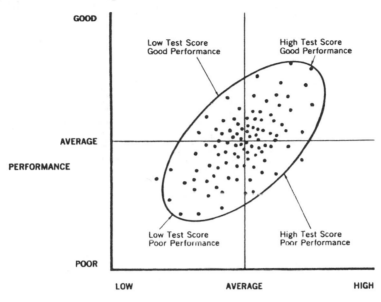

TEST SCORE

impact if the data of the two groups are distributed similarly throughout the scatter plot. The federal government is not concerned with the validity of the test unless there is adverse impact. However, since it does not predict success for anyone, it does not help the employer to select better employees. It should be replaced with a more valid instrument because it detracts from the usefulness of the other parts of the selection procedure. Since it arbitrarily and randomly eliminates good performers at the same rate as the poor performers, it decreases the size of the effective applicant pool that can be considered using other selection techniques. Reduction of the size of the applicant pool reduces the utility of the test, as shown in Figures 14.16 and 14.17.

Figure 13.3 illustrates a test that is valid for both groups but that has an adverse impact against the lower-scoring group. If the test is used to select from the top down, there is an adverse impact that would lead to a prima facie case of discrimination. (In this context, *discrimination* is a neutral word reflecting the differences in hiring rates. There is no suggestion that the difference in employment rates is intentional.)

It would appear that an adequate rebuttal to the prima facie case is that the test is valid for both groups individually and for the applicant pool as a whole. However, these figures oversimplify the situation. The methods for dealing with

Figure 13.2
Fair, Not Valid

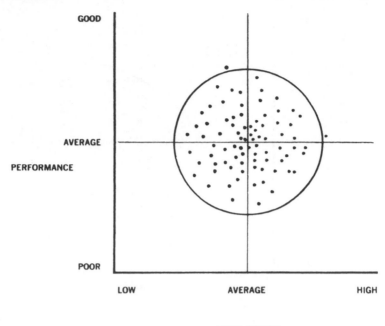

TEST SCORE

this kind of result are fuel for ongoing controversy. The data are never as clear-cut, and the interpretation depends on the definition of fairness that is adopted. A thorough discussion of the issue is beyond the scope of this volume.

Figure 13.4 illustrates a test that is valid for both groups but unfair to the lower-scoring group because their performance is as good as the performance of the higher scorers, although they score poorly on the test. This condition could exist when the members of one group are typically poor test-takers compared with the members of the higher-scoring group. Some attempts have been made to equalize the test-taking ability of the groups by special training programs. The members of the lower-scoring group have a smaller chance of being selected than the members of the group that tests better, although they are just as qualified.

Since the purpose of the test is to select those who are likely to perform well, adjustments that equalize the predicted performance would be justified. However, score adjustments are forbidden under the provisions of the Civil Rights Act of 1991. Such procedures for correcting the situation, although statistically sound, are unpalatable to members of the higher-scoring group, who believe that their superior test performance is a sign of superior worth.

Figure 13.5 illustrates the situation in which the test is not an adequate predictor of success. The test discriminates unfairly against the lower-scoring group

Figure 13.3
Fair, Valid for Both Groups

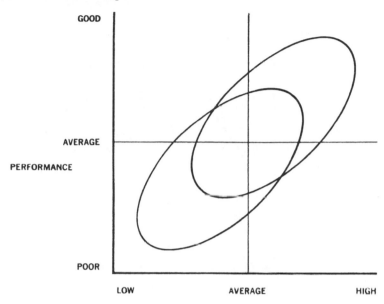

TEST SCORE

but does not help the employer to select better employees from either group. Without validating the test, one can never be sure that this unfortunate situation does not exist.

Figure 13.6 illustrates an extreme case in which a test has different levels of validity for the two groups but no difference in job performance. If the test is valid for one group but not for the other, it is said to exhibit single-group validity. If the validity coefficients of both tests are positive but substantially different, the result is called differential validity. The test is fair to members of both groups, since their test performance and job performance are, on the average, about the same. The employer benefits slightly from using the test because, for at least one group, it selects better candidates.

Figure 13.7 represents one of the many complexities of the analysis of fairness. The members of the group for which the test predicts success perform less well on the test than members of the group for which the test is invalid. There is a greater spread of both the work and the test performance of the group for which the test predicts success than for the invalid test. A low cutoff score would benefit the employer by eliminating more poor performers than good performers, but a high cutoff score would favor the group for which the test is not valid.

I have presented the issues here in a simple, schematic form. Real data are

Figure 13.4
Unfair, Valid for Both Groups

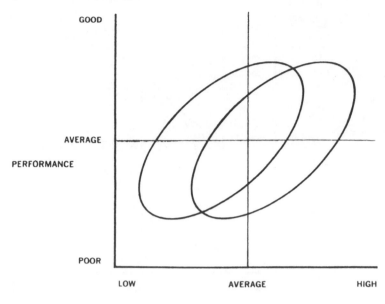

TEST SCORE

not that neat, especially when we must deal with the small samples that are typical of selection research. As Figure 13.7 suggests, the effect of a given selection procedure depends not only on its statistical characteristics but also on how it is used and how it relates to other selection procedures that are used in conjunction with it. These complexities, along with the difficulty of agreeing on socially, politically, and statistically acceptable definition of fairness, will keep the debate alive for a long time.

Myth: *The EEOC requires quotas of private employers.* The EEOC has no jurisdiction over affirmative action in private employment. However, in *Affirmative Action appropriate under Title VII of the Civil Rights Act of 1964*, as amended, it calls for voluntary actions:

1. Training plans and programs.
2. Focused recruiting.
3. Elimination of adverse impact caused by unvalidated selection criteria.
4. Modification of promotion and layoff procedures.

Myth: *An employer must admit to discriminatory practices before undertaking affirmative action.* The same policy statement calls for a reasonable self-analysis, saying:

Figure 13.5
Unfair, Invalid

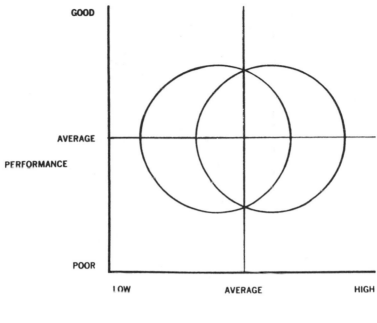

TEST SCORE

In conducting a self analysis . . . persons subject to Title VII should be concerned with the effect on its employment practices of circumstances which may be the result of discrimination by other persons or institutions. . . . It is not necessary for the self analysis to establish a violation of Title VII.

Myth: *Affirmative action policies cause employers to prefer less qualified minorities or women over more qualified white males.* Holzer and Newmark (1996) report on an extensive study of the issues. Here is their *Abstract* in its entirety:

In this paper we use micro-level data on employers and employees to investigate whether Affirmative Action procedures lead firms to hire minority or female employees who are less qualified than workers who might otherwise be hired. Our measures of qualifications include the educational attainment of the workers hired (both absolutely and relative to job requirements), skill requirements of the job into which they are hired, and a variety of outcome measures that are presumably related to worker performance on the job. The analysis is based on a representative sample of over 3,200 employers in four major metropolitan areas in the U.S. Our results show some evidence of lower educational qualifications among blacks and Hispanics hired under Affirmative Action, but not among

Figure 13.6
Single Group and Differential Validity

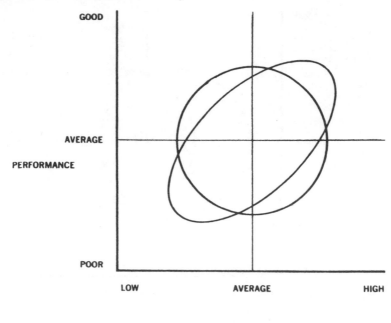

TEST SCORE

white women. Further, our results show little evidence of substantially weaker job performance among most groups of minority and female Affirmative Action hires.

The *New York Times* (1997), in an article that bore the headline "Study of Doctors Sees Little Effect of Affirmative Action on Careers," said in its lead:

In a report certain to fuel the debate over affirmative action, an extensive study of doctors trained at the University of California at Davis over a 20-year period found that those admitted with special consideration for factors like race or ethnic origin had remarkably similar post graduate records and careers to those admitted on academic merit alone.

Although the students admitted with special consideration had trouble with basic science courses and were less likely to graduate with honors, they graduated at essentially the same high rate and followed similar career paths as those who were admitted with the standard credentials. The cohort receiving the special consideration was 54% minority, and 4% of those admitted without special consideration were minority.

Myth: *Goals and timetables are quotas.* The Office of Federal Contract Compliance Programs 60–2.12, *Establishment of goals and timetables*, says:

Figure 13.7
Combination of Differential Validity and Fairness

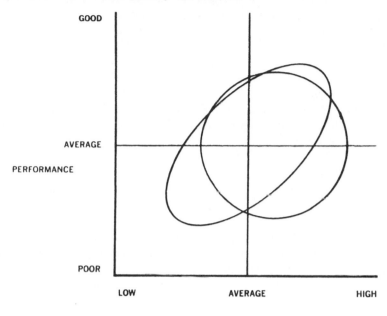

TEST SCORE

Goals may not be rigid and inflexible quotas that must be met, but must be targets reasonably attainable by means of applying every good faith effort to make all aspects of the entire affirmative action work.

Myth: *Removing the most discriminatory items from a test destroys its validity.* As part of a settlement with the Golden Rule Insurance Company, an organization owned and managed by African-Americans, the Educational Testing Service (ETS) removed items from a multiple-choice test of knowledge of insurance law and regulations, thus increasing the number of African-Americans who passed the test and were allowed to sell insurance. Later, ETS representatives expressed regret for their concession, saying that the validity of the test was compromised. Since the test was never validated against performance or any other criterion relating to the protection to the public, the alleged damage to the test has not been demonstrated.

Myth: *If a selection procedure is shown to be adequately valid, the employer may use it despite the adverse impact.* The employer is still obligated to use a less discriminatory procedure if one can be found that serves the employer's needs. Section 3B, *Consideration of suitable alternative selection procedures,* quoted before, emphasizes that the alternative procedures should "serve the user's legitimate interest in efficient and trustworthy workmanship."

Two major impediments to the use of more valid procedures are administrative complexity and costs. Employers are not required to use elaborate and expensive procedures that are not economically justified.

Myth: *The user of oral, rather than written, responses will reduce adverse impact.* A team that assembled a fire scene simulation had the opportunity to compare the written notes of the applicants for promotion with their oral presentations. The results were nearly identical, since the oral presentation was taken directly from their notes.

Myth: *Employers must make a cosmic search to find less discriminatory alternatives.* Section 15B(9), 15C(6), and 15D(8), *Alternative procedures investigated*, all say the same thing:

The selection procedures investigated and available evidence of their impact should be identified (essential). The scope, method, and findings of the investigation, and the conclusions reached in the light of the findings, should be fully described (essential).

All that is required is a reasonable search of the professional literature, which is not so extensive as to be called "cosmic." Test users are expected to consider any alternatives brought to their attention by an interested party. They are not required to listen to every test publisher who claims substantial validity and reduced adverse impact. Reilly (1996) has summarized the available alternatives.

Myth: *Reducing adverse impact will spell the ruination of the American workforce.* Sackett and Roth (1991) report research on the effect of eight different selection methods. The first is "strict top down," which offers the best quality workforce and the greatest adverse impact against low-scoring minorities. Using the Monte Carlo technique, which is a computer simulation of the results that would be obtained under different strategies, they compared the effects of using seven options with the strict top-down procedure. The results varied with the type of selection strategy and the percentage of the applicants who were minorities.

One strategy, *top-down selection within groups*, also called race norming, had been used by the Department of Labor in reporting scores on the GATB. In that procedure, the scores for members of different racial or ethnic groups were based on a comparison with the scores of other members of the same group. Using a strict top-down procedure under these circumstances results in a quota in which the proportion of minority applicants hired equals that of the non-minority applicants. Race norming is forbidden by the Civil Rights Act of 1991.

Other procedures used banding, which is based on the principle that scores that differ by small amounts are essentially the same. Applicants whose scores fall within the band are considered tied. A band is a range of scores that are so close to each other that they are considered tied. (For a detailed discussion of banding, see Zedeck et al. 1996.) In the sliding band procedure, the band from which the applicants are selected shifts downward when a person within that band is selected. The procedure that most benefits the minorities is the sliding band with minority preference within that band when the top scorers are selected.

Sackett and Roth (1991) conclude (p. 239):

[W]e found small differences between different banding approaches in mean test scores of selected individuals. Although strict top-down selection produced the highest mean test performance of any of the selection rules examined, none of the banding procedures produced mean test scores as much as .1 SD lower than top-down selection.

Sackett and Roth point out that selecting randomly from the band does little, if anything, to increase minority or female participation. Giving minority group members preference raises public policy issues and protests from male and non-minority applicants who are passed over. Those who are passed over argue that any deviation from strict rank order is unfair. The counterargument is that precise ranking is a fiction and that there is no noticeable difference in the potential performance of applicants whose scores are virtually the same. It is not my purpose here to resolve such social issues but to articulate and clarify them.

A problem arises when management does not promote one of the higher-scoring applicants. In this case, the high scorer acts as a limit on how much the band can slide, since eventually the upper boundary of the band would slide past the high scorer. If the employer has an option under the rule of three or some similar procedure for skipping over high-scoring applicants, it can be invoked. If there is some compelling reason not to hire or promote the high scorer, the decision maker may justify the decision to eliminate him or her from consideration.

A more radical approach would be to convert the score on the test to a score that reflected the predicted criterion score of the applicants and use that score in the sliding band. Then, a group that is denied access to jobs because of low test scores would have a better chance of being hired if they were evaluated by the best estimate of how they would perform on the job. There would be no rational cause for dissension, since the purpose of the selection procedures is to predict success.

Myth: *White men resist affirmative action and equal opportunity.* Not necessarily. Parker, Baltes, and Christiansen (1997) studied work attitudes of four groups of federal employees. White men did not associate support for affirmative action and equal opportunity with loss of career development opportunities, organizational injustice, or negative work attitudes. Women expressed positive attitudes regarding organizational justice and increased career opportunities.

Implications

Reducing adverse impact without interfering with the rights of other workers or the efficiency and safety of the operations is the basic goal of fair employment legislation. The pressure to improve the quality of tests and to reduce their adverse impact has led to a proliferation of new procedures, discussed in Chapters 2, 3, and 4. The progress in the profession over the past 30 years has been impressive not only in the reduction of impact on a protected group but also in the improvement in the quality of the workforce. One often overlooked benefit of this movement is the entry into the labor pool of minorities and women whose talents in earlier times would have been stifled in jobs that were below their capacities.

Affirmative action, properly construed, is also good business. Through training, focused recruiting, elimination of adverse impact caused by invalid selection procedures, and the improvement of promotion and layoff procedures, employers can enhance the quality of their workforces while serving the objectives of citizens who have previously been discriminated against. (Accommodations required for hiring the disabled are discussed in Chapter 17.)

The ethical principles address some issues relevant to reducing adverse impact. Ethical Standard 1.10, *Nondiscrimination*, states: "In their work-related activities, psychologists do not engage in unfair discrimination based on age, gender, race, ethnicity, national origin, religion, sexual orientation, disability, socioeconomic status, or any basis proscribed by law."

Ethical Standard 1.14, *Avoiding harm*, approaches the same point from a different angle: "Psychologists take reasonable steps to avoid harming their clients, research participants, and others with whom they work, and to minimize harm where it is foreseeable and unavoidable."

Chapter 14

Statistics

BACKGROUND

This chapter is intended to make you a user of statistics, but not a statistician or psychometrician. I explain what to look for in a statistical study and how to interpret results. It is like working with an accountant on your income tax. You need to know what records to keep, what questions to ask, and how to check the results for reasonableness. Nevertheless, you don't have to be a CPA.

The mathematics of statistics can be threatening to the person whose last exposure to computations that are more complex than balancing a checkbook in high school. The selection of statistics and their computation are best left to a discussion with a professional statistician who is familiar with testing issues. During litigation, the statisticians for both sides can argue the mathematics and fine points of the analysis. Interested parties who are not statisticians can protect themselves if they understand the logic behind what was done so that they can interpret the outcomes.

Purpose

There are two basic types of statistics, descriptive and inferential. Descriptive statistics organize a massive set of data to make it understandable. The most common descriptive statistics used in testing are the mean, standard deviation, and correlation coefficient. Fair employment issues add the concepts of selection rate and impact ratio. Of course, there are many others, but since they are rarely used to evaluate fair employment issues, I do not discuss them here.

In reducing data to manageable dimensions, some information is lost in the interest of clarity. Scatter plots (correlation diagrams) such as those later in this chapter, graphs, and tables sometimes give a clearer picture than the statistics that compress the data to a few numbers.

Inferential statistics are used to make quantitative statements about the likely characteristics of a population based on observations of a sample, particularly the difference between two populations or the association between two or more sets of scores. (*Score* is a generic term for a number assigned to measure an attribute of an individual, such as test score, age, and employment status.) The inferences are never certain; it is always possible that the vagaries of chance and mismeasurement will operate to mislead. Further, the choice of the sample, the hypothesis being tested, and the statistical procedures used influence the nature and usefulness of the generalizations.

The best-known and simplest statistic is the arithmetic mean, which everyone has used countless times by adding up scores and dividing by the number of scores. The other measures of central tendency that you have heard of, the median and the mode, are virtually never used in this context, and so I do not discuss them.

The next most important statistic, the standard deviation, is the most stable and useful measure of variability. It appears in the formula for Gauss' normal curve, also known as the normal or bell-shaped curve (from its shape). In the mathematical normal curve, 34% of the scores lie between one standard deviation and the mean.

The other major descriptive statistic is the correlation coefficient, a measure of the association between two sets of scores on the same subjects. Because the meaning of the correlation coefficient is not obvious from the procedures for computing its value, I have prepared Figures 14.1–14.11 to demonstrate visually what the correlation coefficient means. The size of each circle is proportional to the number of subjects whose scores fall in each cell. The swarm of dots is more dense toward the center because the mathematically perfect sets of scores follow the normal curve, which has the greatest concentration of entries near the mean and tapers off as the distance from the mean increases.

The angled lines are regression lines. To predict the criterion score on the vertical axis, (ordinate) from the performance measure on the horizontal axis (abscissa), draw a line up from the test score to the regression line and then horizontally to read the score on the performance measure. The vertical row of dots gives a visual display of the error inherent in the prediction at a given test score. As the correlation increases, error decreases until, with the unattainable correlation of 1.00, there is no error.

Correlation diagrams are often represented by ovals that include most of the data. They give a misleading impression because the eye (or the mind) tends to fill in the area uniformly, leaving the impression that there are fewer cases concentrated in the center and more on the outer fringes than is actually the case. (Please keep this point in mind when reviewing the figures used to illustrate the relation between fairness and validity in Chapter 13.)

The scales need some explanation. They are based on standard scores com-

Figure 14.1
Correlation Diagram (r = 0.00)

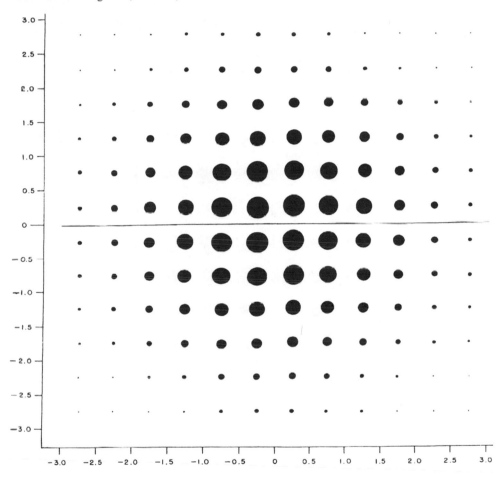

Figure 14.2
Correlation Diagram (r = 0.10)

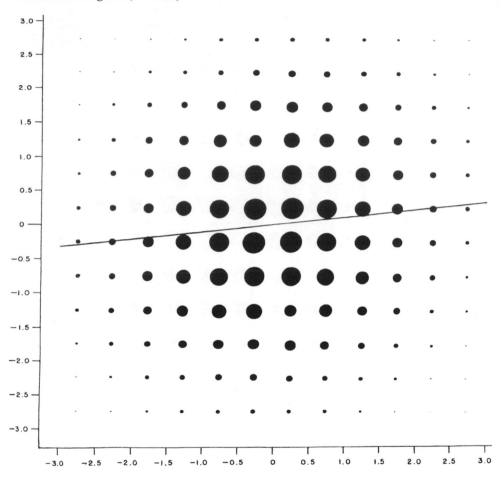

Figure 14.3
Correlation Diagram (r = 0.20)

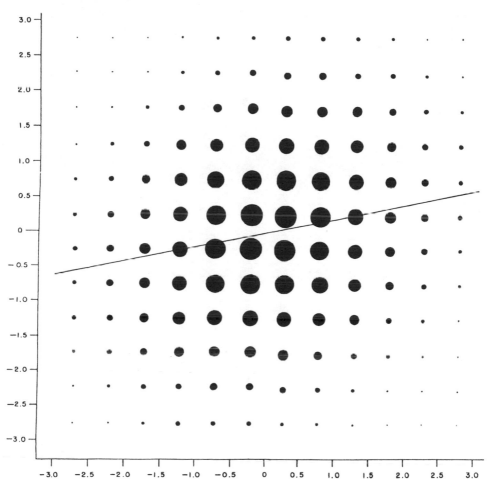

Figure 14.4
Correlation Diagram (r = 0.30)

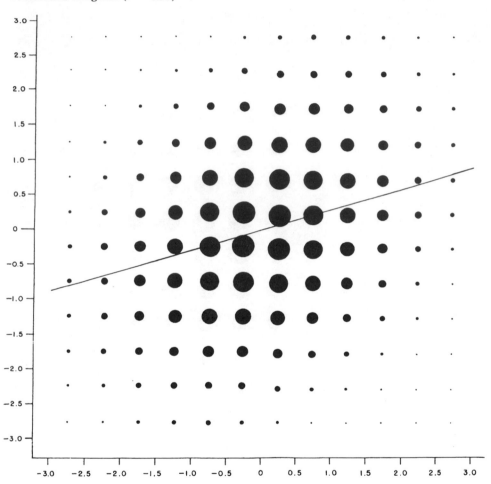

Figure 14.5
Correlation Diagram (r = 0.40)

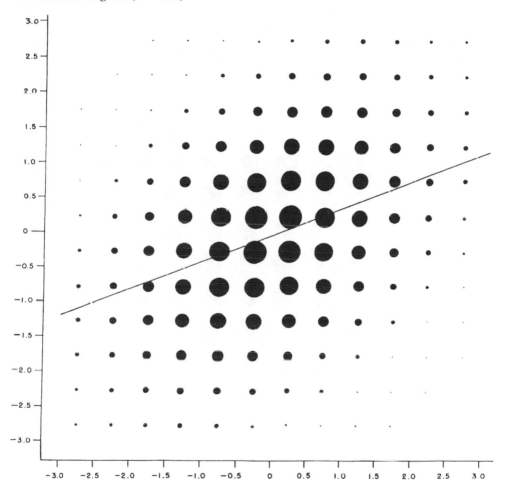

Figure 14.6
Correlation Diagram (r = 0.50)

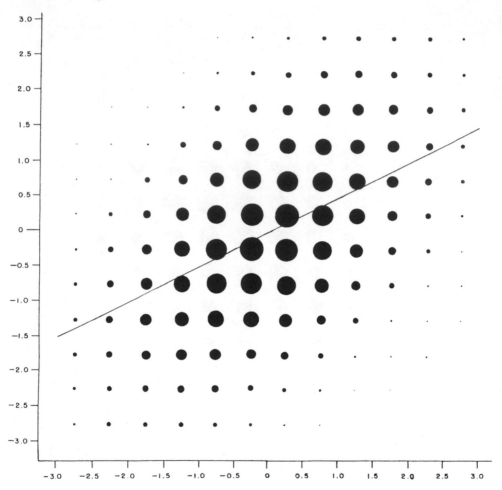

Figure 14.7
Correlation Diagram (r = 0.60)

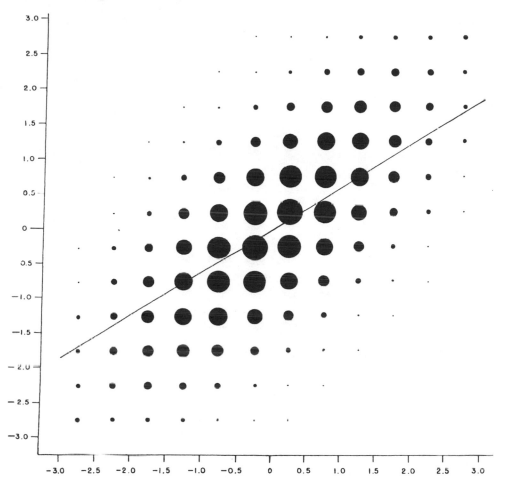

Figure 14.8
Correlation Diagram (r = 0.70)

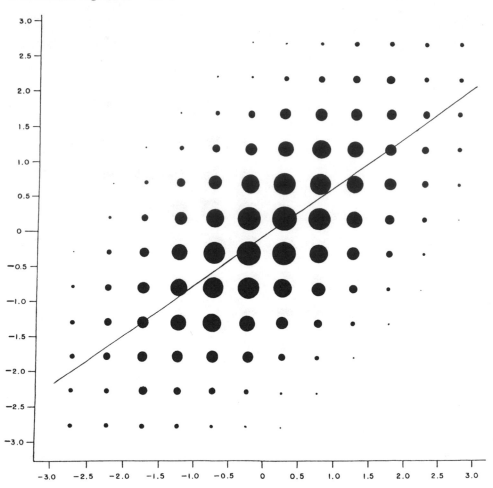

Figure 14.9
Correlation Diagram (r = 0.80)

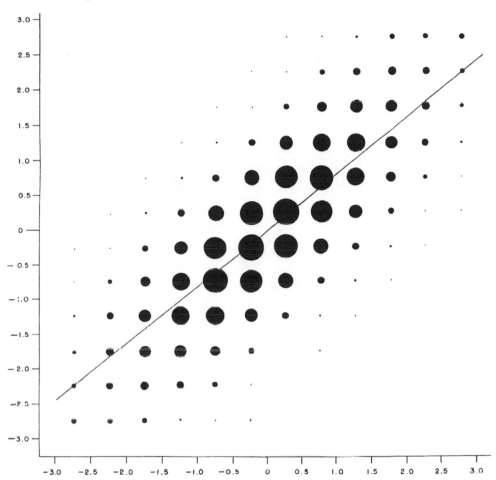

Figure 14.10
Correlation Diagram (r = 0.90)

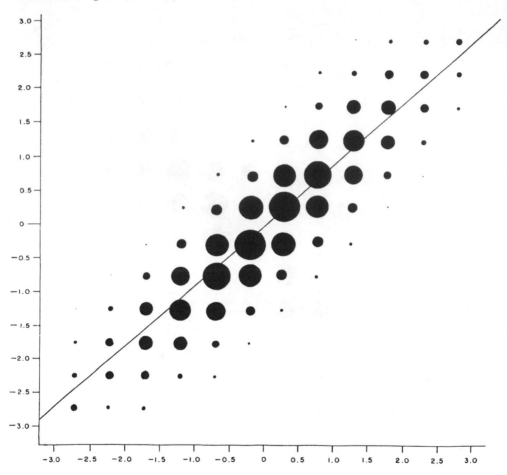

Figure 14.11
Correlation Diagram (r = 1.00)

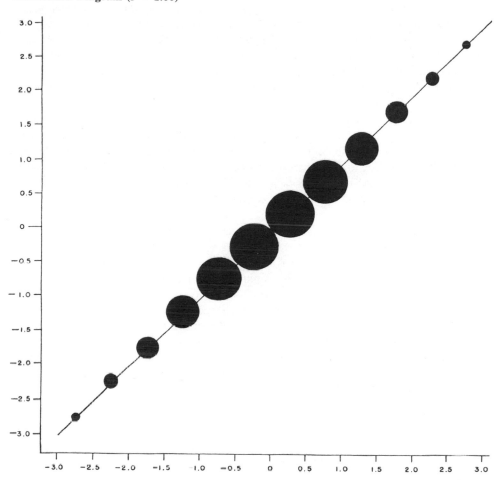

puted by dividing the difference between the score and the mean by the standard deviation. This computation puts all the scores on the same footing, so that correlation diagrams can meaningfully be compared visually. Otherwise, the results would look different when, for example, height and weight are correlated by using inches and pounds rather than centimeters and kilograms, although the underlying phenomena are the same.

Since it is sometimes awkward to use such small numbers as appear in the diagrams, half of which are negative, many other standard scores give the same results but with a different scale. They are computed by multiplying the standard scores by a constant and adding another constant. The best-known standard score is used to report scores on the SAT, with the mean set at 500 rather than 0.0, the standard deviation at 100 rather than 1.0, and a range of 200 to 800. A person with minimal training in mathematics can easily replace the standard scores in the diagrams with the obtained scores to make the result more understandable.

Inferential statistics make it possible to support or to negate generalizations about a population based on the scores of a sample. If the whole population is measured, there would be no need for inferential statistics. What you would see is all that there is to see. There would be no need to speculate about the scores of the population since the data for the whole population are already on hand. Since it is never possible to get scores on the entire population, inferences must be drawn from samples.

Ideally, the samples would be random samples from the population, but there is no such thing as a random sample of a nontrivial population. (It might be possible to define a population as all the children in Ms. Jones' third grade class and compute statistics on their height and weight, but the results would be trivial.) A random sample is one that satisfies two conditions. First, each member of the population must have an equal chance of being chosen. Second, the selections must be independent; that is, the probability of one member's being chosen must not influence the likelihood of any other member's being chosen. The description of the steps in choosing a random sample is deceptively simple, but none can be carried out in the real world. They are:

1. Define the population.

2. Identify all the members of the population.

3. Collect the data from a random sample.

Define the population. There is always something arbitrary about the definition of the population. One cannot define the population of applicants for the next examination to be given by civil service. Some applicants do not know themselves if they are going to take the examination until they arrive at the testing site, and some leave without completing it. I was once involved in a project to sample the opinions of social workers. It was impossible to complete the project because there are so many different types and levels of social workers, and different organizations assign different classes of work to different employees with the same titles and education.

Identify the members of the population. It is not possible to locate all the residents of even a small town. People move in and out at will. People are born, die, or become incapable of participating in the study even while the members of the population are being enumerated.

Collect the data from a random sample. All inferential statistics are based on the deceptively simple premise that the sample was drawn randomly from the population. However, just as there is no way to identify a nontrivial population, there is no such thing as a random sample of whatever population can be identified. The classic way to select a random sample is to assign a unique number to each member of the population and select the sample using a table of pseudorandom numbers. (They are pseudorandom numbers because they are generated by a computer. Once the procedure for selecting the numbers is established, the resulting numbers, although they appear to be random, are already completely determined when the seed number is inserted. However, they are close enough to being random to satisfy the severest critics.) Even if it were possible to select such a sample, it would not be possible to collect data from them all. Some would exercise their legal right to refuse. Others would be out of town, in the hospital, or simply ornery.

If the failure to achieve randomness has no pattern, there is little problem in using the sample, but the sample may not be random. Does this mean that statistics based on samples are useless? Not at all, but it does mean that judgment must be applied to the statistics based on an understanding of the population and the sample drawn from it.

Often, the only available sample comprises those who apply for a job. Immediately the question arises, "Who is an applicant?" The *Uniform Guidelines* address this issue in Q&A 15, which is discussed in Chapter 12. Often, in fair employment studies, the results are projected to future applicants, who could not be identified even if it were possible to enumerate the present population. Economic conditions change, and the demography of the applicants with them. The applicants for secretarial positions to one large employer shifted over the years from older, experienced, less well educated applicants, to younger college graduates. Since then, with the change in opportunities and aspirations of women as a result, in part, of Title VII, the mix has changed again and will probably change in the future as attitudes change, and technology advances.

A frequent problem is the disappearing sample. Tables referring to the same sample sometimes report different numbers. Columns of figures do not always add up to the reported total. Sometimes, the differences are understandable. Applicants are eliminated, drop out, or produce unscorable data and have to be eliminated. The researcher should account for every change in the sample, not only to check on accuracy but also to temper the conclusions drawn from samples that shrink in unexplained ways.

This discussion does not mean that because it is impossible to identify all the members of the population or to draw a random sample from it, no conclusions can be drawn. It means that examining the definitions and makeup of both the population and the sample is essential for the researcher and for the user of the research results and to assess the adequacy of generalities that can be made from the data.

The next step is to analyze the data and draw conclusions. Inferential statistics follow what appears to be a twisted logic. First, statisticians assume that there is no difference between the scores of two groups or that there is no association between two sets of scores. This is called the null hypothesis. Then they attempt to reject the null hypothesis. If they do, they conclude that probably there is a difference or association between the groups. If they do not reject the null hypothesis, they conclude that they have "failed to reject" it rather than accept the conclusion that there is no difference or association. The conclusion is based on the premise that there could still be small, undiscovered differences or associations. However, in real life, someone has to make a decision or take action, so they sometimes tacitly accept the null hypothesis and move on. For example, if there is not an adequate correlation between the test and the criterion, the likely decision is to drop the test or at least not to defend it if it has an adverse impact.

The null hypothesis is the object of study by a twelve-member task force of the American Psychological Association, which advocates a more flexible approach to arriving at conclusions. The task force does not recommend scrapping the null hypothesis. Instead, it recommends different strategies for different circumstances. The following description of the assessment of adverse impact combines the test of the null hypothesis with the 80% rule of thumb to help to determine whether or not there is an impact against one group.

Although the *Uniform Guidelines* emphasize the analysis shown in Chapter 12, based on the 80% rule, the courts have also looked at the significance of the difference in the hiring rates of the minority and non-minority applicants. The basic analysis is Chi-Square, which is illustrated by the data shown in Table 11.1, further pursued in Table 14.1.

The purpose of Chi-Square is to compare the actual number of applicants hired with the number that would be expected if the selection rates were exactly equal. Since 53 of the 343 applicants were hired, the percent hired is 15.5% (100 × 53/343). If exactly 15.5% of the 142 Hispanic applicants were selected, 22.1 (142 × 1.55) would have been hired. The observed number is 12. The expected number hired in each of the four cells is computed the same way. This analysis gives a graphic picture of any disparity in hiring rates.

A one-tail test is used because the issue is whether or not the Hispanics are hired at a lower rate than that for the whites. They would not sue if they were

Table 14.1
Computation of Adverse Impact and Chi-Square

	Hispanic	White	Total
Hired	12	41	53
(Expected)	(21.9)	(31.1)	
Not Hired	130	160	290
(Expected)	(120.1)	(169.9)	
Total	142	201	343
	8.5	20.4	

Hiring rate = 15.5% [100 (53/343)]; Adverse impact = 41.6% [100 (8.5/20.4)]; Chi-Square (with Yates' correction) = 8.20%; Significance p = .0022% (one-tailed test).

hired at a higher rate. The two-tail test addresses the question whether or not the two are different, which is not relevant to this issue.

Chi-Square is used to determine the likelihood that the observed differences arose solely because of random sampling error. Chi-Square, with Yates' correction, is 8.2 for these data. (Yates' correction compensates for the slight error that comes from using an approximation rather than a mathematically exact formulation in computing the significance level. It is especially important when the samples are small. Yates' correction gives results very close to Fisher's exact test, which is seldom used because the numbers involved become immense, even for a computer. As the name implies, Fisher's exact test gives a precise analysis of the data. It does not imply that the conclusions are necessarily correct.) A difference as large as the one obtained here would occur by chance variations in the sample in favor of the whites only 0.22% of the time. This is substantially below the conventional 5% level of significance. This result leads to the inescapable conclusion that Hispanics are hired at a lower rate than that of the non-Hispanic whites.

Another form of analysis is used when the data are continuous, as would be the case in test scores. The significance depends on the size of the samples, the differences between their means, and their standard deviation. Figures 14.12 through 14.14 illustrate the point. They show the results where the difference between the groups is 1.00, .50, and .25 standard deviations, respectively. As the difference between the groups becomes smaller, the p value becomes larger; that is, the likelihood of failing to recognize a difference becomes greater. As the number of cases increases, the likelihood of concluding (correctly) that there is a difference between the two groups increases.

Figures 14.12–14.14 illustrate the influence of sample size and the amount of difference in scores for determining the significance of difference between means. The distributions are drawn to scale so that the area under each curve is proportional to the sample size. To simplify the exposition, the spread of

Figure 14.12

Significance of Difference between Means of Equal-Size Samples (Difference = 1 Standard Deviation)

n = 16
p = .01
(1/100)

n = 32
p = .0002
(2/10,000)

n = 64
p = .00000002
(2/100,000,000)

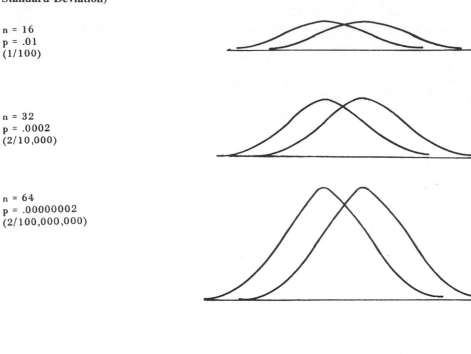

n = 128
p = .00000001
(1/100,000,000)

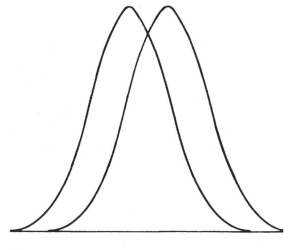

Figure 14.13

Significance of Difference between Means of Equal-Size Samples (Difference = ½ Standard Deviation)

n = 16
p = 18
(18/100)

n = 32
p = .05
(5/100)

n = 64
p = .005
(5/1000)

n = 128
p = .00006
(6/100,000)

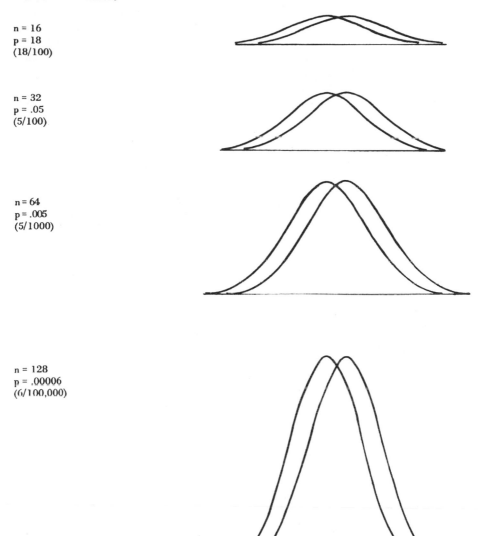

Figure 14.14
Significance of Difference between Means of Equal-Size Samples (Difference = ¼ Standard Deviation)

n = 16
p = .5
(1/2)

n = 32
p = .33
(1/3)

n = 64
p = .16
(1/6)

n = 128
p = .05
(1/20)

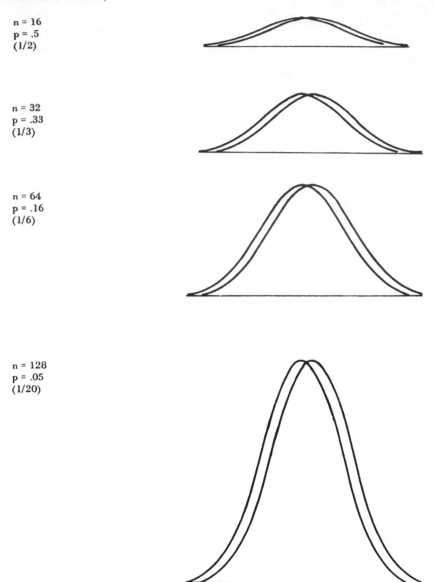

scores (standard deviation) of each group is the same. With real data, the relative size of the two groups and the standard deviations may easily differ. The statistics of a test of significance automatically take any differences into account.

The importance of sample size can be observed by reading down each set of figures. As the number of cases increases, the level of significance decreases. That means that the likelihood that the observed differences are the result of chance variations resulting from sampling errors decreases as the sample size increases, while the difference between the means of the two groups remains constant.

The importance of the size of the difference between the groups is observed by comparing the diagrams for the same number of cases from figure to figure. Where the sample size is held constant, and the differences between the groups are larger, the level of significance is smaller. With a large enough sample, almost any difference will be significant.

The diagrams also illustrate that, even when the differences are large and significant, the scores for the two groups overlap considerably. This overlap is important to the understanding of the meaning of significance, since with large samples, a small difference, with substantial overlap, may be significant.

The diagrams and the associated significance levels relate to a one-tail test. The one-tail test addresses the question, Are the scores of the group with the higher scores significantly greater than those of the low-scoring group? The two-tail test addresses the question, Are the scores of the two groups significantly different (without regard to which is greater)? The two-tail test is appropriate in the exploratory phase of a research study. For example, the developer of a new personality test may want to know whether or not men and women answer differently, without having enough information on hand to predict that either will score higher than the other.

In fair employment litigation brought by minority applicants, the issue is clearer. The question is, Are the non-minority applicants chosen at a higher rate than that of the minorities? If so, there may be a prima facie case of discrimination, which then triggers an investigation of the job relatedness of the selection procedure.

Myth: *To show adverse impact, there must be a statistically significant difference at the 5% level between the two groups being compared.* Q&A 18 says:

Q. Is it usually necessary to calculate the statistical significance of differences in selection rates when investigating the existence of adverse impact?

A. No. Adverse impact is normally indicated when one selection rate is less than 80% of the other. The federal enforcement agencies will normally use only the 80% (4/5ths) rule of thumb, except where large numbers of selections are made.

This provision has been all but forgotten. Some people rely on a 5% level of significance to decide for them. If the difference is significant at the 5% level, they conclude that there is a real, meaningful difference, and if it is not significant, they conclude that the two groups are the same. Dissatisfaction with this interpretation has led a committee formed by interested statisticians to propose a better formulation. The results of their deliberations are not available at this writing.

Several points must be made here. First, the 5% level of significance is itself arbitrary. It has been around for a long time, but it has no inherent virtue over 4% or 6% or some other value except that it is a conveniently rounded number. In the history of statistics other levels have been used, and some are still popular, such as 1% or 2%.

Second, the level of significance of differences between two groups depends on the size of the difference, the number of cases in each group, and the statistic used. The point is addressed in Q&A 24:

Q. Why do the Guidelines rely primarily upon the 4/5ths rule of thumb rather than tests of statistical significance?

A. Where the sample of persons selected is not large, even if a large real difference between groups is likely not to be confirmed by a test of statistical significance (at the usual .05 level of significance). For this reason the Guidelines do not rely primarily upon a test of statistical significance, but use the 4/5ths rule of thumb as a practical and easy-to-administer measure of whether differences in selection rates are substantial.

Courts have recognized this problem in cases where there were so few black applicants that, though no blacks were hired, the difference was not statistically significant, by noting the "inexorable zero."

Myth: *When there is no statistically significant difference between two samples at the .05 level of significance, they are the same.* In fact, two populations are never the same. If they were momentarily the same, someone would enter or leave one of them in the next few minutes, and they will no longer be the same. However, action must be taken based on the available information. Whether or not the two samples are to be treated as if they are the same depends on the additional information, the costs of making error, and the history of the issue.

Myth: *The use of a more stringent level of significance in analyzing adverse impact, for example, 1%, would be more conservative and therefore more scientific and more appropriate.* Despite the principle established in the Q&A 20 earlier, people still use statistical significance to establish or refute a claim of adverse impact, so some further discussion is called for. Using a lower level of significance reduces the likelihood of committing the Type I error, that is, concluding that there is a difference between the two groups when, in fact, there is none. A person using this standard says, in effect, "There is no certainty in this kind of data, so I will take the chance of concluding that there is a difference when there really is none, and I will accept this slight risk of misleading myself and my audience so that we can move ahead in the 95% of the cases where there really is a difference. If the cost of an error to my reputation or to society

Table 14.2
Type I and Type II Errors

	Difference Exists	No Difference Exists
Difference Found	Correct Conclusion	Type I Error
No Difference Found	Type II Error	Corrrect Conclusion

is high, I may decide to be more conservative and adjust the level of the Type I error to a lower figure, say 2% or 1%." The issue is illustrated in Table 14.2.

As the likelihood of the Type I error decreases, the likelihood of a Type II error increases. So being conservative, that is, insisting on a low likelihood of a Type I error, increases the likelihood that a true difference would be overlooked. If an error is to be made, employers would prefer to see the Type II error, and the plaintiffs would prefer the Type I error. In any event, decisions should be made by looking at all of the data and surrounding circumstances, not just at the numbers.

The fundamental problem is sample size. Let us suppose that a mustachioed stranger in a tattersall vest approaches you on a Mississippi side-wheeler and proposes that you engage in a game of chance. He will flip his own coin and call the toss. He calls "heads" and wins. No reason to be suspicious. That happens 50% of the time by chance. He calls "heads" again and wins. This happens 25% of the time. He wins a third time. The probability is down to 12.5%. He wins again, $p = 6.25\%$. When he wins a fifth time, $p = 3.125\%$, a person dedicated to the 5% level of significance finally concludes that something is wrong. Even when the coin actually has two heads, with very small samples, the likelihood of the Type II error is huge.

Myth: *"Statistics prove that..."* Statistics never proved anything. Statistics provide useful, often essential information, but in themselves they never prove anything. The results are ultimately couched in terms of probabilities, so they may reflect an atypical fluke. Ultimately, someone or some group must decide what the statistical results mean and what action should be taken. Nothing is foreordained because statistics come out a certain way. Computing statistics is a confession of ignorance. Statistical results reduce, but never quite eliminate, that ignorance.

Myth: *A validity coefficient (the correlation between the score on the selection procedure and a measure of performance) is best interpreted as the proportion of the shared variance.* That means that, if the correlation between a test and a criterion is 0.50, the test accounts for only 25% ($0.50^2 = 0.25$). This statement is mathematically correct, but it is meaningless to anyone who has not had two courses in statistics, including analysis of variance. Brogden (1946) showed more than 50 years ago that the correlation coefficient shows directly the amount of improvement the use of a test would make in improving the quality of those who are selected.

The relationship is easily shown by Figures 14.15 and 14.16, which illustrate the effect of selecting from the top of a group of test scores when there is a correlation of 0.50. We would like to hire only those above the horizontal line, the best performers. Their average is shown by the distance A. However, the best we can do is to select the top scorers on the test. Their average is represented by the distance B. Brogden showed that the ratio B/A is equal to the validity coefficient, .50.

Figure 14.15 shows the effect of using a test with a validity of .50 to select the top 16% of the applicants. Figure 14.16 illustrates the effect of hiring 50% rather than 16% of the applicants with the same level of validity. Since the applicants in the top 50% are not as talented as those in the top 16%, the selection of the best half of the applicants from the same pool would not be as effective. The average performances on both the test and the job are substantially lower. For more detail, see Barrett (1996), "Interpreting the Correlation Coefficient."

Myth: *The more significant the differences between two groups or the correlation between two variables, the greater the difference or association between them.* The level of significance in itself tells only the likelihood that the difference or association was arrived at by chance. With large samples, trivial differences or correlations can be significant.

Myth: *Modern computers have virtually eliminated statistical errors.* Computers do not make mistakes. People do. It is amazing how many errors in computation appear in reports of investigations, including those prepared for litigation. I have seen mathematical impossibilities reported with a straight face because no one checked the results, relying with blind, unsupported faith on the computer. Everyone who produces or relies on statistics should check for accuracy and reasonableness. Experience with the relevant data is important; there should be extra checking on results that are unusual.

Myth: *All competent statisticians are equally qualified to consult on fair employment issues.* Although statisticians have much the same training, they are not all equally adept in dealing with issues that arise in fair employment. Some are used to large samples and will advocate statistics that require "only 1,000 cases." Except in some popular civil service jobs and jobs in the armed forces, there are few situations in which employment statisticians can work with 1,000 cases. The U.S. Postal Service (USPS), with more than 800,000 employees, has conducted a study of more than 86,000 cases, but USPS is the largest civilian employer in the country. Many theoretical statisticians are unfamiliar with the complexities and errors that are endemic in personnel records.

Myth: *A sample chosen so that every member of the population has an equal chance of being chosen is random.* That statement is correct as far as it goes, but there is another condition. The choice of one member of the population should be unrelated to the choice of any other member. To illustrate, let us suppose that a researcher wants to estimate the height of a class of students by dividing them into two equal groups and choosing the one to measure by flipping

Figure 14.15
Correlation Diagram Showing Effect of Selecting Top 16% of Applicants (r = 0.50)

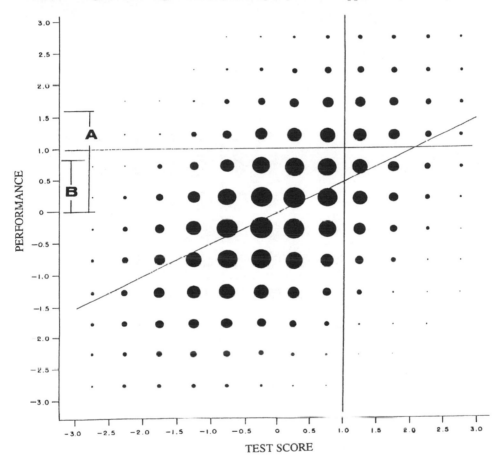

TEST SCORE

Figure 14.16
Correlation Diagram Showing Effect of Selecting Top 50% of Applicants (r = 0.50)

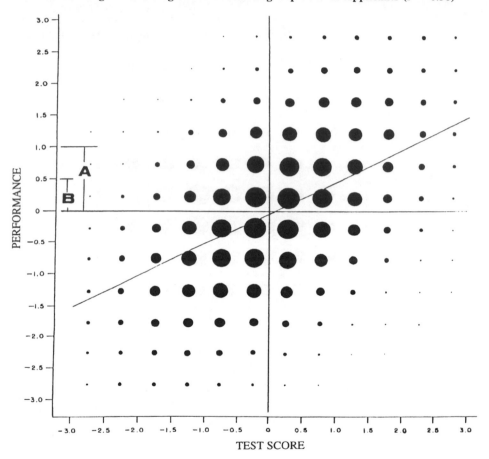

a coin. The first condition is met. Everyone has a 50–50 chance of being chosen. However, suppose it is a gym class in which the pupils line up in order of height, and the researcher divides them at the midpoint. Of the billions of samples that could be chosen, these two represent the most unrepresentative extremes.

Myth: *Reporting data in percentages communicates adequately.* Percentages help to put data on a consistent, easily understood basis. However, percentages can be used to obscure defects in data, particularly small samples. One of my acid-tongued colleagues critiquing a research paper said, "I was very impressed until I realized that 14% was one person." When data are reported in percentages, the number of cases on which the percentages are based should be reported so the reader is not misled by small samples.

Myth: *Statisticians agree on the one correct way to analyze data.* On the contrary, statisticians seldom agree, especially when they are on opposite sides of a case. Statistics is a continually evolving field, partly because, like any field, knowledge grows but also because the high-speed computer places within reach calculations that were too burdensome to be carried out with the mechanical calculators of bygone times. There is no way to resolve the disagreements except to explore the purposes of the studies and evaluate the rationale behind the work. For example, one statistician loaded the dice for his client, the defendant, by insisting on the test of significance despite knowing that with a small sample there is a substantial likelihood of failing to find a difference when one really exists. He also proposed that the adverse impact be statistically significantly more severe than the 80% rule, an unrealistically stringent standard.

Implications

The main purpose of this chapter is to convince the reader who has not had a course in statistics that statistics is a useful tool, but only a tool. The first step in using statistics is to develop a clear understanding of the problem that is being addressed and what you will do depending on what results are obtained.

It is essential to know how the sample on which the statistics are computed relates to the population of interest. This step requires a clear definition of the population, with the rationale behind the definitions being so clear that the relevance is obvious. The reader should know how the sample differs from a random sample and how the differences affect the conclusions. In a complex study, some members of the sample drop out or are eliminated. The reader should know the characteristics of those who dropped out and those who stayed.

Data collection is easily given scant attention because it is so boring, suitable only for the attention of apprentices. Unfortunately, simple errors based on benign ignorance can destroy a study. The data collection should be carefully monitored to make sure that the participants understand what they are to do, why they are doing it, and what will be done with the results. Motivation to give accurate information helps to assure the accuracy of the data, but negative motivation can wreck it. I always appreciated the refusal of a researcher to continue with a study when he learned that instructions had gone out to some raters to subvert the process. He said that getting useful information under those circumstances was like trying to get love under rape.

Once you are convinced that the data are in good shape, descriptive statistical analysis reduces the data from a confusing mass of numbers to a form in which their meaning can be grasped. Reducing data by computing statistics such as the mean, standard deviation, correlation coefficient, and impact ratio always destroys some detail in the interest of organizing the remainder so that it is more understandable. Reducing the data too much eliminates important details that influence the interpretation. Often the detail can be preserved and the results made more understandable by tables or graphs.

At this point inferential statistical analysis is used to give an understanding of how likely the results of the analysis of the sample can be generalized to the whole population of interest. These statistics are then evaluated as a guide to drawing conclusions and taking action. Statistics do not make decisions. People do. Statistics help by providing essential data, but someone has to look at the numbers and the whole research study to make an adequate decision.

Chapter 15

Ethical and Legal Considerations

BACKGROUND

The law and the courts have settled many issues regarding legal behavior of psychologists engaged in developing, validating, and using selection procedures. The practices and standards of the legal and psychological professions generally coincide, but differences in their interpretation and use may cause conflict between professionals. In addition, some specialized ethical concerns confront test developers and users.

Purpose

This chapter is concerned with the specialized issues confronting psychologists in their own practices and with their interaction with attorneys and the courts.

Everyone is bound by the law and ethical standards of behavior concerning courtroom activities. Psychologists in addition are bound by the "Ethical Principles of Psychologists and Code of Conduct" (1992) of the American Psychological Association. They also receive guidance from *Ethics for Psychologists, a Commentary on the APA Ethics Code* (Canter et al. 1994).

The Joint Committee on Testing Practices (Draft 1998) has drafted a statement of *The Rights and Responsibilities of Test-Takers*. The statement of the rights of test-takers is reproduced in Appendix 3. It emphasizes the test user's responsibility to communicate to the test-taker all relevant information that does not compromise the test.

These standards are illustrated for the practice of industrial/organizational psychology in *The Ethical Practice of Psychology in Organizations* (Lowman

1998), a casebook that examines ethical issues in all aspects of industrial psychology. Many of the more than 60 cases are about the practice of testing. They include:

Assessment Techniques

Validation Efforts with Small Sample Sizes

Test Validation Strategies

Avoiding Potential Misuse of Assessment Procedures

Mis-keyed Test Items on Commercially Marketed Tests

Personnel Screening for Emotional Stability

Misleading Reporting of Results

"Realistic Job Previews" and the Selection of Female Employees

Assessment Center Records

Maintaining Confidentiality and Objectivity

The Right Not to Participate in Selection Activities

Misuse of Psychological Services

Confidentiality of Interview Data

Team-Building Interventions

Disposition of Psychological Reports

Avoiding Conflicts of Interests and Roles

Accurately Reporting Research Results

Recording Data without Consent

Avoiding Dual Relationships

Honoring Agreements in Data Collection and Usage

When Testimony Would Be Compelled

Reporting Back Data from Research Studies

Licensing and Credentialing

Questions of Billing, Competence, and Supervision

Accurately and Honestly Marketing Psychological Products

Professional and Scientific Responsibility in Forensic Activities

Evaluating Colleagues' Competencies

Confronting Unethical Behavior

Myth: *Those who are responsible for conducting a study describe and defend what they have done.* The principle of criminal law that accused persons can confront their accusers does not extend to fair employment cases. Employers sometimes engage the ghost expert, who stays in the background, giving advice that affects the conduct of the case. The lawyers' rationale is that they need unbiased information to prepare the best defense. However, the preparation of a case involves selection of the data to be analyzed and the methods of analyzing it. The ghost might try several different approaches, find the one that gives the most favorable results, and suggest to the attorney that another expert be used to conduct only that study and to avoid the other possibilities.

The use of the ghost expert brings the ethics of two professions into conflict. Lawyers say that they are entitled to an unbiased assessment of the situation. Psychologists counter by saying that the clients of ghost experts—generally, defendants—use their services to engineer the most favorable analysis of the data and to limit the plaintiffs' access to relevant information. Psychologists who contemplate serving as ghost experts or who suspect or know that a ghost is haunting the data should be aware that attorneys know about ghost experts and can generally sniff them out. Psychologists can avoid embarrassment by insisting that their names be listed among the potential witnesses. The other side cannot call you unless your client calls you first.

Myth: *Under the principle of discovery, both sides have timely access to the relevant information in the possession of the other side.* A great feature of American jurisprudence is the requirement that those who possess relevant information, usually the defendants, produce it to the opposing side. However, some defendants are experts at delaying the game. I worked on one case in which the court allowed the defendants to stonewall for fifteen years. It was not settled until the judge retired and was replaced by one who acted on the old dictum, "Justice too long delayed is justice denied." The suit was brought against a county that claimed to have lost the relevant test scores. It was the only county in the state that could not find them.

Myth: *Plaintiffs need all the information they ask for.* Plaintiffs' attorneys must prepare detailed and exhaustive requests for production of documents to make sure that they get the information that they need. In response to a suspicion that the defendants may be stonewalling, plaintiffs' attorneys may ask for extremely detailed information. Since they are not always sure what relevant information the plaintiff may have, they legitimately ask for more than they can use to make sure that nothing relevant is overlooked. However, sometimes plaintiffs and their attorneys hope that the administrative and financial burdens placed on the employers will motivate them to settle cases that have little merit. Psychologists have an obligation to make sure that the information sought in their area of expertise is really relevant to the issues at hand and that they are not party to a shakedown.

Myth: *All relevant data are reported.* Sometimes, only the results that serve the interest of the test user are reported. Tests eliminated in experimental batteries because they did not work out are often ignored in the report of a study. Some tables report only the significant, positive results, omitting low and even negative validities. When statistics are corrected for restriction of range or for unreliability, only the corrected and uncorrected data may be reported.

To interpret results of a complex study, one needs all the relevant data so that patterns can be detected and evaluated. It is up to the author of the report to include all relevant data and to give a correct impression of what was done and how things worked out.

Myth: *Studies are performed and reported without bias*. It is only human to collect and present data that support one's point of view. There are countless ways to conduct a study and to analyze and report the results. The awareness of the courts of this problem is exemplified by the Supreme Court in footnote 32 of *Albemarle Paper Company v. Moody*:

It cannot escape notice that Albemarle's study was conducted by plant officials, without neutral, on-the-scene oversight, at a time when this litigation was about to come to trial. Studies so closely controlled by an interested party in litigation must be examined with great care.

Implications

The psychological profession has established a comprehensive code of ethics. Psychologists are responsible for monitoring their own ethical behavior. To assist in this effort, I quote from the American Psychological Association's "Ethical Principles of Psychologists and Code of Conduct" (1992) some ethical principles that are most relevant to the work of psychologists who develop and use employment procedures.

Ethical Standard 1.02, *Relationship of ethics and law*
> If psychologists' ethical responsibilities conflict with law, psychologists make known their commitment to the Ethics's Code, and take steps to resolve the conflict in a responsible manner.

Ethical Standard 1.15, *Misuse of psychologists' work*
> (a) Psychologists do not participate in activities in which it appears likely that their skills or data will be misused by others, unless corrective mechanisms are available.
> (b) If psychologists learn of misuse or misrepresentation of their work, they take responsible steps to correct or minimize the misuse or misrepresentation.

Ethical Standard 1.23, *Documentation of professional and scientific work*
> (b) When psychologists have reason to believe that records of their professional services will be used in legal proceedings involving recipients or participants in their work, they have the responsibility to create and maintain documentation in the kind of detail and quality that would be consistent with reasonable scrutiny in an adjudicative forum.

Ethical Standard 1.24, *Records and data*
> Psychologists create, maintain, disseminate, store, retain, and dispose of records and data relating to their research, practice, and other work in accordance with law and in a manner that permits compliance with the requirements of the Ethics Code.

Ethical Standard 2.09, *Explaining assessment results*

Unless the nature of the relationship is clearly explained to the person being assessed in advance and precludes provision for an explanation of results (such as . . . pre-employment screening), psychologists ensure that an explanation of the results is provided.

Ethical Standard 2.10, *Maintaining test security*

Psychologists make reasonable efforts to maintain the integrity and security of tests and other assessment techniques consistent with the law, contractual obligations, and in a manner that permits compliance with the requirements of this Ethics Code.

Ethical Standard 5.01, *Discussing the limits of confidentiality*

(a) Psychologists discuss with persons and organizations with whom they establish a scientific or professional relationship . . . the relevant limitations on confidentiality.

Ethical Standard 6.08, *Compliance with law and standards*

Psychologists plan and conduct research in a manner consistent with federal and state law and regulations, as well as professional standards governing the conduct of research.

Ethical Standard 6.10, *Research responsibilities*

Prior to conducting research . . . psychologists enter into an agreement with participants that clarifies the nature of the research and the responsibilities of each party.

Ethical Standard 6.11, *Informed consent to research*

(a) Psychologists use language that is reasonably understandable to research participants in obtaining their appropriate informed consent. . . . Such informed consent is appropriately documented.

(b) Using language that is reasonably understandable to participants, psychologists inform participants of the nature of the research; they inform participants that they are free to participate or to decline to participate or to withdraw from the research; they explain the foreseeable consequences of declining or withdrawing; they inform participants of significant factors that may be expected to influence their willingness to participate (such as risks, discomfort, adverse effects, or limitations on confidentiality . . .); and they explain other aspects about which the prospective participants inquire.

(c) When psychologists conduct research . . . [they] take special care to protect the prospective participants from adverse consequences of declining or withdrawing from participation.

Applicants who take a test as part of the employment process have implicitly given their consent to its use. Test-takers should always be given relevant information about the test when it is in their interest to be informed.

Chapter 16

Licensing and Certifying Examinations

BACKGROUND

States require licensing or certification for a variety of professions, from barbering to brain surgery. One of the most significant, the Multi-State Bar Examination, is discussed in some detail as an illustration of the problems that are encountered.

Purpose

Licensing and certifying tests were developed to protect an unwary public from untrained practitioners.

Population

Licenses based on passing examinations are required for jobs from cutting hair to approving plans for a billion-dollar public works.

Measurement and Data Collection Procedure

Licensing and certifying examinations depend heavily on multiple-choice tests of the material taught or judged to be used in the practice. Sometimes, specialist examinations follow general licensing, as when physicians take board examinations in their specialties. Other requirements, including supervised experience, recommendations, and freedom from felony convictions, are not discussed here.

Certifying and licensing examinations arose during a more relaxed era when, for example, young candidates read law under a senior lawyer rather than go to law school. When they were both satisfied that the apprentice had learned the trade, the senior lawyer would sponsor admission to the bar. A court would then admit the new lawyer without any formal standards. This practice was open to broad abuse that led to licensing and certifying procedures that included tests of knowledge but also, depending on the profession, ethical standards, recommendations, and other screening devices.

This reliance on certifying or licensing professionals has led to the abdication of responsibility by some universities. I once heard the dean of a state law school, the only law school in that state, testify that the school sometimes let marginal students through and counted on the bar examination to catch its mistakes. Measurement psychologists have known for a long time that multitrait, multimethod appraisals give the best results. The faculty of the law school has three years to watch students perform in a variety of courses taught by different professors in different ways. They are in a much better position to judge the fitness of their students than a three-hour multiple-choice examination. Some more reasonable states automatically admit all graduates from the state law school.

Some states, particularly California, face a proliferation of marginal law schools, whose graduates may be inadequately trained. The state bar association has developed a simulation test in which the candidates are given a day to examine the kinds of materials that a lawyer might have available in preparing a case, for example, a letter from a client stating a problem, access to relevant (and irrelevant) decisions, and a law library. Candidates write a draft of a letter advising the client, which is evaluated on content, thoroughness, and organization. The answers are graded based on the applicant's ability to counsel the client. The applicants are given a detailed description of the standards.

Myth: *Licensing and certifying tests must meet the standards of the Uniform Guidelines.* Although to practice, many professions one must be licensed or certified, courts have generally ruled that these examinations are not employment tests as defined in Title VII. Minorities have all but given up trying to compel the legal profession to meet the standards that the law imposes on others.

Myth: *One must have a license to practice psychology.* In most jurisdictions psychologists are certified, not licensed. New York, like other states, requires certification, not licensure. The state does not limit the practice of psychology as the practice of medicine is limited, because there is no feasible way to distinguish between the counseling of psychologists and that of ministers, divorce lawyers, social workers, and many others who deal with their clients' emotional problems. To call oneself a psychologist or to use certain titles with the same "psycho-" root, one must go through the certifying procedure. The *Uniform Guidelines* set no standards for psychometricians who build tests, and one need not be certified to testify, since courts have their own procedures for deciding whether or not a witness can testify as an expert.

Myth: *Examinations like the bar examination are needed to maintain the standards of the profession.* The standards of the medical-profession are the highest in the world, but medicine has no equivalent of the bar examination. Medical students are tested regularly, and those who fail an examination repeat the course until they show their mastery of the subject. Most medical students who stick with it are eventually awarded their degrees.

Myth: *The passing score is set to eliminate the unqualified.* In some states the pass rates on the bar examination are remarkably similar from year to year. The passing score is set to eliminate the same proportion of the applicants, no matter whether or not the cohorts differ from year to year in their competence. There is no systematic showing that the passing score sets a level of competence that protects the public. In fact, there is contrary information. The *1986 Bar Examination Statistics* does not report passing scores, but the differences in the pass rates must reflect more than the differences in the legal preparation. The pass rates for the bar examination as a whole, including locally made essay tests, are reported in Table 16.1.

Of the 12,543 who took the Multi-State Bar in California, only 4,798, or 38%, passed. The denial of opportunity to practice of 62% of the applicants is draconian, especially in the light of the 64% passes rate for the entire country.

Myth: *Bar examinations are professionally developed.* Testimony in *Pettit v. Gingerich* gives an insight into how casually some bar examinations are written:

Question: How is it decided . . . which subjects will be given on a given examination?

Answer: Well, it is generally at a meeting, at which time the format of the previous examination is discussed. . . . Generally it is a consensus thing. What we discuss [is] what was omitted last time, what should be included this time.

There is no mention of any exploration into what lawyers do or what they need to know to do it. The process is known in the Beltway by its acronym, BOGSATT (Bunch Of Guys Sitting At The Table). There has never been a comprehensive description of the job of lawyers used to develop and validate the bar examination.

Myth: *The content of the bar examination is race-neutral.* Not according to some black lawyers who describe themselves as people lawyers concerned with divorces, tenant rights, criminal defense, and the like. They claim that there is a bias in the questions toward the kind of law practiced by the item writers, who are from the larger, mostly white law firms specializing in the law of the more affluent members of society.

Myth: *The sole purpose of licensing examinations is to protect the public from inadequately trained practitioners.* In one state, the pass rates are so close over the years that the only difference seems to come from the number of tied scores near the point of cut. It is difficult to prove, but cynics might say that the purpose of the exam is to limit the competition.

Myth: *Licensing examinations are justified because they force the applicants to study.* Candidates may have to open dusty old books, but forcing study is not

Table 16.1
Pass Rates for 1986 Bar Examination

Pass Rate	Frequency
90–100	2
80–89.9	16
70–79.9	16
60–69.9	13
50–59.9	2
40–49.9	4
30–39.9	2
Total	55

the purpose of the examination. If a profession is concerned with the currency and completeness of its members' knowledge, there are better means of making sure that they are up-to-date, such as requiring refresher courses.

As just about everyone has experienced, crammed material that is not used is soon forgotten. Senior, successful lawyers like to boast that they would not pass the bar examination because they have forgotten the issues that are not part of their practice. If it were truly job-related, they should expect to pass.

Myth: *Licensing and certifying examinations test for core information.* I once reviewed some sample items intended to illustrate the type of questions that would be used for a certifying test in a major state. The answer to one question required the identification of a psychological term that was so obscure that it appeared once in the indexes of ten consecutive issues of the *Annual Reviews of Psychology*. Can anyone seriously believe that knowledge of esoterica can help to identify sympathetic, competent psychotherapists?

The bar examination has asked for the definition of obscure Latin terms that are rarely used and can be easily looked up. Cram courses coach candidates in taking multiple-choice examinations, a skill that has no later surrender value.

Myth: *The bar examination is content-valid.* Certifying examinations are never justified on the grounds that they predict success in the profession. The claim is that they measure information needed to perform adequately, but that claim is never checked empirically. There is no description of the job of the young lawyer who is eligible for admission to the bar. There has never been a showing that it meets professional standards.

One standard for content-valid tests is that competent people should pass and that incompetent should fail. Without peeking at the scoring key, I answered correctly 62% of 51 consecutive questions taken from the Multi-State Bar Examination, although I had my only law course in 1948. As part of my professional work, I have learned about civil rights law and picked up by osmosis a working knowledge of the Rules of Federal Procedure, neither of which was covered in the questions I answered. I answered using my general knowledge and my experience with the characteristic deficiencies of bad items. A score of 62% is passing in some states, but I would not be qualified to write your will.

Myth: *The bar examination tests knowledge of the law.* Sometimes it does, but not always. The first two questions that I encountered related to the description of real property in deeds. One piece is described as, "All of my property known as 44 Main Street, Midtown, United States, being one acre." The question further stated that the property at 44 Main Street covered 7/8 of an acre. I chose the wanted answer that said that the deed was "sufficient because the discrepancy is not fatal." My rationale is that there is no perfectly accurate measure of an area, and besides, "7/8th of an acre" is obviously an approximation, as is "one acre." There can be only one property at 44 Main Street, and, having brought and sold several houses, I knew that there is a map of the property in the tax assessor's office. It seemed that the property was sufficiently defined.

The second piece of property was described as, "All that part of my farm, being a square with 200-foot sides, the southeast corner of which is the north line of my neighbor, Julia Brown." After trying for a minute to decipher this description, I was correct in my judgment that it was "insufficient because of vagueness."

Perhaps I did better than my score shows, because there is some doubt about the correctness of the wanted answers. The best way to establish the correctness of the scoring key is to ask a panel of experts to study the test and verify the correctness of the scoring key. An evaluation of the Multi-State Bar Examination prepared for the National Conference of Bar Examiners reported that the members of the expert panel, acting independently, averaged 14% errors. The candidates had an error rate of 36%, only 2.6 times as many errors as the experts. Even after discussion, the panelists disagreed with the scoring key in 5% of the items, casting further doubt on the scoring key.

Myth: *Certifying examinations do not need to be validated using criterion-related validity or construct validity.* Certifying examinations, of which the Multi-State Bar Examination is a prominent example, hide behind the disclaimer that they focus "not on prediction, but on the applicant's current skill or competence in a specific domain." But they never demonstrate that the test measures current skill or competence. The more appropriate model than predictive validity is concurrent validity, but they never study that either. The good reason is that there is no way to test those who fail. However, there are different passing scores in different states, and some are low enough that the use of corrections for restriction of range would provide interpretable results.

The real reason, I am sure, is that the results would be shockingly bad. Competent, experienced lawyers state with no shame that they probably could not pass the bar examination since they have forgotten what they do not use. If it is true that currently practicing attorneys would fail, and there is no demonstration that the test scores are related empirically to competence in the practice, what good is the test?

Implications

Earning a license or certificate is essential for those who want to practice in many professional and subprofessional lines of work. Examiners are typically not trained in psychological measurement. The result is that the public is not as well protected from incompetents as it deserves to be, and potentially competent practitioners are denied the opportunity to use the information that they have amassed, often after years of study.

Chapter 17

Americans with Disabilities Act and Age Discrimination in Employment Act

BACKGROUND

Title VII of the Civil Rights Act of 1964 is the main fair employment legislation, but there are two other significant laws, Americans with Disabilities Act and Age Discrimination in Employment Act. They protect the disabled worker and workers over 40 years of age, respectively.

Purpose

The purpose of the Age Discrimination in Employment Act (ADEA 1967) is to end discrimination based on age of those between 40 years of age and normal retirement age of 65. The purpose of the American with Disabilities Act (ADA 1990) is to provide better access of the disabled to work.

Population

ADEA covers all persons more than 40 years old up to 65 who are applicants or current employees. The EEOC applies the same rules to enforcement of ADEA as it has to Title VII of the Civil Rights Act with respect to the validation of the selection procedures, but the 80% rule does not apply to ADEA actions. Thus, the *Uniform Guidelines* and the *Questions and Answers* have the same force for adjudicating the validity of selection procedures in age discrimination cases as they do for discrimination based on race, ethnicity, or sex. There is no need for further discussion of ADEA.

ADA covers all persons with physical and mental disabilities, visible or hidden. ADA was passed because Congress determined that many employers discriminated against the disabled in employment decisions and actions. They suffered from both intentional exclusion and overprotective laws. Congress passed Title I of ADA to eliminate discrimination in employment by setting enforceable standards.

ADA operates under a completely different set of rules than Title VII and ADEA because the issues and the solutions are different. The rules of dealing with the disabled are complicated by the need to balance two rights, the right of the employer to know about the disability to be able to accommodate it, if possible, and the right of privacy of the disabled person who may feel sensitive about the condition.

Disability is any mental or physical impairment that substantially limits one or more major life activities, a record of having a disability even if the applicant is presently free of disabilities, or being regarded as disabled. The employer is bound to explore the disability and its effects on the work and make a genuine effort to come to a mutually satisfactory resolution with the applicant or employee. Any person who is not personally disabled but whose activities are limited by the need to care for a protected person is also covered in some respects. For example, the employer must arrange for a spouse to be free to take a disabled person for treatment.

Disabilities may be visible or unseen. Visible conditions include blindness, deafness, and loss of a limb or loss of use of a limb. Other disabling conditions may not be visible, such as asthma, heart disease, and neurological impairment. To be covered, the disability must be relatively permanent. Pregnancy, broken bones that are knitting, or even a long convalescence are not disabilities. To qualify under ADA, the disability must interfere with major life activities such as caring for oneself, walking, hearing, speaking.

To qualify as a disability, mental and psychological conditions must be the result of an impairment such as emotional illness or learning disabilities. Low intelligence that does not result from some impairment is not a disability. Mere deviations from the norm, such as heavy drinking, pedophilia, kleptomania, compulsive gambling, homosexuality, and the like, are not included (these are sometimes called Jesse Helms' hit list). Advanced age without disabling conditions is not a disability covered by ADA.

Those who are known to have had a disability that has been cured, such as alcoholism, psychiatric disorders, or physical conditions such as heart disease, are also protected by ADA. A person with a condition incorrectly considered by some as being disabling, such as controlled epilepsy, is also covered.

My discussion follows the psychological principle of going from the known to the unknown, so the description of ADA generally parallels that of Title VII and the *Uniform Guidelines*.

Recruitment. There is no requirement that the employer make a special effort to recruit the disabled. Employers are encouraged to recruit protected applicants under both laws.

Position description. A job description is the beginning of wisdom in validation studies under Title VII. ADA relies on position descriptions. (A *position* comprises the duties performed by one person. A *job* is a collection of positions that are sufficiently similar to be treated alike.) The key word distinction is *similar*. Positions in the same job may differ enough to make a difference in the employment of the disabled. Some executives prefer to type their own letters, so limitations on a secretary's typing may not be important. A row of radial drill presses may all look alike, but if the operator of one must climb down into a pit to accommodate long work pieces, that one position may not be accessible to someone with limited mobility.

Part of the purpose of the position description is to distinguish between essential and marginal functions. A function is essential if the position exists to fulfill the function, a limited number of employees can perform the function, or it is highly specialized. Marginal functions are those that are unimportant or can be assigned to the incumbent in another position. Once it is established that the disability impedes the performance of an essential function, the employer and the applicant try to negotiate a mutually acceptable accommodation. It is expected that the marginal functions will be eliminated, modified, or assigned to someone else.

Job descriptions are typically out-of-date. To expect an up-to-date position description for each position in an organization is unrealistic. However, when a position becomes available, a description of the features that are relevant to the work of the disabled can be prepared.

Qualified applicant. ADA applies only to qualified applicants; there is no requirement to hire the unqualified. However, the decision that an applicant is not qualified must not be made lightly. The employer should have and apply job-related standards of skills, abilities, education, and experience. Employers are permitted to establish qualification standards that protect workers from substantial harm or threats to health and safety of the worker and others who may be affected.

Identifying the disabled. An employer is expected to notice and respond to visible disabilities but must be careful about disabilities that are not readily observable. The interviewer may not ask whether the applicant has, or has a history or record of, a disability or medical condition. It is appropriate for the interviewer to describe the selection procedures and the work requirements. The interviewer may ask whether or not there is any reason the applicant cannot perform on either the selection procedures or on the job. If the disabled person does not respond, the employer is not required to make accommodations. If the response is positive, the two parties work out a mutually agreeable solution.

A basic vehicle for identifying the disabled and keeping a record of the results is the application blank. Although employers must not ask direct questions about the applicant's medical history, they can ask about job-related experience gained in a non-job setting or the ability to meet licensing requirements. For example, it is permissible to ask if the applicant has a driver's license if driving is required by the job. It is not permissible to ask, ''Can you see well enough to drive?''

Reasonable accommodations. Employers are required to make reasonable accommodations in selecting and employing disabled applicants. Selection procedures may be modified to permit the disabled to show what they can do. Modifications may include reading instructions or test items, allowing more time, or allowing the applicant to respond orally to a written examination. Employers should be very sure in the use of the realistic job preview as a self-screening device that the descriptions of the demands of the job are realistic and describe reasonable expectations.

Reasonable accommodation relating to the work means that the employer does not have to make an accommodation if it causes "undue hardship." The determination of undue hardship includes consideration of cost and disruption or fundamental changes in the work. The size of the employer and structure of the operation are also considered. The employer must examine each situation on a case-by-case basis. It is sensible to document the reasons for any adverse decisions.

Some accommodations are:

Making existing facilities accessible.

Modified work schedule.

Adjustment of testing and training requirements.

Providing special equipment.

Medical examinations. Job offers must be made before a physical or medical examination. It is permissible to make a job offer contingent on a medical examination if the same requirement extends to all applicants. Medical information must be stored separately from other personnel data and be accessible only to supervisors who need the information to make accommodations and to safety and first-aid staff.

A sensitive issue regards the communication of medical information to others. For example, a worker might ask for the reasons for changing the job to accommodate the disabled person. If the disabled person resists the communication of the information, it is best to consult an attorney who specializes in the field before proceeding.

Myth: *An employer who does not hire an adequate number of disabled workers must demonstrate the job relatedness of the decisions.* The number of disabled recruited, hired, or promoted is not an issue in ADA. It is not necessary to keep records on disabled applicants or to be concerned with any statistical disparity in hiring rates. Of course, if there is some charge of unfairness to a disabled applicant or employee, a history of accommodation to the disabled puts the employer in a favorable light.

Myth: *If two applicants for a position meet minimum qualifications, and one is disabled, and the other is not, the employer must hire the disabled applicant.* No. The employer is free to choose the more qualified candidate. The decision should take into account the reasonable accommodations and should be documented.

Myth: *ADA is a field day for lawyers and plaintiffs.* Soon after ADA was enacted, I conducted a half dozen seminars for a large human relations consulting organization. I was told that the attendance was greater than usual and that the reviews were favorable. I sat back, waiting for inquiries. None came. I can only conclude that organizations sophisticated enough to send representatives to such seminars are sophisticated enough to deal with ADA without any help or fear of litigation.

Myth: *The costs of ADA are exorbitant.* A large employer recently reported that the cost of accommodations under ADA was less than $300 per hire, a trivial amount.

Myth: *Those with AIDS or who are HIV positive are not protected.* So long as they can work with reasonable accommodation, AIDS patients and those with HIV are protected.

Myth: *It is possible to modify tests to make them operate the same for the disabled as for those who are not impaired.* No one has developed a correction formula to make the scores comparable to those produced under standard conditions. If tests are used with changes in time limits or other conditions of administration, the results can be interpreted only subjectively.

Courts differ widely in their treatment of applicants for licensing or bar examinations. Some order that dyslexic applicants be granted extra time; others order no accommodation. A case in point is that of a law student with dyslexia who, after he failed the bar examination, was denied his request for twice the usual time. The attorney for the defendant suggested that reading at a normal rate might be a legitimate qualification for becoming a lawyer. This rationale misses the point. The purpose of the bar examination is to determine whether or not applicants know enough law to practice. It is up to employers to determine whether slow readers can meet their production standards.

Implications

Both ADEA and ADA benefit employers by bringing into the workforce qualified applicants who might otherwise be overlooked. The benefit to the older workers and the disabled is obvious. The taxpayer benefits because such workers contribute taxes rather than being a potential drain on the system.

Despite original forebodings, both laws seem to be working well. The accommodations that must be made in selection and in operations appear to be minimal, especially when compared with the increased talent in the labor pool.

Chapter 18

Implications

BACKGROUND

Most chapters in this book ended with a statement of implications. Here are some of the more general implications I hope you will take with you.

Adverse impact. Determining whether there is adverse impact against a minority depends, in the first place, on the identification of the race of each applicant. The *Uniform Guidelines* identify five racial/ethnic groups as the basis for computing adverse impact. However, the federal government permits people to identify themselves with more than one race, reflecting the reality of the racial mixing that continually takes place.

The simplest and most direct way of determining adverse impact once the applicants are sorted out by race is to construct a table such as Table 12.1. Before assembling the numbers, it is essential to look at the jobs that are covered and the methods of counting the applicants and those who are hired or promoted. Statistical tests of significance are not called for in the *Uniform Guidelines*, but if someone insists, it is not hard to find a statistician who can compute them for you if you do not know how. Generally, adverse impact is not a borderline issue. A real difference will jump up and hit you in the face. When numbers are small, consideration of the history of similar tests may help to clarify the issue.

You don't have to be a specialist to know good tests from bad. Psychometricians frighten off interested nonspecialists by an emphasis on statistics and arcane descriptions of what they are up to. However, most of the issues in employment testing can be understood by anyone who looks carefully at the important steps in the process of developing and validating tests. Some basic questions that apply to all tests are:

Are the objectives of the selection procedure articulated?

Is the job description adequate?

Is an adequate portion of the job covered by the selection procedure?

Is the selection procedure administered and scored properly?

Is the passing score set at the appropriate level?

Does the selection procedure meet empirical standards?

To establish content validity, you need satisfactory answers to some basic questions:

Is the wanted answer correct?

Is each distractor acceptable?

Is there a clear link between the wanted answer and work performance?

Would the applicant be expected to act in conformity with the response?

Would the applicant need to apply the knowledge immediately on appointment?

How important would the ability to respond be to successful job performance?

Does the selection procedure provide adequate background information?

Do applicants have adequate backgrounds to respond?

Empirical demonstrations of criterion-related validity are more complicated, but, fortunately, they are generally done more carefully and reported in more detail that the content validation studies. Here, too, there are some straightforward questions that should be answered in the report:

Are the jobs studied in the research representative of the jobs sought by the applicants?

Is the sample of research subjects representative of the population who take the test?

Does the criterion accurately measure the relevant work behaviors of the sample subjects?

Do the results show that the selection procedure would lead to a useful improvement of the quality of the workforce?

There are also questions that help to evaluate the usefulness of any selection procedure that do not relate directly to its validity:

Would competent journeymen perform well on the selection procedure?

Would those without adequate training or experience perform poorly on the selection procedure?

Is the test free from the effect of extraneous influences, such as favoring the testwise or using inappropriate language?

Is the selection procedure free of bias?

Would the employer benefit from training the applicants to take the selection procedure?

Does the item require a constructed response?

Use of selection procedures. For all procedures, valid or invalid, it is important to understand if they meet these standards:

What role does each selection procedure have in the entire process?

How are decisions made using the selection procedure?

Is the process fairly applied to all applicants?

Does the procedure foster the goal of an integrated, effective workforce?

Affirmative action is good business. Affirmative action is not quotas. Full affirmative action programs emphasize many procedures that will improve the quality of the workforce, starting with an active recruitment of qualified applicants of all races and ethnic groups and both sexes. Affirmative action then calls for a redesign of the work to take into account the capacities of those who may have to make up for an inferior education. Finally, affirmative action includes the targeting of training programs to maximize the skill level and contribution of the trainees. In this context, there is an effort to increase the representation of women and minorities at all levels in the organization.

To profit from the increased use of tests, the employer does not need to adhere rigidly to the top-down selection procedure illustrated in Figures 14.15 and 14.16. Note that near the point of cut, there is a large spread in the expected performance. Here other procedures come into play. Furthermore, Figures 14.15 and 14.16 are misleading, because it has been commonly observed that blacks typically score one standard deviation below whites, but their performance is only one-half a standard deviation below that of the whites. That means that accepting black applicants with slightly lower test scores would not result in any decrease in performance.

Fair employment is good business. Progressive employers have used validated testing for many years for one simple reason. It pays off. Many adopted validated selection procedures because of the effectiveness of work done by military psychologists during World War II. Returning to a peacetime economy, some veterans and civilians applied the skills they had learned working for the armed forces. Academic programs in industrial psychology taught a new generation of psychologists the techniques of test development and validation. Passage of Title VII and other fair employment laws and the promulgation of guidelines and professional standards motivated test users to improve their procedures.

The payroll is their largest controllable cost for most organizations. Countless reports of research document the improvement of the safety and efficiency of the workforce because of the use of improved selection procedures. An early article even told how the introduction of testing improved the quality of the applicants, probably because applicants who recognized their limitations avoided the hassle and humiliation of failing a test. Realistic job previews discourage those who are unsuited for the work and forewarn the rest who are less likely to be disappointed by unsuspected drawbacks of the work.

The focus on validity in the *Uniform Guidelines* has encouraged employers to improve their selection procedures and thus enhance the safety and efficiency of the organization and to reduce the cost of doing business. They have also profited form the new availability of talented minorities and women who were previously ignored or relegated to positions beneath their capacities. Women who two generations ago would have been top-notch secretaries make a greater contribution as lawyers and managers and in other higher-level positions. The need for diversity in the workplace has encouraged reconsideration of what makes the ideal employee. Employers have profited from the emphasis on the talents of the disabled rather than on their disabilities.

The Glass Ceiling Commission (1995) concluded (p. 14):

[A] growing body of evidence . . . indicates shattering the glass ceiling is good for business. Organizations that excel in leveraging diversity (including hiring and promoting minorities and women into senior positions) can experience better financial performance in the long run than those which are not effective in managing diversity.

Cox and Smolinski (1994) cite a Covenant Investment Management study that:

rated the performance of the Standard and Poor's 500 companies on factors relating to the hiring and advancement of men and women, compliance with EEOC and other regulatory requirements, and employee litigation. Companies which rated in the bottom 100 on the glass ceiling earned an average of 7.9 percent return on investment, compared to the average return of the 18.3 percent for the top 100.

You can legislate morality. There is nothing so powerful as an idea whose time has come, and legislation can move it along. One of the most galling aspects of Jim Crow legislation was the restriction on public accommodations. Black business or pleasure travelers had to locate the few black hotels or restaurants that catered to blacks or stay with members of a network.

Although local acts of discrimination continue, no hotel or restaurant has an announced policy of refusing to serve minorities. Lester Maddox, later the one-term governor of Georgia, handed out pickax handles to help his white patrons at the Pickrick Restaurant maintain his policy of racial segregation in his restaurant. No one does that anymore. George Wallace, who vowed to stand at the schoolhouse door to prevent desegregation, subsequently modified his stand. The laws and customs reflect and lead to the progress that has been made.

The government supports fair employment. Many laws, some of which predate the landmark Civil Rights Act of 1964, have repeatedly strengthened the federal position of fair employment. Chief Justice Burger is quoted as saying that the *Griggs* decision was the most important in the term in which it was handed down. President Bush is quoted similarly as saying the Americans with Disabilities Act was the most important law that he signed into law that year.

The Civil Rights Act of 1991 extended the coverage of the earlier laws. It specified the damages in cases of intentional discrimination in employment, strengthened the obligations of the burden of proof of employers in defending their tests, facilitated prompt and orderly resolution of challenges, and extended protection for government employees. Title II of the act, called the "Glass Ceiling Act of 1991," created a Glass Ceiling Commission to make recommendations concerning eliminating artificial barriers to the advancement of women and minorities and foster advancement to management and decision-making positions in business. The only major exceptions are the controversial set-asides in government contracting and the modification of test scores on the basis of race.

One reason it has been possible to legislate morality is that the laws reflected changes in attitudes. For example, some department stores would have been willing to hire minority salesclerks except for fear that racist customers might take their business elsewhere. When they all had to hire minorities, the presumed competitive disadvantage disappeared. Similarly, some purveyors of public accommodations wanted the minority business but were afraid to be first.

Times have changed. Lewis (1996) writes:

"We believe that no particular background . . . enjoys inherent advantages or possesses the secret of success," says the I.B.M. employment brochure before explaining how far the company has come in hiring minorities. And it has! In 1962, I.B.M. employed 1,250 minorities and women, or 1.5% percent of its work force. In 1995, I.B.M. employed 19,400 minorities and women, constituting 18.2 percent of its work force. Of its managers, 3,500 are women and 2,000 are minorities.

The Glass Ceiling Commission (1995, p. 154) reports:

Between 1982 and 1992, the proportion of women holding the title of Executive Vice President rose from 4 percent to 9 percent. In that same period, the proportion of those at the Senior Vice Presidential level rose from 13 percent to 23 percent.

The commission reports (p. 148) the results of a survey by Korn/Ferry International: "Almost 93 percent of the 439 senior women surveyed in 1992 felt that a glass ceiling for women still exists."

On the other hand, 96% of these 439 executives believe that women are continuing to make progress in business. The majority of those surveyed in 1982 expect that women will constitute 20% of their company's senior management by the year 2000.

Forty-five percent of all senior executive women surveyed said that they aspired to a higher-level office, and 14% of all aspired to be CEOs. Two-thirds of women in the sample do not think that male backlash has increased now that more women are in competitive positions with men. On the other hand, a quarter of the women in the survey felt that ''being a woman/sexism'' was the biggest obstacle they have to overcome, and 59% of the survey participants have personally experienced sexual harassment on the job.

Progress has been made, but there is still a long way to go. Improved selection procedures are part of what is needed.

Appendixes

Appendix 1

Role of the Equal Employment Opportunity Commission

The Equal Employment Opportunity Commission's mission is to ensure equality of opportunity by vigorously enforcing federal legislation prohibiting discrimination in employment. It uses investigation, conciliation, litigation, coordination, regulation in the federal sector, education, policy research, and provision of technical assistance to achieve this end.

It enforces:

Title VII of the Civil Rights Act of 1964

Equal Pay Act

Age Discrimination in Employment Act

Rehabilitation Act of 1973

Title I of the Americans with Disabilities Act

Civil Rights Act of 1991

The text of these laws is reproduced in the EEOC publication *Laws Enforced by the U.S. Equal Employment Opportunity Commission.*

The EEOC publishes an *Annual Report*, which covers:

The commission's authority

Enforcement data

Private sector enforcement and compliance activities

Federal sector programs

Enforcement litigation

Legal guidance and coordination

Communication, education, and technical assistance.

It promulgates, from time to time, notices on selected topics in Enforcement Guidance (Number 915.002). Among them are:

Workers' Compensation and the ADA, 9/3/96

The Effect of Representations Made in Applications for Benefits on the Determination of Whether a Person Is a ''Qualified Individual with a Disability'' under the American with Disabilities Act of 1990 (ADA) (2/12/97)

Americans with Disabilities Act and Psychiatric Disabilities

Nonwaivable employee rights under EEOC enforcement statutes (4/10/96)

Policy Statement on Mandatory Binding Arbitration of Employment Discrimination Disputes as a Condition of Employment (7/10/97)

ADA Enforcement Guidance: Disability-Related Question and Medical Examinations

For additional information you may call EEOC's Publication Distribution Center toll-free on 1–800–669–EEOC. The TDD number is 1–800–800–3302. Or you may write to the Office of Communication and Legislative Affairs, EEOC, 1801 L Street, NE, Washington, DC 20507.

For information on filing a charge with EEOC, you may reach the field office that has jurisdiction in your area by calling 1–800–669–4000. The EEOC World Wide Web address is http://www.eeoc.gov.

The *Equal Employment Opportunity Commission Charge Process* is presented in Figure A.1.

Figure A.1
The Equal Employment Opportunity Commission Charge Process

Title VII	Age Discrimination in	Americans with	Equal Pay Act (EPA)
Prohibits discrimination	Employment Act (ADEA)	Disabilities Act (ADA)	Prohibits discrimination
on basis of race, color,	Prohibits discrimination	Prohibits discrimination	in the payment of wages
sex, national origin,	on basis of age—protects	against an individual with	based on sex
and religion	persons 40 and older	a disability	

Act of Prohibited Discrimination in:
Hiring, Assignment, Promotion, Discipline, Wages, Layoffs, Discharge, Benefits,
and Terms and Conditions of Employment

▼

Employee, Former Employee, or Job Applicant
FILES CHARGE
Within 180 days
(Jurisdiction without State or Local Fair Employment Practices Agency (FEPA))
Or
300 days
(Jurisdiction with FEPA)

(If EEOC Processes) ▼ deferred to ▶ **FEPA**

Notify Respondent
(Employer, Union, Employment Agency)
Within 10 Days of Charge

▼

Interview Charging Party (CP) and CP Witnesses

▼

Send Respondent Request for Information
(may include on-site interview)

▼

Analyze Respondent's documents and Interview Respondent's witnesses
(possible subpoena of Respondent for information)

▼

Investigator analyzes all evidence and drafts Investigative Memoranda
summarizing evidence

▼

Pre-Determination Interview
(with party that decision will probably rule against)

▼

EEOC Issues Letter of Determination

▼ ▼

No reasonable cause   **Reasonable cause determination**
(no further EEOC involvement)   (EEOC will attempt to settle charge
informally through conciliation)

▼   ▼   ▼

CP has Right to File in Court—   **Successful**   **Unsuccessful**
De Novo Trial   **Conciliation**   **Conciliation**

▼

EEOC or CP has Right to
File in Court—De Novo Trial

Appendix 2

Content Validation Form II

Selection Procedure as a Whole
(The answer to each of these questions should be *Yes* or *Does not apply*.)

Are the objectives of the selection procedure articulated?
  Are objectives described in the report?
  Are objectives relevant to employer's needs?
  Is the procedure planned to conform to Title VII of the Civil Rights Act of 1964,
    Americans with Disabilities Act, and Age Discrimination in Employment Act?
  Is the procedure planned to conform to professional and ethical standards?

Is the selection procedure subject to content validation?
  Does the procedure measure content, not a construct?
  Is the procedure designed to measure prerequisite work behavior or KSAs?

Is the job description adequate?
  Does the job description cover job duties, their importance and complexity?
  Is the job description up to date?
  Does the position description (relative to hiring disabled applicants) comply with
    ADA?

Is an adequate portion of the job covered by the selection procedure?
  Does it, combined with other procedures, measure the most important content of
    the job?

Is the selection procedure administered and scored properly?
  Is the administration adequately monitored?
  Are the tests secure?
  Is the scoring procedure verified as accurate?
  Is adequate accommodation made for disabled applicants in the content of the
    selection procedure, its scoring, and administration?

Is the passing score set at the appropriate level?
    (No passing score.)
    Does the passing score conform to reasonable expectations of proficiency?
    Is the passing score modified for disabled applicants?

Does the selection procedure meet empirical standards?
    Is it reliable?
    Does it discriminate between levels of performance?
    Is its weight in the battery appropriate?
    Does internal statistical analysis support the use of the selection procedure?

Item-by-Item Analysis
(Questions that focus on multiple-choice tests may be adapted to other selection procedures. The preponderance of responses should be positive.)

Is the wanted answer correct?
    Is the source up to date?
    Does the wanted answer conform to accepted practice?
    Is the correct answer supplied?

Is each distractor acceptable?
    Is the behavior or knowledge presented incorrect under all reasonable circumstances?
    Is there a clear distinction between the distractor and the wanted answer?
    Is the distractor likely to attract responses?

Is there a clear link between the wanted answer and work performance?
    Does correct behavior follow from the wanted answer?
    Is the response relevant to important work behavior?

Would the applicant be expected to act in conformity with the response?
    Does the answer show that the applicant would be able to perform adequately?
    Would applicants be motivated to act in congruity to the response?

Would the applicant need to apply the knowledge immediately on appointment?
    Would the applicant be required to perform adequately without further training?
    Would the knowledge be used by incumbents at this organizational level?
    Would the new incumbent work without benefit of close supervision?

How important would the ability to respond be to successful job performance?
    Would there be serious consequences for safety or efficiency if the applicant does not have the information or skills needed to respond?

Does the selection procedure provide adequate background information?
    Does the stem or introduction correctly provide all the needed information?
    If the question is a simulation, does it communicate the needed information?

Do applicants have adequate backgrounds to respond?
    Can applicants be expected to have the necessary education?
    Can applicants be expected to have the necessary training or experience?

Supplementary Indications of Content Validity
(The preponderance of responses should be positive.)

Would competent journeymen perform well on the selection procedure?

Would those without adequate training or experience perform poorly on the selection procedure?

Is the test free from the effect of extraneous influences?
> Would applicants who are not testwise be likely to do well as well as they should?
> Are the language and mathematics demands of the test commensurate with those required by the job?

Is the selection procedure free of bias?
> Are selection procedures of this kind free of a history of discrimination against minorities or women?
> Would the content of the selection procedure be acceptable by minorities or women?

Would the employer benefit from training the applicants to take the selection procedure?
> Are the skills that would be taught related to work behavior?

Does the item require a constructed response?
> Is it sufficient that the applicant recognize rather than construct a response?

Appendix 3

The Rights and Responsibilities of Test-Takers

As a test-taker, you have the right to:

1. Be informed of your rights and responsibilities as a test-taker.
2. Be treated with courtesy, respect, and impartiality, regardless of your race, gender, age, disability, religion, ethnicity, national origin, and sexual orientation.
3. Be tested with measures that meet professional standards and that are appropriate for you, given the manner in which the test results will be used.
4. Be informed prior to testing about the test's purposes, the nature of the test, whether test results will be reported to you, and the planned use of the results, when not in conflict with the testing purposes.
5. Know in advance when the test will be administered, when test results will be available, and whether there is a fee for testing services that you are expected to pay.
6. Have your test administered and your test results interpreted by appropriately trained individuals.
7. Know if a test is optional and to learn of the consequences of taking or not taking the test.
8. Have test results explained promptly after taking the test and in commonly understood terms.
9. Confidentiality about your results to the extent allowed by law.
10. Present concerns about the testing process and receive information about procedures that will be used to address them.

Bibliography

Affirmative Action appropriate under Title VII of the Civil Rights Act of 1964 as amended, 29 CFR 1608, EEOC.

Affirmative Action Guidelines, January 19, 1979, *Federal Register*, Vol. 44, No. 14, pp. 4423–4430.

Age Discrimination in Employment Act (1967), 29 U.S.C. 621–634, P.L. 90-202.

Albemarle Paper Company v. Moody, U.S. S.Ct. (1975), 422 U.S. 405.

American Psychological Association. (1992). "Ethical Principles of Psychologists and Code of Conduct." *American Psychologist*, Vol. 47, pp. 1597–1611.

Americans with Disabilities Act of 1990 (P.L. 191–336), ADA as amended, 42 U.S.C. 12101 *et seq.*

Anastasi, A. (1982). *Psychological Testing*. New York: Macmillan.

Ash, P. (1989). *The Legality of Pre-Employment Inquiries*. Park Ridge, IL: London House.

Barrett, R. S. (ed.). (1996). *Fair Employment Practices in Human Resource Management*. Westport, CT: Quorum Books.

Boston Chapter NAACP, Inc. v. Beecher (1975), 421 U.S. 910.

Bridgeman, P. (1924). *The Logic of Modern Physics*. New York: Macmillan.

Brogden, H. (1946). "On the Interpretation of the Correlation Coefficient as a Measure of Predictive Efficiency." *Journal of Educational Psychology*, Vol. 37, pp. 65–76.

Burns, W. C. (1996). Personal communication.

Byham, W. (n.d.). Personal communication.

Canter, M. B., Bennett, B. E., Jones, S. E., and Nagy, T. F. (1994). *Ethics for Psychologists: A Commentary on the APA Ethics Code*. Washington, DC: American Psychological Association.

Cascio, W. F. (1982). *Applied Psychology in Personnel Management*, 2nd ed. Reston, VA: Reston Publishing Company.

CFR 1981 and 1983.

City of New York. Department of Personnel. (1970). Promotion to Lieutenant (P.D.), Exam No. 9580, February 28.

Civil Rights Act of 1964, Title VII, 42 U.S.C. 2000e *et seq.*, P.L. 88–352.

Civil Rights Act of 1991, P.L. 102–166 (C.R.A.).

Cox, T., and Smolinski, C. (1994). *Managing Diversity and Glass Ceiling Initiatives as National Economic Imperatives.* Ann Arbor: University of Michigan. Paper prepared for the Glass Ceiling Commission. On file.

Cronbach, L. J. (1970). *Essentials of Psychological Testing.* Evanston, IL: Harper and Row.

EEOC (n.d.). *Affirmative Action appropriate under Title VII of the Civil Rights Act of 1964.*

EEOC (n.d.). *The EEOC and Affirmative Action.* EEOC Office of Communication and Legislative Affairs.

EEOC (n.d.). *Legislative History of Titles VII and XI of the Civil Rights Act of 1964.* Washington, DC: U.S. Government Printing Office.

EEOC (1965). *Guidelines on Employment Testing Procedures.* Washington, DC: EEOC.

EEOC Enforcement Guidelines on Preemployment Disabilities-Related Injuries and Medical Examinations under the Americans with Disabilities Act of 1990, Number 915.002. Washington, DC: Author.

Equal Employment Opportunity Act of 1972, 42 U.S.C. 2000e 88–352.

Equal Employment Opportunity Coordinating Council. (n.d.). *Policy Statement on Affirmative Action.* Appendix, *Uniform Guidelines.*

Equal Pay Act of 1963, 29 U.S.C. 201 *et seq.*

Executive Order 11246 30 FR 12319, 12935, 3 CFR 1964–1965, CMR, p. 339.

Eyde, L. D., Nester, M. A., Heaton, S. M., and Nelson, A. V. (1994). *Guide for Administering Written Employment Examinations to Persons with Disabilities, PRDC 94–11.* Washington, DC: U.S. Office of Personnel Management, Personnel Research and Development Center.

Fowler, L. N., and Fowler, O. S. (1969). *Phrenology: A Practical Guide to Your Head.* New York: Chelsea House.

Frederiksen, N. (1986). "Toward a Broader Conception of Human Intelligence." *American Psychologist,* Vol. 41, No. 4, pp. 445–452.

Gael, S. (1993). *Job Analysis: A Guide to Assessing Work Activities.* San Francisco: Jossey-Bass.

Gaudet, F. J., and Caril, A. R. (1957). "Why Executives Fail." *Personnel Psychology,* Vol. 10, No. 1, pp. 7–21.

"Giant of Exam Business Keeps Quiet on Cheating." (1997). *New York Times,* September 28, p. 1.

Glass Ceiling Commission. (1995). *Good for Business: Making Full Use of the Nation's Human Capital.* Washington, DC: Author.

Griggs v. Duke Power Co. (1971), 401 U.S. 424.

Hanson, M. A., and Ramos, R. A. (1996). "Situational Judgment Tests." In R. S. Barrett (ed.), *Fair Employment Practices in Human Resource Management.* Westport, CT: Quorum Books. pp. 119–124.

Hogan, R. (1996). "Personality Assessments." In R. S. Barrett (ed.), *Fair Employment Practices in Human Resource Management.* Westport, CT: Quorum Books, pp. 144–152.

Holzer, H., and Newmark, D. (1996). *Are Affirmative Action Hires Less Qualified? Ev-*

idence from Employer-Employees Data on New Hires. Cambridge, MA: National Bureau of Economic Research, Working Paper Number 5603.

Joint Committee on Testing Practices. (1998). *The Rights and Responsibilities of Test-Takers.* Draft. Washington, DC: Author.

Kirkpatrick, J. J., Ewen, R. B., Barrett, R. S., and Katzell, R. A. (1968). *Testing and Fair Employment.* New York: New York University Press.

Klein, S. (1982). *An Evaluation of the Multistate Bar Examination.* Chicago: National Conference of Bar Examiners.

Latham, G. P., and Sue-Chan, C. (1996). "A Legally Defensible Interview for Selecting the Best." In R. S. Barrett (ed.), *Fair Employment Practices in Human Resource Management.* Westport, CT: Quorum Books, pp. 134–143.

Lewis, M. (1996). "Rainbow, Inc." *New York Times Magazine,* December 8, p. 32.

Lowman, R. L. (ed.). (1998). *The Ethical Practice of Psychology in Organizations.* Washington, DC: American Psychological Association Books.

Miner, J. B. (1985). "Sentence Completion Measures." In H. J. Bernardin and D. A. Bownas (eds.), *Personality Assessment in Organizations.* New York: Praeger.

National Conference of Bar Examiners. (1987a). *Multi-State Bar Examination Questions, IX.* Columbia, MO: Lucas, p. 136.

National Conference of Bar Examiners. (1987b). *1986 Bar Examination Statistics.* Repr. from *The Bar Examiner,* Vol. 56, No. 2.

Office of Federal Contract Compliance Programs. (1995). 41 CFR Paragraph 60–2.12.

Oncale v. Sundowner Offshore Services, S.Ct. No. 96–568.

Parker, C. P., Baltes, B. B., and Christiansen, N. D. (1997). "Support for Affirmative Action, Justice Perceptions, and Work Attitudes: A Study of Gender and Racial-Ethnic Group Differences." *Journal of Applied Psychology,* Vol. 82, No. 3, pp. 376–389.

Pearson, K. (1931). *Tables for Statisticians and Biometricians.* Part 2. London: Biometric Laboratory, University College, pp. 78–109.

Petit v. Gingerich. (n.d.). District Court, Maryland Civil Actions 72–964–13.

Policy Statement on Affirmative Action. (n.d.). Equal Employment Opportunity Council.

Questions and Answers to Clarify and Provide a Common Interpretation of the Uniform Guidelines on Employment Selection Procedures. (1979). 41 F. R. 11916, March 7.

Reilly, R. R. (1996). "Alternative Selection Procedures." In R. S. Barrett (ed.), *Fair Employment Practices in Human Resource Management.* Westport, CT: Quorum Books, pp. 208–221.

Sackett, P. R., and Roth, L. (1991). "A Monte Carlo Examination of Banding and Rank Order Methods of Test Score Use in Personnel Selection." *Human Performance,* Vol. 4, No. 4, pp. 279–295.

Salyards, S. D., and Normand, J. (1996). "Employment Drug Testing." In R. S. Barrett (ed.), *Fair Employment Practices in Human Resource Management.* Westport, CT: Quorum Books.

Schmitt, N. (1996). "Validity Generalization." In R. S. Barrett (ed.), *Fair Employment Practices in Human Resource Management.* Westport, CT: Quorum Books.

Schmitt, N., Borman, W. C., and Associates. (1993). *Personnel Selection in Organizations.* San Francisco: Jossey-Bass.

Schneider, B., and Schmitt, N. (1986). *Staffing Organizations,* 2nd ed. Glenview, IL: Scott, Foresman.

Seberhagen, L. W. (1996a). "How Much Does a Test Validation Study Cost?" In R. S.

Barrett (ed.), *Fair Employment Practices in Human Resource Management*. Westport, CT: Quorum Books.

Seberhagen, L. W. (1996b). "A Modern Approach to Minimum Qualifications." In R. S. Barrett (ed.), *Fair Employment Practices in Human Resource Management*. Westport, CT: Quorum Books.

Society for Industrial and Organizational Psychology, Inc. (SIOP). (1987). *Principles for Validation and Use of Personnel Selection Procedures*. 3rd ed. College Park, MD: Author.

Standards for Educational and Psychological Testing. (1985). Washington, DC: American Psychological Association.

Sternberg, Robert J., and Williams, Wendy M. (1997). "Does the Graduate Record Examination Predict Meaningful Success in the Graduate Training of Psychologists?" *American Psychologist*, Vol. 52, No. 6, pp. 630–641.

Stokes, G. S., and Toth, C. S. (1996). "Background Data for Personnel Selection." In R. S. Barrett (ed.), *Fair Employment Practices in Human Resource Management*. Westport, CT: Quorum Books, pp. 171–182.

Teal v. Connecticut (1982), 457 U.S. 440.

"Technical Recommendations for Psychological Tests and Diagnostic Techniques." (1954). *Psychological Bulletin*, Vol. 51, No. 2, Part 2, pp. 1–38.

Torby, George R., Eyde, Lorraine D., Primoff, Ernest S., and Hardt, Robert H. (1976). Job Analysis of the Position of New York State Trooper. New York State Police, Albany. Mimeo, p. 111.

Uniform Guidelines on Employee Selection Procedures, 29 CFR 1606 (1978).

United States v. New York State Police (1978), 82 RFD 1.

U.S. Civil Service Commission. (1976). *Job Analysis of the Position of New York State Trooper*. Washington, DC.

U.S. Department of Labor, Employment Standards Administration, Office of Federal Contract Compliance Programs, Transmittal Number 207, December 13, 1995.

Wards Cove Packing Co. v. Antonio (1989), S.Ct. No. 87–1387.

Washington v. Davis (1976), 426 U.S. 229.

Zedeck S., Cascio, W. F., Goldstein, I. L., and Outtz, J. (1996). "Sliding Bands: An Alternative to Top-down Selection." In R. S. Barrett (ed.), *Fair Employment Practices in Human Resource Management*. Westport, CT: Quorum Books, pp. 222–234.

Name Index

Subject Index

Question and Answer Index

Uniform Guidelines Index

About the Author

RICHARD S. BARRETT is Principal of Barrett Associates, a consulting firm specializing in fair employment issues. He has held professorships at New York University and Stevens Institute of Technology. Dr. Barrett has also testified in cases argued before the Supreme Court and worked for the Equal Employment Opportunity Commission, where he participated in writing the *Uniform Guidelines on Employee Selection Procedures.* He has authored, coauthored, and contributed to ten previous books.

DATE DUE

BENJAMIN
BANNEKER
AMERICAN SCIENTIFIC PIONEER

SPECIAL LIVES IN HISTORY THAT BECOME

Signature LIVES

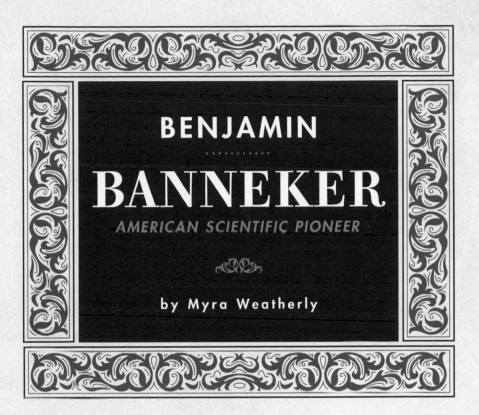

BENJAMIN
BANNEKER
AMERICAN SCIENTIFIC PIONEER

by Myra Weatherly

Content Adviser: Gwen Marable,
Banneker family descendant,
and Board Member,
The Friends of the Benjamin Banneker
Historical Park and Museum, Oella, Maryland

Reading Adviser: Susan Kesselring, M.A.,
Literacy Educator, Rosemount–Apple Valley–Eagan
(Minnesota) School District

COMPASS POINT BOOKS MINNEAPOLIS, MINNESOTA

Compass Point Books
3109 West 50th Street, #115
Minneapolis, MN 55410

Visit Compass Point Books on the Internet at *www.compasspointbooks.com*
or e-mail your request to *custserv@compasspointbooks.com*

Editor: Nick Healy
Page Production: Bobbie Nuytten
Photo Researchers: Kelly Garvin and Svetlana Zhurkin
Cartographer: XNR Productions, Inc.
Library Consultant: Kathleen Baxter

Art Director: Jaime Martens
Creative Director: Keith Griffin
Editorial Director: Carol Jones
Managing Editor: Catherine Neitge

Library of Congress Cataloging-in-Publication Data
Weatherly, Myra
  Benjamin Banneker : American scientific pioneer.
     p. cm.—(Signature lives)
  Includes bibliographical references and index.
  ISBN 0-7565-1579-3
  1. Banneker, Benjamin, 1731-1806. 2. Astronomers—United States—
Biography—Juvenile literature. 3. Scientists—United States—Biography—
Juvenile literature. 4. Mathematicians—United States—Biography—
Juvenile literature. 5. African American scientists—Biography—Juvenile
literature. 6. African American mathematicians—Biography—Juvenile
literature. I. Title. II. Series.
  QB36.B22W43 2006
  520.92—dc22   2005028708

Signature Lives

REVOLUTIONARY WAR ERA

The American Revolution created heroes—and traitors—who shaped the birth of a new nation: the United States of America. "Taxation without representation" was a serious problem for the American colonies during the mid-1700s. Great Britain imposed harsh taxes and refused to give the colonists a voice in their own government. The colonists rebelled and declared their independence from Britain—the war was on.

Table of Contents

1 BANNEKER'S BOLD DECLARATION

Chapter

❦

On August 19, 1791, a man named Benjamin Banneker sat down to write a letter. This ordinary act would hardly seem noteworthy, except that the person writing the letter and the one who would receive it were both so extraordinary. Banneker addressed his letter to Thomas Jefferson, the man who had written the Declaration of Independence in 1776 and who was by then serving as secretary of state.

In the Declaration, Jefferson had explained why the colonies needed to break from Great Britain, and it set forth the principles of freedom and equality that would guide the new nation. Now 15 years had passed, and Banneker was challenging Jefferson to live up to his words and to ask his country to do the same.

Benjamin Banneker penned a famous letter challenging one of the United States' Founding Fathers, and he gained fame as an almanac maker.

Thomas Jefferson was U.S. secretary of state from 1790 to 1793.

Writing such a letter was a bold move for Banneker, a self-educated man and the son and grandson of former slaves. He was a free black person in a time of slavery. He was a tobacco farmer of modest means who had spent most of his life on family land near the Patapsco River in Maryland, not far from the present-day city of Baltimore. Yet he lived a life of unusual achievement, and he would become perhaps the best-known African-American in the early history of the United States. He was a skilled astronomer and mathematician, and he would later be well-known as a producer of almanacs, books that were important sources of information, entertainment, and education for early Americans.

Banneker's original idea was to compose a cover letter to send along with a handwritten copy of his then-unpublished almanac. In his letter, he explained that he took up his pen "in order to direct to you as a present, a copy of an [Almanac] which I have calculated for the succeeding year. ... This calculation, Sir, is the production of my arduous study, in this my advanced stage of life." Banneker went on to inform Jefferson that the almanac was already in the hands of a publisher, who was considering whether to print and sell the book.

Banneker's fascination with astronomy fueled his desire to create an almanac that would be as good as one written by any formally educated scientist. In colonial times, almanacs were popular reference books. They provided all sorts of useful information for daily living. People read almanacs to find out when the sun and moon would rise and set, which served as a way for people in households without clocks to keep track of time. Almanacs also provided the best predictions for the weather and eclipses. Farmers looked to almanacs to help decide the best dates to plant and harvest. Sailors relied upon what they could see in the night skies to help them navigate the seas. Inaccuracies in an almanac could leave people lost and confused.

Banneker hoped that many people would benefit from his almanac. But he realized his potential readers would not include many of his fellow African-

>
>
> *An almanac is a book of tables, including a calendar of months and days with astronomical data and calculations. The first printed almanac was produced in Germany in 1457, and by the late 1700s, almanacs included other useful information, such as articles, letters, poems, and weather predictions.*

Americans. The more than 100,000 enslaved people living in the state of Maryland lacked the necessary skills and opportunities to read an almanac. Few slaves ever learned to read and write. Generally, they were not allowed to go to school, and they did not have the chance to use their minds to the full potential. Being a slave meant a life of forced labor and little free will.

Although he had lived his entire life in freedom, Banneker wondered why slavery was allowed to exist in a nation that had so recently won its freedom from tyranny. In his letter, he posed that question to Jefferson. Banneker likened the conditions of the colonists under British rule to the enslavement of black people in the United States. He challenged Jefferson to think back to the time when Britain imposed "a variety of dangers" and "a state of servitude" on the colonies.

Although Jefferson was a slaveholder, he had written famously in the Declaration of Independence that "all men are created equal" and that they are granted by "their Creator" such basic rights as "life, liberty and the pursuit of happiness." With the American Revolution won, Banneker did not understand how some Americans could be slaves when the nation was founded on the idea that all people are equal. He accused Jefferson and the other Founding Fathers of not fulfilling their pledge to

Traders captured African people, transported them to America, and sold them into a life of slavery.

preserve the rights of all Americans.

Banneker did not mince words. In his letter, he decried "how pitiable it is ... that you should at the same time be found guilty of that most criminal act" of holding innocent people—even newborn children—in the captivity of slavery. The lengthy letter included a plea for Jefferson to provide "aid and assistance" in getting rid of "absurd and false ideas" that one race was superior to another, as many white Americans believed at the time.

Banneker concluded the letter with the sort of parting salute common to the era. He wrote "Your most Obedient humble Servant" and signed his name. He mailed off the letter and a copy of his almanac.

He would not have to wait long for a reply.

The secretary of state received Banneker's letter exactly a week later—on August 26, 1791—and within four days, he sent a polite reply. In the short letter, Jefferson seemed to agree with Banneker that slavery was unjust.

No body wishes more than I do to see such proofs as you exhibit, that nature has

*given to our black brethren, talents equal
to those of the other colors of men, and that
the appearance of want is owing merely to
their degraded existence.*

With these words, Jefferson was saying that
Banneker provided proof of the potential of black
people. He seemed to be acknowledging that the
system of slavery was what held black people back—
not a lack of natural ability. That was an important
distinction at the time because the way many people
justified slavery was to claim that African-Americans
were somehow lesser beings than white people.

Jefferson expressed his own wish that, in time,
black Americans would be treated better. He wrote
that he hoped a system would be put into place "for
raising the condition of both their body and mind
to what it ought to be." Jefferson noted that he had
"taken the liberty" of sending a copy of Banneker's
almanac to the Royal Academy of Sciences in Paris
as an example of the talents of black people. There
was also the possibility the academy would publish
Banneker's work.

Nothing would come of Jefferson's effort. No reply
from Paris has been found among Jefferson's papers,
and the academy's surviving records do not indicate
that Banneker's manuscript was ever reviewed. But
Banneker would soon see his almanac published, and
new editions would follow in coming years. He would

Thomas Jefferson was among the most admired of the Founding Fathers. He was the primary author of the Declaration of Independence, the country's first secretary of state, and the third U.S. president. Jefferson declined to reveal his birthday (April 13, 1743) to officials who desired to celebrate the date. He repeatedly answered that the only birthday he recognized was that "of my country's liberties," or Independence Day. On July 4, 1826, the 50th anniversary of approval of the Declaration of Independence, Jefferson died at Monticello, his Virginia home.

find a large audience of readers, and he would publish his exchange of letters with Jefferson in a 1793 almanac. Those letters would later be used by people in the antislavery movement to promote their cause.

Slavery continued for decades to come, long past the deaths of Jefferson and Banneker. And racial discrimination would long be a problem in the United States, even though the country was founded on the notion of equality. Still, Banneker's life and work served as evidence of human potential. And his important accomplishments demonstrated a genius that shone through—despite his lack of a formal education and despite the fact that he lived in a country that did not allow black people, whether enslaved or free, the same opportunities afforded to whites.

With little more than borrowed books and determination, Banneker achieved greatness as a mathematician and astronomer. His self-taught expertise as a surveyor led to his important role in the planning of Washington, D.C., which had been designated as the site of the nation's new capital. His almanacs became widely read and well-liked, and they made his name known to, and respected by, many Americans.

Many of his accomplishments were all but forgotten for more than 150 years, but in recent times, Banneker's work as a scientist has been newly recognized and admired. His letters, surviving journals, and other important documents have helped modern historians learn more about him as a person, as well as about the political and social times in which he lived. Today, Banneker is remembered as a brilliant thinker and scientist far ahead of his time. ॐ

Benjamin Banneker became widely known in colonial America.

2 AN EXCEPTIONAL FAMILY

Chapter

⤛⤜

On November 9, 1731, a child was born on a farm in the valley of Maryland's Patapsco River. The parents, Mary and Robert, named their son Benjamin, and he began life as a part of an exceptional family. At a time when most black people in colonial America were held as slaves, members of Benjamin's family were free. This is because of a powerfully influential person in his early life: his grandmother Molly Welsh, whose personal history shaped her family's future.

Welsh was a white woman who was born and raised in England. As a young girl, she was a servant for a family in a small village in the English countryside. A dairy maid, Molly worked long and hard milking cows to earn barely enough money to pay for her food, clothes, and lodging.

A female convict is sold as an indentured servant after being transported from England to the American colonies.

A woodcut showing a 17th century English milkmaid

Something happened in 1682 that changed her life. Welsh said that while she was milking a cow, the animal gave a kick and turned over an entire pail of milk. Her angry employer did not believe her story. He insisted that it was not an accident and claimed she had stolen the milk. For this offense, the man had his servant arrested. At that time in England, a person found guilty of such theft could face death by hanging on the gallows.

A court found Molly guilty, taking the word of the employer over that of his young worker. But before pronouncing the death sentence, the judge turned to a provision of English law known as "calling for the book." This meant that the prisoner would be presented with a book. If she could read, which would indicate some potential in her, the penalty would be reduced. Rather than hanging, she would face forced emigration to an English colony, where she would have to spend a certain number of years of unpaid servitude. In Molly's case, the Bible was placed before her, and she read it with ease. The judge handed down the sentence—seven years of servitude in the Maryland colony.

Molly Welsh was shipped off across the Atlantic Ocean. Her fellow travelers included teachers, farm laborers, house servants, carpenters, and masons—all seeking

When Molly Welsh arrived in the New World, Cecil Calvert governed the colony of Maryland from his home in England. Calvert, the second Lord Baltimore, founded the colony in 1634 out of a desire for profit and a hope to create a haven for Catholics who were being persecuted in England. In 1649, Maryland passed an act that promised religious freedoms. The colony then attracted Puritans and Quakers, in addition to Catholics and Protestants In 1688, five years after Welsh's arrival, Quakers made the first written protest against slavery in the colonies.

opportunity in the colonies. For the former milkmaid and others, it was a treacherous voyage. The Atlantic crossing took as much as four months, depending on the weather. The ships were small. Greedy ship owners crowded their passengers into tiny, rat-infested quarters. Many people starved to death or died from smallpox or other diseases before reaching shore. Molly's ship dropped anchor at the mouth of the Patapsco River in the Maryland colony in 1683.

A tobacco farmer with a plantation on the Patapsco River took Welsh as an indentured servant. She worked for seven years without pay to compensate for the cost of her voyage and living expenses. After earning her freedom, Welsh decided to establish a farm of her own. To do so, she rented a small piece of land in the Patapsco Valley. After clearing the land, she planted tobacco as well as some corn. She became a successful farmer and set aside enough money from her profits to purchase the land.

As a landowner and farmer working on her own, Welsh needed assistance with her crops. She decided to purchase slaves to help with the labor. She was opposed to slavery, but she decided she had no other choice if she wanted to keep her farm. According to the history handed down in the family, Welsh purchased two slaves in 1692 "from a ship anchored in the Bay."

The two men were very different from each other. One—whose name has not survived—proved to be strong and adaptable. He felled large trees to increase the amount of land for farming. He helped in the construction of a new tobacco barn as well as with other chores. The other worker was not as strong or as adaptable as the first. Welsh assigned him the lighter tasks. Gradually, she managed to communicate with him. He told her that his name was Banneka. He claimed to be an African tribal prince who had been captured by slave traders. According to one description passed down from generation to

Many tobacco farms in the American colonies depended on slave labor.

generation, he was "a man of bright intelligence, fine temper, with a very agreeable presence, dignified manners, and contemplative habits."

Within a few years, most likely in 1696, Welsh freed the men. Then she did a very dangerous thing. She married Banneka. Marriage put the couple at great risk of losing their freedom and land. Colonial laws governing interracial marriage were strict. In several of the British colonies in North America, including the colony of Maryland, it was against the law for a white woman to marry a black man.

Mindful of drawing attention to her marriage, Molly took her husband's name, embraced his heritage as her own, and withdrew from her white neighbors. Together, they led a quiet life on their remote tobacco farm. Their hardworking existence paid off. The farm prospered and so did their family. The couple had four daughters, the second of which was born around 1700 and named Mary. She would grow up to become the mother of Benjamin Banneker.

Benjamin would never know his grandfather. Banneka died around 1720, leaving Welsh and her children to run the farm. Mary helped out by taking the tobacco crop to the nearby river landing to sell to passing merchants. She also assumed much of the responsibility for rearing her younger sisters.

In 1730, Mary married a freed African man from

Guinea. He had been baptized into the Church of England and given the name Robert. At the time of his baptism, he also received his freedom. Having no surname (last name) of his own, he took his wife's.

Historical records show three different spellings for the last name used by generations of this family. Welsh took Banneka as her last name. Mary and Robert used Bannaky as their last name. Benjamin eventually changed the spelling to Banneker, apparently at the suggestion of a schoolmaster he came to know.

As newlyweds, Mary and Robert lived on Welsh's farm. They helped with the tobacco crops and put aside any money they could, hoping to buy their own land. Soon they bought 25 acres (10 hectares) of wooded land called Timber Poynt. Since the land was near Welsh's farm, they continued to live with her while they worked their own land. Benjamin grew up under the influence of strong women such as his mother and grandmother.

> *While he did not know his grandfather, Banneka, the African prince forced into slavery, Benjamin Banneker grew up hearing stories about him and his African ancestry. Family members recalled how Banneka's astonishing ability to predict the weather helped them produce a stronger tobacco crop, and they told of how he devised a way of irrigating plants in the field. When Benjamin later demonstrated a talent for science, people figured he had inherited it from his grandfather.*

3 THE GIFTED CHILD

❦

In his early years, young Benjamin spent a great deal of time with his grandmother, Molly Welsh. This arrangement worked well for Benjamin's parents because it allowed them more time for farmwork and other tasks. Benjamin proved to be an amazingly bright boy and quickly became his grandmother's favorite. She had a major impact on the education of her grandson.

Welsh taught Benjamin in part through stories and conversation. She captivated him with tales about his grandfather Banneka's royal African background. These pieces of family history—along with information from Benjamin's father, a former slave who carried his own connections to Africa—linked Benjamin to the history, culture, and wisdom of

A rural cabin in colonial America, like the one Benjamin's father built for his family

Africa. Benjamin never forgot the lessons passed on to him by his grandmother and father. Many people credited his knowledge of, and interest in, the stars and the weather to their early influence.

Welsh taught him to read and write at an early age. Every Sunday, she had Benjamin read to her from her Bible, her most prized possession and the only book she owned. At age 5, Benjamin could read from the Old and New Testaments. He even memorized Biblical passages and recited them for family members. He developed a style of speech and writing far beyond what was typical for the son of tobacco farmers. Those who knew him said he could answer questions with the knowledge and manner of an educated adult.

More than anything else, it was Benjamin's mathematical ability that set him apart. At age 6, he could help neighbors with their accounts. He awed those around him by not only sorting out the figures but remembering each person's numbers later. His memory seemed amazingly deep and accurate, and throughout his lifetime, Benjamin never lost his gift of recall.

Benjamin grew up with the feeling that he was special. His parents, Robert and Mary, appreciated his intellect. However, they kept him grounded in reality. They taught him that mathematical skills and beautiful handwriting did not produce tobacco

or provide food. He worked the farmland just like everyone else in his family, and as he grew older, he would have to take on more and more of the never-ending chores of a tobacco farm.

Tobacco crops required a lot of labor because leaves had to be dried and processed before they were sold.

Benjamin's father had long dreamed of owning a piece of land not far from the original family farm. The property, called Stout, was situated on high ground with a stream running through it. On March 10, 1737, Robert got that land, exchanging 7,000 pounds (3,150 kilograms) of tobacco for the property. It was not unusual for people to use tobacco like money. At that time, the crop had value that was as reliable as any other sort of currency.

Robert purchased Stout jointly in his name and in the name of his son, Benjamin. The deed stated that the tract was sold "and confirmed unto them … their heirs and assigns forever one hundred acres of land." Robert knew the importance of owning land, and he wanted to make sure that when he died, the farm would go to his son without question. With the signing of the deed, a former slave and his 6-year-old child—the grandson of an African prince—became owners of not a small plot, but a large farm of 100 acres (40 hectares). This was an impressive achievement. The family's move meant Benjamin would live away from his grandmother's farm for the first time.

Tobacco leaves left to cure on a Maryland farm

Robert faced the task of making the newly acquired property suitable for homesteading and tobacco growing. He began by removing underbrush and clearing trees. He lost no time in planting crops the first year. Benjamin helped in the planting of corn and tobacco. That first summer, the vegetable garden yielded beans, cabbage, potatoes, onions, and squash.

Following the fall harvest, Robert turned to constructing a one-room log cabin for his family. The dwelling had a root cellar for storing food and, most likely, a loft for sleeping space. Robert cut trees on the land to get the logs and sealed them with clay on both sides to keep out the winter's cold and summer's heat. Since he could not afford glass for the windows, Robert used wooden shutters that could be closed against the cold and rain. A large stone fireplace, used for heating and cooking, occupied one wall.

Furniture for the cabin had to be made. Since nails were scarce, Robert fastened the furniture by using wooden pegs. He made an all-purpose table and stools in this manner. Mary collected the downy feathers from the fowl on their property and made feather mattresses. She placed the fluffy mattresses atop the wooden slabs that served as beds. The simple cabin met the basic needs of the Bannaky family, which now, in addition to Benjamin, included three daughters—Jemima, Minta, and Molly.

In the 18th century, maintaining a profitable

tobacco farm required a lot of hard work, even under the best of circumstances. But it was even harder for the few free black farmers, who had to do all the work themselves while many white farm owners used slave labor. Beginning in early spring and lasting until harvest time, the cultivation of tobacco dominated the family members' lives from dawn until dusk. With each passing year, Benjamin and his sisters did more to assist in the fieldwork and chores.

From spring until midsummer, the Bannaky family seeded, planted, replanted, weeded, and waged a constant battle with insects. Benjamin spent his time picking destructive insects—such as aphids, cutworms, slugs, and tobacco caterpillars—from the plants. Each August, Robert and his family cut

Tobacco was packed into barrels and rolled to the market.

the plants. Then they collected the stalks of tobacco leaves and hung them in a tobacco barn to dry for about six weeks. The final steps in the harvest included stripping the leaves from the stalks, tying the leaves into bundles, and packing the bundles into hogsheads, which were barrels used for transporting and shipping tobacco.

Tobacco farming consumed much of Benjamin's boyhood. While he worked diligently with his hands, his brain was hard at work making up and solving problems in mathematics. For instance, to satisfy his own curiosity, Benjamin calculated that the entire process of tobacco growing included at least 36 different operations.

Somewhere around the age of 9, Benjamin had the good fortune to attend a nearby small country school recently established by members of a group called the Society of Friends, also known as Quakers. The movement began in England. Many Quakers came to the colonies around the same time Molly Welsh had. A large number of them settled in Maryland and Pennsylvania, believing these colonies would be open to the Quaker ideas of equality and justice. The one-room Maryland schoolhouse where Benjamin attended class was one of many small schools started by Quakers for poor children.

A Quaker schoolmaster-farmer ran the school. Because children helped their families with the

In the 17th century, Englishman George Fox founded a group called the Society of Friends, or the Quakers. They were also known as Dissenters because their practices differed from other Protestants. In church worship services called meetings, Quakers used no pulpits or songs. Sermons were delivered by members of the group who felt moved to speak. In the latter part of the century, the movement expanded across the Atlantic Ocean. Quakers affirmed the equality of all people, regardless of race, station in life, or sex. They opposed violence and war, and members believed in helping the less fortunate.

planting and harvesting of crops, they attended school only during the winter months. Also, the schoolmaster needed to tend to his own crops. Students sat on hard benches in the unheated room. The schoolmaster provided instruction for several white and two or three black children. Jacob Hall, a classmate and lifelong friend, later recalled Benjamin's consuming interest in learning. He said that as a boy, Benjamin was not particularly fond of children's games. One account quotes Jacob as having said, "All he liked was to dive into books."

Attending school opened up new worlds for Benjamin. Although he displayed mathematical skills earlier, he studied arithmetic in a formal setting for the first time under the Quaker schoolmaster. And through his exposure to many fine books, his reading took on a new dimension. The teacher, astonished by Benjamin's unusual intelligence, supplied college-level books from his personal

Some Quakers taught black children how to read and write.

library to advance the boy's education. Benjamin's reading included translations of works by ancient Greeks, histories of ancient Rome, and publications by mathematicians.

After a year or two of formal schooling, demands of farmwork made it impossible for Benjamin to attend classes. He would not return to school again, but that did not stop him from learning. He never lacked opportunities to use his mind and his hands. He devoured books for the rest of his life, and his surroundings became his classroom, as he studied the weather, animal life, and astronomy. His mechanical skills equaled his mathematical ability, and he eventually used his knowledge to create things few people would have thought possible. ✍

4 DOING DIFFICULT WORK

Chapter

❧⟨∾⟩❧

As Benjamin Banneker moved into his teen years, he took on an ever-increasing load of work on his family's farm. Many of his daytime hours were filled with caring for the tobacco crop and keeping up on other chores. He had to take advantage of opportunities to read and learn in his little free time.

The Patapsco River valley was dominated by tobacco farming. Benjamin's family lived near a small village called Elkridge, an important place for local farmers. A British visitor noted, "This village does not deserve noticing on account of its size, as it contains only about 15 houses, 2 stores, and a few shops, but for being a place of business long before Baltimore was inhabited." Area farmers brought their tobacco to Elkridge, where a great volume of the crop was sold and shipped down the river, bound for markets faraway in Europe.

There was a downside to the success of the tobacco crop, and that was its long-term damage to the soil. Growing the same crop year after year was hard on the soil, and tobacco was harder on it than many other plants. Tobacco drained nutrients from the earth, creating the possibility that someday crops would fail.

Benjamin realized this, as had his father and grandfather before him. But farmers in the area did

Banneker's family farm was located in an area later incorporated as Oella, Maryland.

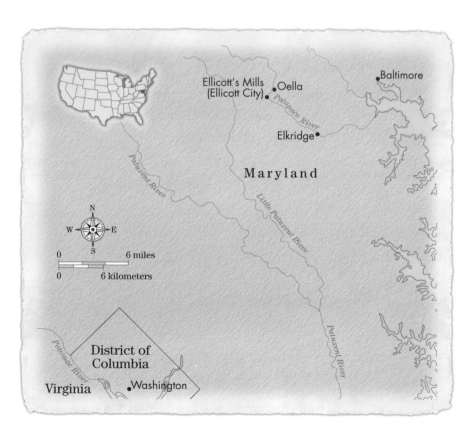

not believe they had any good option other than continuing to plant tobacco. After all, tobacco was valuable, and farmers had easy access to people who wanted to buy the crop. Switching to another crop would have been risky. If, for example, a family decided to raise grain, there was no local mill to buy the product and make it into flour. The farmers would have to ship their crop to distant mills. Benjamin's family, like others, stuck with tobacco and did what they could to care for the soil.

While the farm absorbed much of his time, Benjamin's mind continued to be hungry for other knowledge as he grew into adulthood. He studied the world around him and the skies, in part because anything he might learn could help him better care for the land and the crops. "The soil I work with and the stars up there are all part of the same thing. They were both made for a purpose, and the purpose was good," he said.

Watching the movement of the sun and stars was also more than idle study for Benjamin. Like most people of the era, he looked to the skies to determine something very basic to daily life: the time of day. His workday began when the sun came up. When the sun was high overhead, it was time for the noon meal. When the sun went down, it was time to quit working.

The concept of time had fascinated Benjamin since he was a child. He had never actually seen a clock, although they were nothing new to the world. European monks had developed the first mechanical clocks during the 13th century. But in colonial America of the 1750s, only wealthy people owned clocks or watches. Now in his early 20s, Banneker decided to build a clock of his own. This would be no simple task.

For starters, he had no instructions to guide his work. He had to figure out how a time-keeping device worked before he could create one. People who knew Banneker reported later that the young man had seen only two timepieces in his life. One was a sundial; the other was a pocket watch.

According to a statement he made to his neighbors, Banneker borrowed a pocket watch— from whom it is not known—to use as a model for his clock. He approached the project as if it were a puzzle. At first, he wound the watch and observed the movement of its hands. He knew that to learn why the watch ticked and to see why it moved with precision would mean taking it apart. But he worried that he might destroy the inner workings of the watch by taking it apart. He finally pried open the back of the watch. The tiny gears and other working parts remained intact.

His extraordinary abilities to observe and recall served him well. Banneker examined the intricate mechanism of the watch, and he made detailed

To build his clock, Banneker had to first make all of the working parts.

drawings of each tiny gear, wheel, and pin. Once he understood the workings of the watch, he had to figure out how to make the parts bigger for a clock. He labored long hours on his clock, after having worked all day in the fields. Using his mathematical skills, he reproduced the watch pieces in perfect scale. He carved each piece by hand, using wood he had collected and treated to prepare for such a use. After months of carving, he assembled his clock. The parts fit together perfectly. His new clock worked, and its iron bell chimed on the hour.

Word of Banneker's creation spread all over Patapsco Valley in southeastern Maryland and beyond. Scores of people came to his cabin wanting to see the wooden clock that ran and kept accurate time. They wanted to meet the clockmaker, too.

The person they found was a confident and well-spoken man of 22. Banneker was 5 feet 9 inches (175 centimeters), which was taller than average for that time, and he had a striking head of dark hair— loose curls that were considered a result of his multiracial heritage. In time, his hair would turn gray, and by his later years people would remark on his "mass of white ringlets." Banneker had the lean build of his father and grandfather, and he would later write that his skin was "in that colour which is natural to them of the deepest dye."

Completed in 1753, Banneker's clock continued to operate for decades. Visitors to his home in 1790 recalled that "at their request he gave them an account of its construction." Banneker explained that he produced the clock using "inferior tools" and only "a borrowed watch" as a model. He felt himself "amply repaid" for the time and labor spent in constructing the clock "by the precision with which it marked the passing time."

Six years after building his wooden clock, Banneker suffered a major loss. His ailing father died July 10, 1759. According to the terms of the deed, Benjamin became the sole owner of the farm called Stout, without any shares going to his mother or sisters. At age 28, he assumed full responsibility for running the farm.

With the help of his mother, who was still active in her 60s, he continued to grow tobacco. Records show that he owned two horses and several cows. He maintained a number of beehives and cultivated a large garden to raise vegetables for the family's own

Banneker's work on his farm included beekeeping.

use and for sale.

Most likely, Banneker's grandmother, Molly Welsh, had died by this time, but surviving records of the period include no record of her death. Records do indicate Banneker's sisters married and moved to nearby farms. For a decade or more after the death of his father, he lived alone with his mother.

At the age of 32, Banneker made a noteworthy purchase. He bought his first book, a used edition of the Bible. On the inside, he inscribed: "I bought this book of Honora Buchanan the 4th day of January, 1763, B.B." He also wrote in the Bible: "Benjamin Banneker was born November 9th, in the year of the Lord, God, 1731, and Robert Banneker departed this life July the 10th, 1759."

Farmwork dominated Banneker's life through his late 20s and early 30s, and his intellectual pursuits apparently took a less important role for a period of several years. The tobacco crops demanded attention, and the ongoing strain on the soil continued to cause concern.

Banneker's life was in many ways solitary. It seems he did not have any close friends at this time, although he interacted with some of the other farmers in the valley and with traveling tradesmen. Banneker would never marry and have a family of his own. He derived pleasure from his musical interests. He loved to sit outside his cabin in the twilight,

Today a historical marker stands on the site of Banneker's farm, where a museum has been built to tell his story.

playing his banjo, violin, or flute. He also filled his free hours by reading his Bible and figuring out mathematical puzzles.

Banneker's life might have gone on this way for many years if not for a major change that came to the Patapsco River valley. This change would affect the future of farmers in the area, and it would introduce Banneker to new opportunities to learn and use his gifts to their full potential. ৩৯

Chapter

5 A CHANGE IN THE VALLEY

&c&x&o

In 1771, Benjamin Banneker was 40 and seemed content—or at least preoccupied—with his secluded life of peace and quiet in the Patapsco Valley. According to one description, the wilderness around the Banneker farm at that time remained:

> covered with great trees, the growth of centuries; oaks of different sorts, hickory, maple, gum, ash, chestnut, and all other varieties common to the climate. In the midst of this forest on level ground were the dogwood, the red bud, spice bush, prickly ash, alder, elder, and other shrubs, clustered so closely together, it was often necessary for men, when exploring the ground, to cut away a path with axes.

The Ellicott family brought new industry to the region of Maryland where Banneker had long lived and farmed.

It may not have seemed like a place that was ripe for major change, but that was what came with the arrival of some new faces in the winter of 1771. A pair of Quakers named John Ellicott and Andrew Ellicott III, along with a large work crew, came to the valley and set up temporary lodgings along the Patapsco River, less than a mile from Banneker's farm. Then the Ellicott brothers went to work.

Banneker's new neighbors had brought with them new and improved methods of farming as well as new business enterprises that would affect all of Maryland and eventually the nation. Their arrival not only changed the landscape and helped farmers, but also put new energy into Banneker's life.

The Ellicott brothers came to southeastern Maryland from Bucks County, Pennsylvania. However, the history of the Ellicott family in America began in the early 1700s, when wool manufacturer Andrew Ellicott, with son Andrew II, left Devonshire, England, bound for North America. They settled in Pennsylvania and endured the ups and downs like many people did when they came to the colonies.

Soon after arriving in Pennsylvania, Andrew Ellicott II married a local woman, Ann Bye. They became parents to five sons—Joseph, Andrew III, Nathaniel, Thomas, and John. When Andrew II died in 1741, he left his wife and young children in dire

A 1700s mill where grain was ground into flour

circumstances. As the boys grew older, they were placed with other families to learn various trades.

Joseph Ellicott, eldest of the sons, lived with a millwright, whose job was to grind wheat into flour. Joseph learned how the process worked and how to repair gristmills, the places where grain was ground into flour. Gristmills were built alongside streams or rivers, where the current would turn a large waterwheel and power the machinery inside the mill. A series of rods and gears used the energy of the waterwheel to turn a grindstone, which crushed grain into flour. The flour was, of course, important for making bread and many other staples of the colonists' diet.

Before the age of 21, Joseph used his knowledge to his own profit. With the help of his four brothers, he built a gristmill for a local businessman. The Ellicott brothers soon became known for their mechanical skills. Joseph would eventually gain significant wealth, but it did not come at first through his milling knowledge. In 1766, he was informed that he had inherited property from his great-grandfather in Cork, Ireland. Without wasting any time, Joseph traveled to Ireland to claim his inheritance. After selling the large Irish estate for a huge sum, he returned to Pennsylvania a wealthy man.

Joseph decided to use his fortune to fund milling operations for himself and his brothers. They looked to the nearby colony of Maryland as a possible site for a new mill. The Ellicotts traveled on horseback through the Maryland wilderness, seeking a good spot to build. They needed a site near a river with a current strong enough to power the machinery, and they wanted the land to be suitable for growing grain.

Baltimore was a growing city and seaport in the mid-1700s.

They planned a large operation, and to sell their flour they needed to be near a major seaport.

The Ellicotts found an ideal mill site near the falls of the Patapsco River. The property, located 10 miles (16 kilometers) west of the newly settled city of Baltimore, provided everything they had been looking for. But getting to and building on the bottomland, which was called The Hollows, would be no easy task.

In January 1771, John and Andrew Ellicott, accompanied by hired workers from Pennsylvania, began cutting a path through the wilderness to the river. They started from an existing road 5 miles (8 kilometers) outside of Baltimore and moved toward their planned building site. Cutting through woods and over rocky hills was extremely difficult, and the group encountered other challenges. According to an account recorded in a family history: "Wolves howled in the night a short distance from their camp, and at times they had to fight off wildcats." Weeks later, the new trail reached the land on which the mill would be built.

This would be no ordinary milling operation. The Ellicotts had purchased a vast amount of land stretching across a large piece of the Maryland colony. The land included 2 miles (3.2 km) of riverbank along the Patapsco. The brothers would in time clear large fields and plant them with wheat, and they would build two large milling facilities.

Word of the land sale and conquest of the terrain spread from one farm or plantation to another. Rumors and questions abounded. Why had these strangers come? What did they plan to do with all the land and the huge amount of equipment? Curious neighbors watched and guessed and waited.

Banneker was one of the many keeping a close eye on the work in progress. Fascinated by the size and complexity of the project, he spent more and more time at the construction site. He had never seen construction on such a large scale. The tools being

Peter DeAnna's mural, Building of Ellicott Mills

used and the size of the machinery intrigued him. After a lifetime of a quiet existence, it was strange to hear the constant sounds of construction. Banneker watched the valley transform before his eyes.

Meanwhile, the newcomers revealed their plans to build a series of gristmills. At first, the area farmers, including Banneker, were puzzled. Where would these men get corn and wheat to grind? The only commercial crop grown in the valley was tobacco. But in time, the farmers saw how the Ellicotts were providing them an opportunity to change crops and to give the soil a break from the damaging tobacco plants.

At first, Banneker shied away from talking to his new neighbors, but they soon learned about him. The

Ellicotts needed a local source to provide food for the laborers until such time as they could produce their own. The brothers made arrangements to buy food from Banneker and his mother. Mary was over 70 years old then, but she agreed to provide food supplies for the workers. Almost every day, she delivered large amounts of poultry, vegetables, fruit, honey, and other farm products to the boardinghouse where the laborers lived. Soon Banneker and his mother became well-known figures in the growing Ellicott community.

After several years of slow and difficult work, an impressive structure—named Ellicott's Lower Mills—was completed in 1774. The stone structure stood one-and-a-half stories high and contained five pairs of large millstones. Banneker often visited the new mill. He had seen smaller mills that ground grain for family use, but never one like the Ellicotts'.

The Ellicotts had devised machines to do almost all the work. A belt with scoops moved the grain through the mill, doing the jobs of many laborers.

Soon after the completion of Ellicott's Lower Mills, Joseph Ellicott established his own milling enterprise—Ellicott's Upper Mills—a few miles above the Lower Mills. The mill was equipped with the same innovative machinery used in the Lower Mills. Joseph also built a mansion that became the conversation piece of the region. The residence featured a large, round clock near a third-floor window so passersby could see the time of day.

Another machine, called a "hopper boy," raked ground meal from the loft into a chute. There were machines that unloaded the grain, lifted it up, emptied it onto the millstones, poured the flour into barrels, and loaded the barrels onto wagons to be sent to market. Workers brought the grain to the mill and transported the flour to market. Mechanics kept the complicated machinery in working order.

After building their mill, residences for their families, and a boardinghouse for the workers, the Ellicotts added a general store. The opening

The Ellicott Store became a gathering place for people who lived nearby.

of Ellicott & Co. helped change the area's economy. The store sold food, hardware, and other goods. People traveled long distances to shop at the store.

Benjamin Banneker and his mother were among the first customers at Ellicott & Co. Surviving ledgers show that Mary purchased "a pair of shoes on October 4, 1774 ... for which she paid cash the next spring." Benjamin bought "paper, ink, gunpowder, sugar, molasses, cloth, and other necessities."

Soon the store became a popular meeting place for the valley's farmers—including Banneker. He enjoyed listening to the conversations swirling around him. The topics ranged from crops and weather to politics and world events. Before long, Banneker—quiet by nature—joined in the conversations. His talent for conversation was described "as being of the first order and he was encouraged to visit the store frequently."

In the mid-1770s, Banneker kept up with the fast-moving events occurring in the colonies while picking up supplies at the store. He also devoured the newspapers, hungry for up-to-date information regarding the unrest in the colonies, which in 1775 sparked the first battles in the Revolutionary War. Very little fighting would take place on Maryland soil. However, Baltimore built ships and armaments for the colonial forces. During the struggle for independence from England, free black people were

exempted from military service. Banneker's life remained much the same as the war went on.

During the Revolutionary years, Banneker became friends with George Ellicott. George was the son of one of the founders of the mill. George had been only 12 years old when he moved with his family to Maryland, and he was just 18 when he first met Banneker, then 47 years old. Despite their age difference, the men shared many interests— especially mechanical and scientific ones. They would often meet at the Ellicotts' store to talk, and occasionally George visited Banneker in his cabin. George introduced Banneker to the latest books and ideas about astronomy—a subject that would dominate Banneker's later years. 𝒮𝒽

Banneker followed news of the Revolutionary War, such as the Battle of Concord.

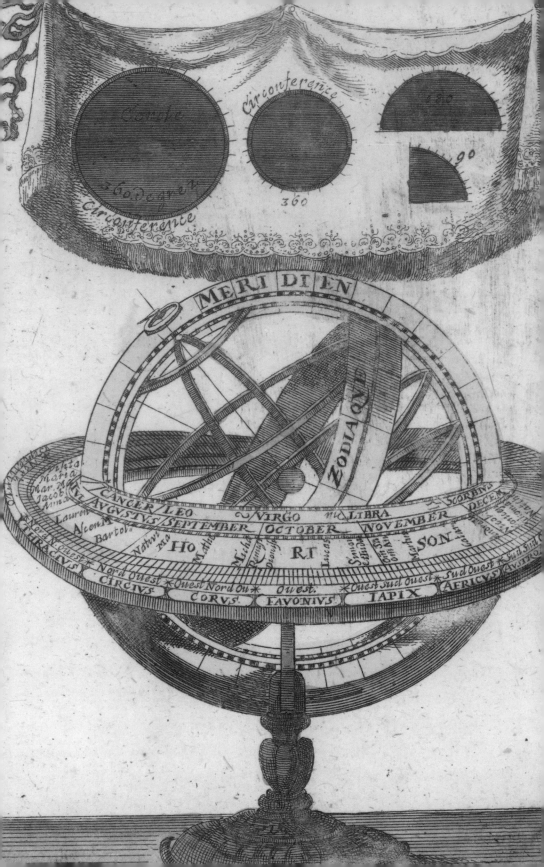

6 A NEW ENERGY FOR LIFE

୧୧୧୬୬

In 1783, Americans celebrated the signing of the Treaty of Paris, which brought an official end to the Revolutionary War. Although fighting had stopped two years earlier, the peace treaty between Great Britain and its former colonies recognized that a new country had been born. Benjamin Banneker was proud to be a citizen of the United States of America. Nonetheless, he was weary of the fact that slavery had not ended.

Now 52 years old, Banneker had reached old age, considering that the average life span for a man of his day was 35 years. But he had not lost his zest for learning. He put new energy into his pursuits outside of farming, and the Ellicotts continued to play a defining role in his growth as a person and in the development of his genius.

The friendship of George Ellicott had a great effect on Banneker in his later years. George's daughter, Martha Tyson, later recalled: "There was an ... empathy between one of the younger members of the Ellicott family and Banneker. That was my own father, George Ellicott." George was a gifted young man, as Banneker had once been. Tyson said of her father, "That he had much energy and capacity we may know from the fact that the present road from Frederich to Baltimore was surveyed and laid out by him when he was seventeen years old." She noted that her father was fond of teaching astronomy to others. In George Ellicott, Banneker had found someone with common interests, especially in literature and science.

Banneker, who had always wondered about and carefully observed the stars, took advantage of the astronomy lessons that Ellicott offered. Filled with awe, Banneker studied the details of the heavens through Ellicott's telescope, and he thirsted for more knowledge of the stars, planets, comets, and asteroids. Astronomy dominated his thoughts and journal writings for the rest of his life.

At times, Banneker's study was hampered by Ellicott's long absences from home on company business. Also, Banneker had a tobacco farm to run. His mother had died during the war years, leaving

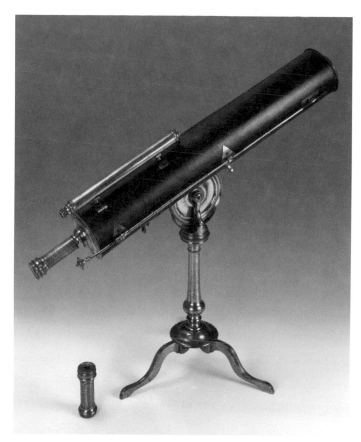

*A reflecting
table telescope,
a type used by
astronomers of
the 1700s*

him little time for leisurely pursuits. Left alone in the
world, Banneker added cooking and other household
chores to his workload.

In the fall of 1788, an event occurred that
cemented the new direction of Banneker's life.
George Ellicott arrived at Banneker's door with
some of his astronomy texts and instruments.
He offered to loan them to Banneker, explaining
that the increasing demands of his work at the

prospering mills left little time for stargazing.

Ellicott departed with a promise to return soon to teach Banneker how to use the instruments. Banneker was left with a telescope mounted on a stand, a set of drafting instruments, and a small pile of books. In the pages of those books, Banneker would find complex diagrams and text that would in time open up a whole universe to him.

Several days later, Ellicott sent his friend a heavy, oval-shaped gateleg table with drop leaves, which could be left open to create a larger surface or turned down to create a small one. The table had been in the Ellicott family for generations but was no longer being used. Despite its age, the sturdy table provided Banneker with space for the instruments and books as well as a large work surface for his drawings and writings. Ellicott also sent a tin candleholder with a saucer base. According to Ellicott's daughter, once everything was in place, Banneker was pleased "with the way his new acquisitions changed the atmosphere of his home."

Ellicott never found the time to provide the promised guidance, but that did not deter Banneker. With the books, the telescope, and the worktable, he began the study of astronomy. Neglectful of his farm duties, he spent long hours tinkering with the instruments and poring over the volumes supplied by Ellicott. He quickly discovered that mathematics was

a big part of astronomy.

Banneker first tackled Scotsman James Ferguson's *An Easy Introduction to Astronomy.* Ferguson, one of the foremost astronomers of the

Astronomer James Ferguson's writing became a valuable reference for Banneker.

63

German astronomer Johann Tobias Mayer

day, wrote in a simple style with many illustrations.

Banneker grasped the concepts with ease, and he took many notes as he read. He continued his careful study, next reading the *Tables of Tobias Mayer*, which was originally published in Latin. Banneker's copy had some English translations, but he had to teach himself some Latin to fully understand the book's contents.

The source he turned to time and time again was George Leadbetter's *A Compleat System of Astronomy* in two volumes. This comprehensive work provided advanced data not available in the other books. After plowing through the borrowed volumes, Banneker wanted to test what he had learned and to make observations of his own.

Nighttime found the self-taught astronomer with his eye glued to the eyepiece of the telescope, focused on the stars. On the Maryland hillside, the wonder of the sky opened above. There were no artificial lights or smog to blur the view.

As months passed, the study of astronomy came to dominate Banneker's life completely. His interest in farming continued to fade. When he was in the fields, his mind was on the stars. The crops sometimes went untended. The animals sometimes waited for hours to be fed.

Banneker stayed up nights, gazing at the stars from the hillside. At dawn, he dragged himself home and fell upon the bed to sleep. He often spent the afternoons at the oval table, reading, identifying constellations, drawing, and making maps of star patterns. At nightfall, he was back at the telescope.

In 1789, after one year of intense study of celestial bodies, Banneker began work on the mathematical calculations needed to predict an eclipse of the sun. In

Though not the first telescope maker, Italian scientist Galileo Galilei was the first to design and use the telescope to seriously study the heavens. In 1609, Galileo was able to see the craters and valleys on the moon. He discovered four moons orbiting Jupiter. He also found out that Venus has phases like Earth's moon. This meant that Venus and the other planets revolved around the sun— not around Earth, as many then believed. In 1610, Galileo published Starry Messenger, a book about what he had seen through his telescope.

order to calculate the occurrence of an eclipse, he taught himself how to use a mathematical method known as logarithm. Before the invention of pocket calculators, logarithm aided in the difficult task of multiplying and dividing large numbers.

After making his calculations, Banneker made a drawing, called a projection. The projection showed his prediction of the paths the sun and moon would take while in eclipse. After the completion of the projection, Banneker sent the sketch to George Ellicott.

Ellicott carefully reviewed his friend's drawings and measurements. Astonished, he realized that Banneker had made remarkable progress in mastering astronomy on his own. George corrected a small computational error in the drawing before returning it to Banneker.

Ellicott's excitement and admiration pleased Banneker. Not one to let a single error mar his work, he resumed his study of the sky. To Ellicott, he said: "[I]f I can overcome this difficulty I Doubt not being able to Calculate a Common Almanack." Banneker developed a strong desire to produce his own almanac, which would include charts of the stars and information for daily living.

For the next year, Banneker devoted most of his time to calculating an ephemeris for his almanac. An ephemeris is a chart showing positions of the sun, moon, and planets for every day of a year. After completing the difficult calculations, Banneker sent his ephemeris to three different publishers of almanacs. The book was rejected by all three, and now he would have to redo the calculations for the

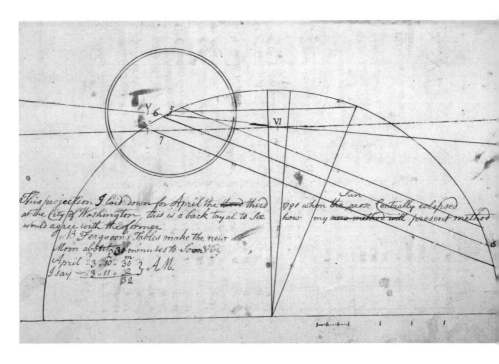

A projection from one of Banneker's astronomical journals

following year.

But something happened that delayed his plans. Banneker, who had hardly ever left the vicinity of his farm, received word that he had been selected to perform an important job for the U.S. government. ✑

7 AN IMPORTANT TASK

಄ೕಷ಄

In July 1790, the Congress of the United States— leading what was still a freshly independent nation— decided where to establish a new capital. Until that time, there had been no permanent capital. The government had moved from city to city over the course of 14 years while Congress debated the question of location. Many different sites were considered and then rejected. One harried congressman suggested, "Perhaps they should put the new capital on wheels and roll it from place to place."

Finally, Congress designated that the capital be built along the Potomac River. This undeveloped area was a natural midpoint between northern and southern states. Maryland and Virginia gave up land

A painting of George Washington (left) and Charles L'Enfant exploring the site of Washington, D.C.

along the Potomac to be used for the capital city.

President George Washington, whose Mount Vernon home was in the area, selected the specific site. Government officials found the marshy wilderness less than impressive, but these conditions did not daunt the president, who had tramped through swamps and marshy areas while training to be a surveyor at age 16. Washington bypassed Congress, hoping to reduce friction and delays, and launched the building of the capital city on January 14, 1791. He appointed three commissioners to oversee the project, and he ordered a survey of the new city to begin.

Washington suggested surveyor Major Andrew Ellicott III to head the project to determine and describe the boundaries of the city that would come to bear the president's name. Washington knew that Ellicott had conducted many precise surveys that established state and territorial boundaries. Washington promised Ellicott, who had served well during the Revolutionary War, that he could choose his own staff.

Major Ellicott began to make preparations at once. He received a notice from Secretary of State Thomas Jefferson that said, "You are to proceed by the first stage to the Federal territory on the Potomac, for making a survey of it." The letter set instructions for laying out 10 square miles (26 square

Major Andrew Ellicott III was chosen to lead the surveying of the nation's new capital.

kilometers) for the federal territory, to be called the District of Columbia.

In addition to field hands, Ellicott needed an assistant to make astronomical calculations, so he asked his cousin George Ellicott to help. Although George had the necessary skills, he was too busy with the expansion of the mills to accept the offer. But, according to one account, he made a recommendation to the major: "Take Benjamin Banneker as your assistant. There's not a better man for the job anywhere."

Major Ellicott chose Banneker, who lacked field experience in surveying but was skilled in astronomy. Banneker accepted the offer. He could hardly believe that he—a farmer 60 years of age, having little education other than what he had learned from borrowed books and his own observation—would have such an important role in the project. Skills in astronomy would be essential because the surveyors would rely on astronomical measurements to keep their bearings in the swamps and dense brush, and to make sure they laid out perfectly square borders for the new district.

Banneker quickly made plans for his trip. His sisters lived nearby and agreed to care for his livestock and keep an eye on his house. George Ellicott's wife helped Banneker pick out suitable clothes, which was important because he would likely be in the company of some of the most important people in the country. After two weeks of planning and preparation, Banneker and Major Ellicott left the Patapsco Valley on horseback. They headed for Alexandria, Virginia, where they planned to set up a base camp for the first phase of the survey. The weary and rain-soaked travelers arrived on February 7, 1791.

Bad weather delayed the start of the project. Ignoring the rain, Banneker explored the streets of Alexandria alone. He enjoyed having a chance

The valley of the Potomac River upstream from the site of the capital

to experience the excitement of a bustling town firsthand. In the meantime, Ellicott made arrangements for establishing the base camp. He purchased equipment and horses, and he hired woodcutters and laborers. After assembling the surveying party, Ellicott fretted and waited for the weather to clear.

When the rain stopped, the survey team got to work. After clearing the ground, they set up tents,

Banneker surveying Washington, D.C.

unloaded the equipment, and finally began laying out the boundary lines.

As Major Ellicott's assistant, Banneker worked in the large observatory tent set up on a high ridge in the forest. The tent had a hole cut in the top for the main telescope called a zenith sector. Banneker was responsible for maintaining the instrument known as an astronomical clock. He constantly monitored the sensitive clock's rate and temperature. He studied the stars at night, making measurements. He recorded the exact time of the measurements as shown on the astronomical clock. After keeping a watchful eye on the clock during the night, Banneker made observations of the sun's position in the sky during the day. Lack of sleep and aching bones did not prevent Banneker from enjoying his job.

The survey was well under way when President Washington chose Major Charles L'Enfant to prepare drawings of the capital grounds and buildings. On March 12, 1791, the *Georgetown Weekly Ledger* announced the arrival of L'Enfant. The article also noted the earlier arrival of Ellicott:

> attended by Benjamin Banniker, an Ethiopian, whose abilities, as a surveyor, and an astronomer clearly prove that Mr. Jefferson's concluding that race of men were void of mental endowments, was without foundation.

In his *Notes on the State of Virginia*, first published in 1787, Jefferson had written about the possibility that blacks were mentally inferior to whites. A few more years would pass before Banneker would send his famous letter to Jefferson, challenging the statesman on this issue.

Late in March 1791, President Washington visited the survey site. Ellicott met with the president,

In recent years, a report of Major Ellicott's expense account for the Washington, D.C., surveying project has come to light. Titled Expenses Incurred in Surveying the Experimental and Permanent Lines of the District of Columbia, the report provides an itemized list of expenditures. The cost from February 1791 through December 1792 totaled $2,986.25. For his work at the Georgetown base camp, Benjamin Banneker was paid $60. This expense account was discovered among Thomas Jefferson's papers.

but there is no record of Banneker participating in this meeting.

Having completed the survey of the Columbia territory, Major Ellicott proceeded to the next phase of the project—the survey of the new city that would hold the Capitol and other government buildings. By this time, Ellicott's brothers had arrived from New York to help. This meant that someone was now available to replace Banneker in the observatory tent. After working day and night, seven days a week for three months, the aging Banneker was physically exhausted. He longed to be home and to return to his latest almanac, which was waiting to be completed. He departed the survey team sometime late in April 1791.

Major Ellicott and his brothers continued to make progress with the survey of the city. However, things were not going so well with the young, arrogant architect hired for the project. L'Enfant's grand building plans for the city and his clashes with officials resulted in his dismissal early in 1792.

The conflicts surrounding L'Enfant gave rise to an often-repeated story that involved Banneker. According to the story, Banneker, having seen the original design for the city only once, re-created it in detail from memory after L'Enfant returned to France with the original plans. This legend has led some people to credit Banneker with a greater

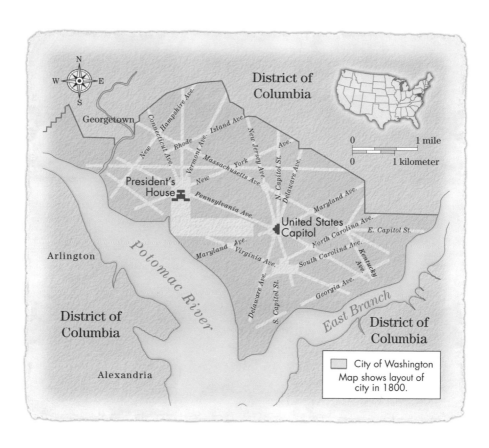

District of
Columbia

Georgetown

Connecticut Ave.
New Hampshire Ave.
Rhode Island Ave.
Vermont Ave.
Massachusetts Ave.
New York Ave.
New Jersey Ave.
N. Capitol St.
Delaware Ave.
Maryland Ave.

President's
House

Pennsylvania Ave.

United States
Capitol

North Carolina Ave.
E. Capitol St.

Arlington

Potomac River

Maryland Ave.
Virginia Ave.
Delaware Ave.
S. Capitol St.
South Carolina Ave.
Georgia Ave.
Kentucky Ave.

East Branch

District of
Columbia

District of
Columbia

Alexandria

0 — 1 mile
0 — 1 kilometer

☐ City of Washington
Map shows layout of
city in 1800.

role in creating the capital city. However, there is no evidence that Banneker contributed anything to the design of the city or that he ever met L'Enfant.

The first streets were laid soon after Banneker worked on surveying the site of the capital.

Modern historians acknowledge that the inaccurate information—the myths surrounding Banneker—resulted in his contribution to the city being overvalued. Unfortunately, those myths sometimes obscure Banneker's greatest genuine contribution to society—the almanacs he would publish in his later years. ✑

Benjamin Bannaker's
PENNSYLVANIA, DELAWARE, MARY-
LAND, AND VIRGINIA
ALMANAC,
FOR THE
YEAR of our LORD 1795;
Being the Third after Leap-Year.

BANNAKER.

PHILADELPHIA:
Printed for WILLIAM GIBBONS, Cherry Street

Chapter

8 ALMANAC MAKER

❧✦❧

Back at home in the Patapsco Valley, Benjamin Banneker felt satisfied with his contributions to the survey and was eager to resume work on his almanac. He had been unable to find a publisher for his earlier almanacs, and creating a new one each year required a great deal of work.

Before settling down to work, Banneker visited George Ellicott. Their meeting was later described by Ellicott's daughter Martha Tyson:

> On his return home, [Banneker] called at the house of his friend George Ellicott to give an account of his engagements. He arrived on horseback, dressed in his usual costume, a full suit of drab cloth, surmounted by a large beaver hat. He

An image of Banneker, with his name spelled differently than was standard, appeared on the cover of one of his popular almanacs.

was in fine spirits, seeming to have been reanimated by the kindness of the distinguished men with whom he had mingled. With his usual humility he estimated his own services at a low rate.

Banneker's next stop was the Ellicott & Co. store. His brief employment with Major Ellicott had taught him the importance of keeping careful records of all observations and calculations. At the store, he bought a bound journal with 300 blank pages of fine handmade paper. The expensive purchase may have signaled Banneker's commitment to his study of astronomy and preparation of a new almanac.

Although his first contacts with publishers had been disappointing, Banneker still held on to his dream. In his work with Major Ellicott, Banneker had used some of the best astronomical instruments and texts of the time. With confidence and renewed energy, he set about producing an ephemeris—the chart showing daily positions of the sun, moon, and planets—for 1792.

By the beginning of June 1791, Banneker had completed a draft of his ephemeris. Hoping to get the greatest possible distribution of his work, he sent a copy of the full manuscript of his almanac to a Georgetown printer and delivered a copy to William Goddard, a well-known printer in Baltimore. Both expressed interest in his work.

Then he waited for word from the publishers regarding his manuscript. During this time, Banneker decided to send a copy of his almanac manuscript to Thomas Jefferson. That decision led to Banneker's now-famous letter challenging Jefferson's views on slavery and race. At the time it was written, Banneker's letter was a bold act but not one that gained attention or prompted action. Banneker complained that black people in America had "long been looked upon with an eye of contempt, and that we have long been considered rather as brutish than human."

In his letter, Banneker flattered Jefferson and appealed to his highest ideals, writing that "you are measurable friendly and well disposed towards us, and that you are willing to lend your aid and assistance to our relief." But he was direct in his challenge to Jefferson, who was then secretary of state and would someday be president. Banneker asserted that all people, regardless of race, are created by "one universal Father" and given the same feelings and capabilities. He said it was the duty of free people who called themselves Christians

> *Benjamin Franklin published his famous Poor Richard's Almanack for 25 years, beginning in 1732. He wrote under the pen name of Richard Saunders, a poor man who needed money to take care of his carping wife. Every issue contained witty advice such as, "A penny saved is a penny earned."*

The final page of Banneker's 1791 letter to Thomas Jefferson

to "extend their power and influence to the relief of every part of the human race." Banneker's long letter also reminded Jefferson of the exact words he had used in the Declaration of Independence—"that all men are created equal"—and asked that he consider again how those words applied to African-Americans. Banneker said he would not suggest what actions Jefferson could take, only that he and other leaders "wean yourselves from those narrow prejudices."

Jefferson's reply expressed his wishes that the situation of black people in America would be improved. Jefferson wrote that "nobody wishes more ardently to see a good system commenced for raising the condition of both their body and mind to what it ought to be." However, he did not promise to take any action.

Their correspondence might have been forgotten, if the letters had not later been reprinted in Banneker's almanacs, which in 1791 were about to find willing publishers. While he awaited word from the two printers who had the almanac in hand, Banneker spoke to George Ellicott about finding an interested printer in Philadelphia. Eager to help, George sent a copy of the manuscript to his brother, Elias Ellicott. Elias, an activist in the antislavery movement, contacted James Pemberton in Philadelphia. Pemberton, president of a Pennsylvania organization dedicated to abolishing slavery, saw this as an opportunity to promote the antislavery cause. He requested another copy of Banneker's ephemeris to send out to reviewers.

Banneker was ill when he received word of

William Goddard was one of the publishers of Banneker's first almanac.

the need for another copy, but he managed to get out of bed and copy his complex handwritten manuscript in a matter of days. George forwarded the copy to Pemberton. After several months, Banneker got word that both William Goddard in Baltimore and Joseph Crukshank in Philadelphia wanted to print his almanac. Banneker was thrilled. However, he now had two publishers fighting over his work. In the end, the publishers compromised, and Banneker saw his work printed in both cities.

Banneker's first almanac went on sale in late December 1791 and sold out quickly. The publishers hurried to print a second edition. *Benjamin Banneker's Pennsylvania, Delaware, Maryland, and Virginia Almanack and Ephemeris For the Year of our Lord, 1792* was a rousing success by the number of copies sold.

In the next few months, Banneker completed an ephemeris for 1793. He had no lack of publishers this time. The new almanac followed the same format as

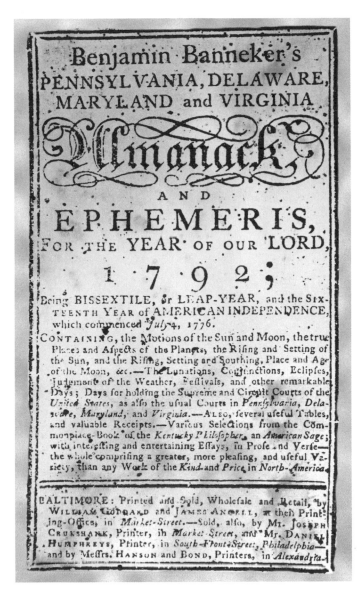

the first, using essays, humor, and practical information along with the ephemeris—except the new almanac had longer stories and essays. The second

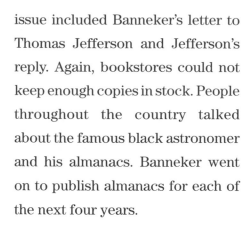

issue included Banneker's letter to Thomas Jefferson and Jefferson's reply. Again, bookstores could not keep enough copies in stock. People throughout the country talked about the famous black astronomer and his almanacs. Banneker went on to publish almanacs for each of the next four years.

The books brought Banneker a great deal of attention. He received letters from readers far and wide, and people even stopped by his home to meet him. He often paused in whatever he was doing, invited the visitor into his cabin, and offered something to eat or drink while they chatted.

Word-of-mouth enthusiasm kept the presses rolling with Banneker's work. People liked the reading matter that came along with his astronomical calculations. Banneker included a wide variety of advice and commentary in essays printed in his almanacs. He wrote a great deal about race and the condition of black slaves in America. For example, the 1796 edition included a preface that stated: "The Maker of the Universe is no respecter of colours; that the colour of the skin is in no ways connected with strength of mind or intellectual powers."

In the 1797 issue, Banneker's advice to readers included a caution about the dangers of smoking. He even crafted poems and shared them with his readers. One such poem read:

> *Behold ye Christians! in pity see*
> *Those Africa sons which Nature formed free*
> *Behold them in a fruitful country blest.*
> *Of Nature's bounties see them rich possest.*
> *Behold them herefrom torn by cruel force,*
> *And doomed to slavery without remorse.*
> *This act, America, thy sons have known*
> *This cruel act, relentless they have done.*

Banneker did not publish another almanac after 1797. His health in his advancing years was not good, and the difficult work of preparing a new book each year was exhausting. But according to his journal, Banneker calculated an ephemeris for each year from 1798 to 1802 for his own enjoyment. ✎

9 BANNEKER'S LAST YEARS

❧❧❧

After his retirement from publishing, Benjamin Banneker lived out his days on the Maryland property he knew so well. When his income from the almanacs ceased, he had to find another way to get by. He had not cultivated crops on much of his land in recent years, and beginning such work again seemed unwise for a man of his age. He tried renting his land to neighboring farmers, but this did not work out.

A series of disturbing incidents marred Banneker's leisurely existence. His journal pages for these years contain examples of unknown persons heard outside his cabin and gunshots fired close to his door. On August 27, 1797, he recorded in his journal, "Standing by my door, I heard the discharge of a gun, and in 4 or 5 Seconds … the shot came rattling

Banneker continued his study and scientific work during his later years.

about me, one or two of which Struck the house." In a journal entry dated April 29, 1798, Banneker tells of two men coming to his cabin and discharging a gun in his presence. "I, being very unwell, could not pursue to find who they were." A few years later, he recorded: "The night of the 27 November 1802 my house was violently broken open and several articles taken."

These incidents quite likely resulted from racial tensions. Banneker's almanacs had made him a well-known and successful black person. He and his almanacs had been celebrated by abolitionists—the people working to end slavery. At the same time, Banneker's success stirred hatred among pro-slavery people. It is also possible that Banneker was being bothered by people who assumed he had amassed large profits from his almanacs and that he kept money stashed inside his cabin. Whatever the cause, these incidents rattled the quiet life that Banneker had known for so long.

He longed for undisturbed solitude to pursue his studies, to read, and to write in his journal. Finally, Banneker and the Ellicotts agreed to a deal that amounted to a delayed sale of Banneker's land, which would relieve Banneker of the strain of working to support himself. The Ellicotts would pay Banneker a share of the sale price each year, and he would continue to live in his longtime home. Upon his

Banneker's handwritten notes in a journal of his nighttime observations

death, the land would go to the Ellicotts. Banneker struggled with the decision to part with the land that his parents had worked so hard to obtain. But the deal made sense. Banneker had no children to take over the farm, and his sisters had married and moved to property of their own.

Completely relieved of farm duties, Banneker entered a calm and peaceful existence. Advancing age curtailed some of his activities, but not his love of learning. He often wrapped himself in his cloak and lay upon the ground at night, taking in the beauty of the skies. He studied his bees' behavior and took great pleasure in watching them at work. He enjoyed having time to record his observations of nature in his journal, also called a commonplace book. His regular routine included a short daily walk.

On the morning of October 9, 1806, he returned from his walk feeling ill. Later that afternoon, he died in his cabin. Benjamin Banneker was 74 years old, a month short of his 75th birthday. His burial took place two days after his death on October 11. The gravesite was a few yards from the home where he had lived most of his life.

Prior to his death, Banneker had arranged for the disposal of his few possessions. The borrowed items—astronomy texts, telescope and other instruments, and the oval table—were returned to George Ellicott. George also received his friend's astronomical journal as well as his personal journal.

Between the Sunday he died and the following Tuesday when his burial took place, Banneker's sisters sorted through his possessions. Household items such as linens, pots and pans, dishes, and cutlery items were shared between the households. Some months prior to his death, Banneker had given a featherbed to one of his sisters. Years later, she felt something hard among the feathers. It turned out to be a purse of gold coins.

On the day he was buried, a mysterious fire destroyed Banneker's cabin. Mourners watched as the small structure, with all its contents, burned to the ground. His wooden clock, pieces of furniture,

Benjamin Banneker

Black Heritage USA 15¢

A postage stamp issued in 1980 honored Banneker's scientific achievements.

his manuscripts, printed copies of his almanacs, and his books were lost in the flames. The fire destroyed many of Banneker's notes and journals, in effect erasing many details of his personal life, his thoughts, and his theories. Banneker's beloved Bible survived the blaze. One of his sisters likely removed it from the house before the funeral. The Bible remained in the possession of a family member for many years, but its whereabouts today are unknown.

On October 28, 1806, almost three weeks after Banneker's death, a Baltimore newspaper ran an obituary. It read in part:

> *Mr. Benjamin Banneker ... was well known in his neighborhood for his quiet and peaceful demeanor, and among scientific men as an astronomer and mathematician. ... Mr. Banneker is a prominent instance to prove that a descendant of Africa is susceptible of as great mental improvement and deep knowledge into the mysteries of nature as that of any other nation.*

Following his death, Banneker's achievements were for the most part forgotten or distorted for a century and a half. Even his grave site was left without a monument marking its place. But modern historians rediscovered Banneker's achievements and went to work in hopes of finding out more about his life.

Between 1983 and 1986, archeological digs discovered the remains of Banneker's home and

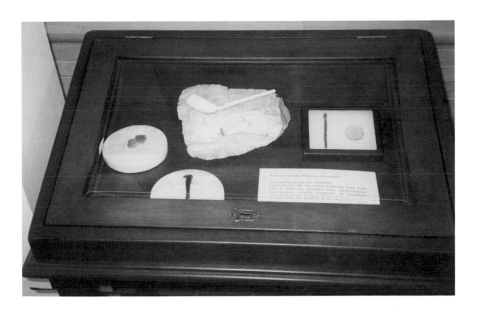

A pipe and other items of daily life were among the artifacts found on the site of Banneker's farm and home.

farm. The project's goal was to recover artifacts and preserve the site of Banneker's home. Hundreds of volunteers spent thousands of hours working in the field and lab.

The Benjamin Banneker Historical Park and Museum opened its doors to the public in 1998, following years of work by a nonprofit group and Baltimore County officials. The museum includes property that was once part of Banneker's farm. Surviving artifacts and ongoing research make it possible for Banneker to be remembered and appreciated for, as one historian put it, "his achievements as a successful American man of science regardless of his race." ✑

BENJAMIN BANNEKER'S LIFE

1731

Born a free black person on November 9 in the Maryland Colony

1737

Parents purchase land near his grandmother's farm near Maryland's Patapsco River

1730

1735

Swedish naturalist Carolus Linnaeus publishes his first work on botanical classification

1738

Englishman John Wesley and his brother Charles found the Methodist church

WORLD EVENTS

1753

Constructs a wooden clock using a pocket watch as a model

1759

Inherits the family farm after his father's death

1755

1759

The British Museum opens in London

1756–1763

The Seven Years' War is fought; Britain defeats France

BENJAMIN BANNEKER'S LIFE

1763

Buys his first book, a
secondhand Bible

1771

Meets the Ellicott
brothers, who moved
to the area to build
flour mills

1760   **1780**

1762

Catherine the Great
becomes empress of
Russia and rules for
34 years.

1768

British explorer
Captain James Cook
leaves England for a
three-year exploration
of the Pacific

1770

Clergyman and chem-
ist Joseph Priestly
gives rubber its name
when he discovers it
rubs out pencil marks

WORLD EVENTS

1789

Calculates his first
ephemeris

1788

Begins studying the
stars after being
loaned a telescope
and several books
about astronomy

1789

The French
Revolution begins
with the storming
of the Bastille prison
in Paris

1788

The *Times* newspaper
in London is founded

BENJAMIN BANNEKER'S LIFE

1791

Surveys the boundary for the new national capital; exchanges letters with Thomas Jefferson; publishes his first almanac

1792

Publishes his second almanac

1790

1791

Austrian composer Wolfgang Amadeus Mozart dies

1793

King Louis XVI and Queen Marie Antoinette are guillotined in Paris during the French Revolution

WORLD EVENTS

1797

Publishes his sixth
and final almanac

1806

Dies at his home on
October 9 at age 74

1800

1795

J. F. Blumenbach
writes his book *The
Human Species* thus
laying the foundation
of anthropology

1802

United States Military
Academy founded at
West Point

DATE OF BIRTH: November 9, 1731

BIRTHPLACE: Maryland Colony

FATHER: Robert (? – 1759)

MOTHER: Mary Bannaky

EDUCATION: Self-taught; briefly attended Quaker school

SIBLINGS: Jemima Lett
Minta Black
Molly Morten

DATE OF DEATH: October 9, 1806

PLACE OF BURIAL: On his property, later incorporated as Oella, Maryland.

FURTHER READING

Altman, Susan. *Extraordinary African-Americans.* New York: Children's Press, 2001.

Harness, Cheryl. *Thomas Jefferson.* Washington, D.C.: National Geographic, 2004.

Hinman, Bonnie. *Benjamin Banneker: American Mathematician and Astronomer.* Philadelphia: Chelsea House Publishers, 2000.

Litwin, Laura Baskes. *Benjamin Banneker: Astronomer and Mathematician.* Berkeley Heights, N.J.: Enslow Publishers, 1999.

LOOK FOR MORE SIGNATURE LIVES
BOOKS ABOUT THIS ERA:

Abigail Adams: *Courageous Patriot and First Lady*
ISBN 0-7565-0981-5

Samuel Adams: *Patriot and Statesman*
ISBN 0-7565-0823-1

Ethan Allen: *Green Mountain Rebel*
ISBN 0-7565-0824-X

Benedict Arnold: *From Patriot to Traitor*
ISBN 0-7565-0825-8

Benjamin Franklin: *Scientist and Statesman*
ISBN 0-7565-0826-6

Alexander Hamilton: *Founding Father and Statesman*
ISBN 0-7565-0827-4

John Hancock: *Signer for Independence*
ISBN 0-7565-0828-2

John Paul Jones: *Father of the American Navy*
ISBN 0-7565-0829-0

Thomas Paine: *Great Writer of the Revolution*
ISBN 0-7565-0830-4

Mercy Otis Warren: *Author and Historian*
ISBN 0-7565-0982-3

Martha Washington: *First Lady of the United States*
ISBN 0-7565-0983-1

Phillis Wheatley: *Slave and Poet*
ISBN 0-7565-0984-X

ON THE WEB

For more information on *Benjamin Banneker*, use FactHound.

1. Go to *www.facthound.com*
2. Type in a search word related to this book or this book ID: 0756515793
3. Click on the *Fetch It* button.

FactHound will fetch the best Web sites for you.

HISTORIC SITES

The Benjamin Banneker
Historical Park and Museum
300 Oella Ave.
Catonsville, MD 21228
410/887-1081
A museum highlighting the life and contributions of Benjamin Banneker

Monticello
931 Thomas Jefferson Parkway
Charlottesville, VA 22902
434/984-9800
The home of Thomas Jefferson

abolitionists
people who supported the banning of slavery

almanacs
publications containing astronomical information
for a given year as well as general information

artifacts
human-made objects found at historical sites

deed
a signed document containing a legal transfer
of property

eclipse
when one object in space blocks light and keeps it
from shining on another object in space

ephemeris
a table that gives information about the sun,
moon, and planets

gristmills
mills for grinding grain

logarithm
a mathematical process used in astronomical
calculations

millstone
circular stone used to crush grain

obituary
a notice of a person's death, usually with a short
biographical account

Chapter 1

Page 10, line 26: Letter from Benjamin Banneker to Thomas Jefferson dated Aug. 19, 1791. Quoted in Charles A. Cerami, *Benjamin Banneker: Surveyor, Astronomer, Publisher, Patriot.* New York: John Wiley & Sons, Inc., 2002, p. 166.

Page 12, line 17: Ibid, p. 165.

Page 13, line 3: Ibid, p. 166.

Page 13, line 7: Ibid, p. 164.

Page 13, line 12: Ibid, p. 167.

Page 14, line 7: Letter from Thomas Jefferson to Benjamin Banneker dated Aug. 30, 1791. Quoted in Charles A. Cerami, *Benjamin Banneker: Surveyor, Astronomer, Publisher, Patriot.* New York: John Wiley & Sons, Inc., 2002, p. 168.

Page 15, line 15: Ibid, p. 169.

Page 15, line 18: Ibid.

Chapter 2

Page 22, line 27: Silvio A. Bedini, *The Life of Benjamin Banneker*, Second Edition. Baltimore: Maryland Historical, 1999, p. 12.

Page 24, line 1: Ibid, p. 13.

Chapter 3

Page 30, line 5: Quoted in *The Life of Benjamin Banneker*, p. 321.

Page 34, line 16: *Benjamin Banneker: Surveyor, Astronomer, Publisher, Patriot*, p. 26.

Chapter 4

Page 37, line 10: Ibid, p. 31.

Page 39, line 16: Ibid, p. 32.

Page 42, line 14: Ibid, p. 34

Page 42, line 18: Ibid, p. 165.

Page 42, line 22: Martha E. Tyson. *Banneker, the Afric-American Astronomer. From the Posthumous Papers of Martha E. Tyson. Edited by her Daughter.* Philadelphia: Friends' Book Association, 1884. Quoted in *The Life of Benjamin Banneker*, p. 44.

Page 44, line 10: Quoted in *The Life of Benjamin Banneker*, p. 48.

Page 44, line 12: Ibid.

Chapter 5

Page 47, line 6: Robert J. Hurry, *The Discovery and Archeological Investigation of the Benjamin Banneker Homestead.* Crownsville, Md.: Maryland Historical Trust Press, 2002, p. 19.

Page 51, line 19: *The Life of Benjamin Banneker*, p. 55.

Page 56, line 4: Ibid, p. 63.

Page 56, line 6: Ibid.

Page 56, line 15: Ibid, p. 62.

Chapter 6

Page 60, line 4: Martha Ellicott Tyson, *Memoir of Benjamin Banneker*, as told to her daughter, Anne T. Kirk. Philadelphia: Friends Book Association, 1884. Quoted in *Benjamin Banneker: Surveyor, Astronomer, Publisher, Patriot*, p. 107.

Page 60, line 9: Ibid.

Page 62, line 19: *The Life of Benjamin Banneker*, p. 84.

Page 66, line 16: Ibid, page 89.

Chapter 7

Page 69, line 9: Joseph J. Ellis, *His Excellency George Washington*. New York: Alfred A. Knopf, 2004, p. 206.

Page 71, line 14: *The Life of Benjamin Banneker*, p. 328.

Page 71, line 26: *Benjamin Banneker: Surveyor, Astronomer, Publisher, Patriot*, p. 130.

Page 75, line 12: *The Life of Benjamin Banneker*, p. 127.

Chapter 8

Page 79, line 10: *Banneker, the Afric-American Astronomer. From the Posthumous Papers of Martha E. Tyson. Edited by her Daughter.* Quoted in *The Life of Benjamin Banneker*, p. 137-138.

Page 81, line 14: Letter from Benjamin Banneker to Thomas Jefferson dated Aug. 19, 1791. Quoted in *Benjamin Banneker: Surveyor, Astronomer, Publisher, Patriot*, p. 163.

Page 81, line 19: Ibid, page 164.

Page 81, line 26: Ibid.

Page 82, line 1: Ibid.

Page 82, line 4: Ibid, page 165.

Page 83, line 5: Ibid, page 166.

Page 83, line 8: Letter from Thomas Jefferson to Benjamin Banneker dated Aug. 30, 1791. Quoted in *Benjamin Banneker: Surveyor, Astronomer, Publisher, Patriot*, p. 169.

Page 86, line 27: *The Life of Benjamin Banneker*, p. 339.

Page 87, line 7: *Benjamin Banneker: Surveyor, Astronomer, Publisher, Patriot*, p. 194.

Chapter 9

Page 89, line 14: Ibid, page 204.

Page 90, line 4: Ibid.

Page 90, line 6: Ibid.

Page 94, line 10: *The Life of Benjamin Banneker*, p. 272.

Page 95, line 13: Ibid, p. 320.

Arebeck, Bob. *Through a Fiery Trial*. Lanham, Md.: Madison Books, 1991.

Bedini, Silvio A. *The Life of Benjamin Banneker: The First African-American Man of Science*. Baltimore, Md.: Maryland Historical Society, 1999.

Cerami, Charles. *Benjamin Banneker: Surveyor, Astronomer, Publisher, Patriot*. New York: John Wiley & Sons, 2002.

Ellis, Joseph J. *George Washington: His Excellency*. New York: Alfred A. Knopf, 2004.

Drotning, Phillip T. *Black Heroes In Our Nation's History: A Tribute To Those Who Helped Shape America*. New York: Cowles Book Company, Inc., 1970.

Graham, Shirley. *Your Most Humble Servant*. New York: Julian Messner, Inc., 1949.

Hurry, Robert J. *The Discovery and Archeological Investigation of the Benjamin Banneker Homestead*. Crownsville, Md.: Maryland Historical Trust Press, 2002.

Levey, Bob and Jane Freundel Levey. *Washington Album: A Pictorial History of the Nation's Capital*. Washington, D.C.: The Washington Post, 2000.

Sobel, Dava. *Longitude*. New York: Walker & Company, 1995.

Myra Weatherly lives in South Carolina. She is the author of many books and articles for children and young adults. For Weatherly, her research for this book resulted in a deeper understanding and appreciation of Benjamin Banneker.